“十二五”职业教育国家规划教材
经全国职业教育教材审定委员会审定
财政部规划中等职业学校财经商贸类教材

外贸单证实务

张　云　　　主　编
王　真　刘　阳　副主编

中国财政经济出版社

图书在版编目（CIP）数据

外贸单证实务／张云主编．—北京：中国财政经济出版社，2015.5（2023.8 重印）
“十二五”职业教育国家规划教材　财政部规划中等职业学校财经商贸类教材
ISBN 978－7－5095－5850－8

Ⅰ．①外…　Ⅱ．①张…　Ⅲ．①进出口贸易－原始凭证－中等专业学校－教材
Ⅳ．①F740.44

中国版本图书馆 CIP 数据核字（2014）第 276278 号

责任编辑：唐　堂　　　　　　　　　责任校对：徐艳丽
封面设计：汪俊宇　　　　　　　　　版式设计：兰　波

中国财政经济出版社 出版

URL：http：//www.cfeph.cn

E－mail：cfeph @ cfeph.cn

社址：北京市海淀区阜成路甲 28 号　邮政编码：100142

营销中心电话：010-88191537　北京财经书店电话：64033436　84041336

北京中兴印刷有限公司印刷　各地新华书店经销

787×1092 毫米　16 开　15.5 印张　374 000 字

2015 年 5 月第 1 版　2023 年 8 月北京第 4 次印刷

定价：36.00 元

ISBN 978－7－5095－5850－8/F・4727

（图书出现印装问题，本社负责调换）

本社质量投诉电话：010－88190744

打击盗版举报热线：010-88191661、QQ：2242791300

编写 说明

本书是“十二五”职业教育国家规划教材、财政部规划教材，经全国职业教育教材审定委员会审定。

进入21世纪以来，我国积极融入贸易全球化进程，对外贸易迅猛发展，目前已成为世界第一出口大国。随着对外贸易的快速发展，外贸分工越来越细化，在整个对外贸易业务中单证工作已成为外贸企业的关键环节。外贸单证操作技能也是外贸人员必须具备的基本技能。为了使中等职业教育能够培养出高素质的制单专门人才，满足外贸企业对单证员的需求，我们根据外贸企业的工作要求，编写了本教材。

本书在编写过程中，通过项目导向，任务引领，以一笔信用证为付款方式的出口贸易合同履行为主线，根据实际业务步骤设计了四个项目，每一个项目又设不同的任务，学生每完成一个任务就学会了一项技能，力求体现职业教育特色，加强实践技能教学，突出学生动手能力的培养，保证职业教育符合实际工作岗位的需要。

本教材在编写过程中主要突出以下几个特点：

1. 采用项目教学，充分体现工学结合。教材通过“项目情境”、“英文储备”、“工作认知”、“工作指导”、“工作演练”、“工作评价”和“项目实训”等环节循序渐进，让学生以职业人身份进行学习，突出了学生的主体地位，让学生在做中学，教师在做中教。

2. 直观性和趣味性强。在相关抽象的理论内容中插入图片、表格、流程图，增强了教材的直观性和趣味性，加大了可操作性。

3. 文字精练、深入浅出、简单易学，适应当前中等职业学校学生的学习特点。

4. 采用大量实际工作案例，体现了教学过程的实践性和职业性。教材中贯穿了各种不同类型的实际工作案例，极大方便了课堂讲授和学生实训，教学资料丰富且符合工作要求。

本教材由青岛外事服务职业学校高级教师张云任主编，王真、刘阳任副主编。参加本书编写的人员有：王真（项目一、二）、刘阳（项目五），张云（项目四），孟静（导论、项目三的运输单据），王海燕（项目三的保险单据），其中山东省食品进出口公司国际结算部中心主任王海燕提供了大量单据资料。全书由张云、王真总纂、定稿。

本课程为72学时，各学校可根据学生的实际情况酌情安排。学时分配见下表（仅供参考）。

学时分配建议

课程内容	学时数		
	合计	讲授	实训
导论　认识外贸单证	2	2	0
项目一　制单依据	10	6	4
项目二　结汇单据	20	10	10
项目三　运输单据和保险单据	14	8	6
项目四　通关单据	14	8	6
项目五　综合练习	12	0	12
合　　计	72	34	38

本书为用书学校任课老师提供了课后练习答案和电子课件，如有需要，请登录中国财经教育网（http：//cjjc. cfeph. cn 或 www. zgcjjy. com）下载。

本书可作为中等职业学校国际商务专业及其他相关专业的教材，同时还可作为外贸行业单证岗位培训和自学用书。

本书在编写过程中，得到了有关外贸公司领导和专家的大力支持与帮助，参阅了有关论著与资料，编者在此深表衷心感谢。

限于编者水平，书中错误在所难免，敬请读者及有关专家批评指正！

编　者
2015年3月

目 录

情境导入

张丽是一名国际商务专业的学生，经学校招生就业处介绍，进入青岛海富贸易有限公司进行一年的顶岗实习，由资深业务员李华指导她的工作。

报到的第一天，师傅李华带着张丽参观了公司的进出口业务部、单证部、储运部、报关报检部等部门，李华对每个业务部门的工作进行了简单的介绍。张丽的实习岗位是单证部的单证员，师傅告诉她单证员的工作贯穿于进出口贸易业务的全过程，需要从业者具备扎实的进出口业务专业知识、熟练的职业技能，在制单业务中务必做到"正确、完整、及时、简明、整洁"。听完师傅的介绍后，张丽深感单证员工作的重要，并充满了信心。

导　论
认识外贸单证

一、外贸单证的含义

外贸单证（Foreign Trade Document）是指国际贸易中处理的各种文件和证明，反映在进出口业务中是指国际贸易中的单据（包括商业发票、装箱单、产地证、保险单、检验检疫证书、报关单、进出口许可证、提单、装船通知、汇票、受益人证书等）和信用证。

在国际贸易业务中，买卖双方凭借进出口业务中的各种单据来相应处理货物的发运、保险、商检、通关和提货、支付等手续。因此，狭义的单证指单据和信用证，广义的则指各种文件和证明。

二、外贸单证的种类

国际贸易中涉及的单证很多，而且每一笔交易所需要的单证也不尽相同，但总的来说，可以分为以下几类：

（一）根据贸易双方的工作责任划分

（1）进口单证：进口地企业及有关部门涉及的单证，如进口许可证、合同、信用证、进口货物报关单等。

（2）出口单证：出口地企业及有关部门涉及的单证，如出口许可证、出口货物报关单、商业发票、包装单据、保险单据、合同、信用证、汇票、运输单据、装船通知等。

（二）根据单证的用途划分

（1）资金单据：汇票、支票、本票等用以取得款项的凭证。

（2）商业单据：商业发票、包装单据。

（3）货运单据：各种运输方式单据的统称，如海运提单、航空运单、铁路运单、邮政收据等。

（4）保险单据：保险公司出具的保险单、保险凭证。

（5）官方单据：官方机构出具的单据和证明，如许可证、原产地证明、品质证书、卫生证等。

（6）附属单据：寄单证明、寄样证明、装运通知等。

三、外贸单证的作用

（一）单证是国际结算的基本工具

国际贸易中的商品买卖，在实际业务中主要表现为单据的交换。卖方提交单据，代表交付货物，买方付款赎取单据，代表买到货物。在国际贸易结算中，无论采取何种支付方式，买卖双方都要发生单据的交接。

资料卡

在国际结算的三种主要方式中，信用证以银行信用作为保证付款的支付方式长期以来一直处于主导地位，我国出口企业的使用率高达50%～60%。国际商会《跟单信用证统一惯例》第五条“单据与货物、服务或履约行为”规定：银行处理的是单据，而不是单据可能涉及的货物、服务或履约行为；第十四条“单据审核标准”规定：按指定行事的指定银行、保兑行（如有的话）及开证行须审核交单，并仅基于单据本身确定其是否在表面上构成相符交单。

与此同时，国际贸易中货物的单据化为货物买卖时货权的过渡与转移带来了便利。因此，现代贸易又称为单据买卖的贸易。

（二）单证是履行合同的必要手段

在国际贸易中，买卖双方相隔遥远，在大多数情况下，货物与货款的对流并非直接进行，而必须通过单证作为交换的手段。在出口贸易合同履行过程中的单证，一般可以分为两类：一类具有商品属性，代表商品；另一类具有货币属性，它们有的直接代表货币，有的为货币的支付做出承诺或做出有条件的保证等。每种单据都有其特定的功能。它们的签发、组合、流转和应用反映了合同履行的进程，也反映了买卖双方权责的产生、转移和终止。由此可见，单据是履行合同的必要手段。

（三）单证工作是出口企业经营管理的重要环节

单证工作贯穿于合同履行的全过程，在合同履行的不同阶段都会有相应的单证出具、组合和流通。合同的内容、信用证条款、货源安排、检验检疫、租船订舱、报关、交单议付等出口业务管理问题，都集中在单证上反映出来。单证工作还涉及业务工作管理中很多具体的问题，因此出口企业必须认真及时处理单据流通过程中出现的各种问题，以保证及时足额地收汇。

（四）单证工作是政策性很强的涉外工作

外贸单证工作是一项政策性很强的涉外工作，体现着平等互利和按国际惯例办事的政策精神。出口单证为涉外商务文件，必然体现着国家的对外政策，因此必须严格按照国家有关外贸的法规和制度办理。例如，进出口许可证关系到国家对某些进出口商品的计划管理，甚至还会涉及两国之间的贸易协定。出口单证既是收汇的依据，当发生贸易纠纷时，又是处理争议、解决索赔的依据和法律文件。

四、缮制单证的基本要求

单证工作分为审证、制单、审单、交单与归档五个环节。总要求是“四个一致”，即单单一致、单证一致、单同一致、单货一致。单单一致、单证一致是信用证业务最基本、最重要的要求，是卖方安全收汇的保障，但在实际业务中卖方还必须做到单据与所交的货物一致以及单据与货物买卖合同一致。

（一）审证

在收到信用证后，即着手审证。通知行审核信用证时重点审核开证行的资信状况、信用证的密押情况及偿付条款等；出口企业主要审核信用证条款是否与合同相符，如有不符或不能接受的条款需要及时提出，要求对方修改。

（二）制单

制作单证原则上应做到“正确、完整、及时、简明、整洁”。

1. 正确

正确是出口单证工作的前提和核心，是安全收汇的保证。正确包括两个方面的内容：一方面要求各种单据必须做到单证相符、单单相符、单货一致；另一方面，要求各种单据必须符合有关国际惯例和进出口国家有关法律法规。

2. 完整

提交的单据必须完整，它是银行审核的重要部分，一般包括三个方面的内容：

（1）单据的内容完整。任何单证都有其特定的作用，而这些作用有时通过其特定的格式、项目、内容、文字、签章等表现出来。如果格式不当、项目漏填、内容不完整、文字不全、签章遗漏，就不能构成一份有效的文件，也就不能被银行接受。

（2）单据的种类完整。信用证中所要求办理的各种单据必须齐备，不能遗漏，如有遗漏银行肯定会拒付。

（3）单据的份数完整。信用证中会明确规定提交的单据以及单据的数量，提交时应严格按照要求提供相应份数的正本或副本。

3. 及时

及时是指进出口单证工作时间性很强，必须掌握装运期、交单期及信用证的有效期等，做到及时出单。

4. 简明

单证内容应按照信用证的规定和国际贸易惯例填制，力求简明。这样不仅可以减少工作量，提高工作效率，而且有利于提高单证的质量和减少单证的差错。

5. 整洁

单据的布局要美观、大方，其格式的设计和缮制应力求标准化和规范化。如果说正确和完整是单证的内在质量，那么整洁则是单证的外观质量。单证是否整洁，不但反映出制单人的业务熟练程度和工作态度，而且还会直接影响出单的效果。

（三）审单

全套单据缮制完后应先预审。一般以发票为中心，以信用证为依据，严格仔细审核，做到单证、单同、单单一致。

（四）交单

交单是议付与结汇的基础，一个企业只有按时交单才能实现顺利结汇的目的。预审无误后，应严格按信用证或合同规定的期限及时交单，防止逾期交单，影响结汇。

（五）归档

进出口单证是涉外的单据文件，交单后还可能发生退单、拒付、索赔与仲裁，因此应保存一份完整的副本归档，做好索引，以备查阅。这也是单证工作中重要的一环。

五、出口业务单据流程图（见图1）

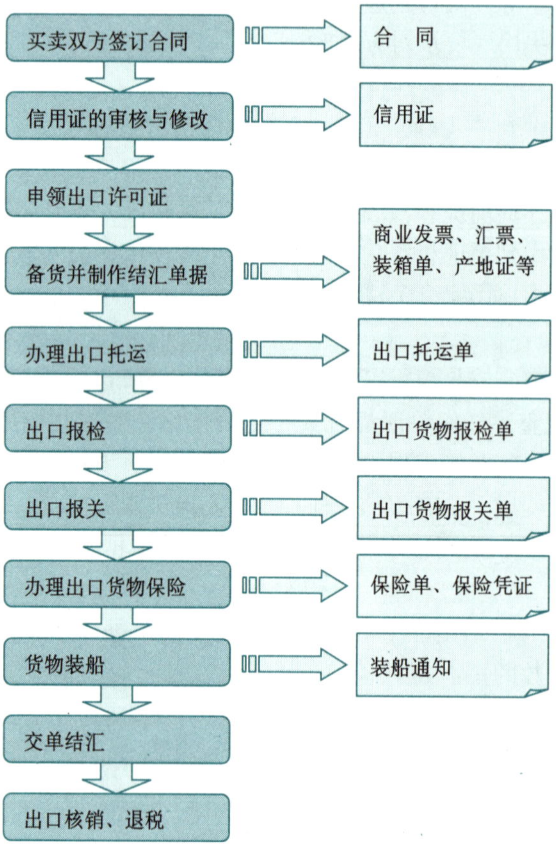

图1　国际贸易出口业务基本流程

项目一

制　单　依　据

项目介绍

在国际贸易中，买卖双方通过交易磋商，最终达成交易，签订合同。然后根据外贸合同约定的条款履行合同，其中可以选取汇付、托收或信用证方式来支付货款。本书主要以信用证为例讲解单据的制作。

学习目标

知识目标

- □ 熟悉合同的形式和基本构成。
- □ 熟悉信用证的定义、特点、种类及流程。
- □ 掌握合同和信用证的主要条款。

能力目标

- □ 能够根据买卖双方的交易磋商内容，制作外贸合同。
- □ 能够根据合同条款的信息，审核信用证，找出问题条款并提出修改意见。

德育目标

培养学生一丝不苟的工作作风和团结协作的职业守则。

项目情境

张丽实习的青岛海富贸易有限公司是一家主要经营食品进出口的国际贸易公司，与荷兰的 FUTURO 公司有着长期的业务合作关系。现在，荷兰 FUTURO 公司需进口一批食品青岛春卷，2013 年 3 月 27 日来函与青岛海富贸易有限公司进行磋商，双方意见达成一致后，师傅李华起草了这批食品的销售合同，并让张丽于 4 月 12 日传真给了荷兰 FUTURO 公司，4 月 12 日收到了对方签好的合同，一个月后收到了对方银行开来的信用证。师傅李华要求张丽认真阅读合同和信用证的相关条款，根据合同审核并修改对方开来的信用证。

英文储备

Contract	合同
Sales confirmation (S/C)	销售
Commodity	商品，货物
Quantity	数量
Unit price	单价
Amount	金额
Packing	包装
Shipping marks	唛头
Insurance	保险
Letter of credit (L/C)	信用证
Issuing bank	开证行
Beneficiary	受益人
Applicant	开证申请人
Port of loading	装运港
Port of discharge	卸货港
Description of goods	货物描述

任务分解

为了完成制单依据项目的学习，具体可分解为以下两个任务：

(1) 缮制外贸合同。

(2) 审核、修改信用证。

任务一 认知外贸合同

【工作认知】

一、认知合同的基本内容

在国际贸易的交易磋商过程中，当一方的发盘被另一方接受后，贸易合同即告成立，买卖双方就建立了合同关系。

（一）合同的形式

合同的形式一般情况下有口头合同和书面合同两种。在国际货物买卖中，我国不允许书面形式以外的合同形式。

在进出口贸易中，合同的书面形式主要包括：销售合同（Sales Contract）、销售确认书（Sales Confirmation）、协议（Agreement）、订单（Order）、备忘录（Memorandum）和意向书（Letter of Intent）等。

（二）合同的基本构成

合同一般由三部分构成，即约首、本文、约尾。

1. 约首

合同的约首是合同的序言部分，通常包括合同的名称、编号、日期、地点和买卖双方的名称、地址、电话、传真等。

2. 本文

合同的本文是合同的主体部分，通常包括合同的各项条款：品名、品质、数量、价格、包装、交货时间、装运港和目的港、支付方式、保险、检验检疫、索赔、仲裁和不可抗力条款等。

3. 约尾

合同的约尾是合同的结尾部分，通常包括合同签订的时间和地点、买卖双方签字及合同适用的法律惯例等。

（三）合同样章

合同样章如下所示。

销 售 合 同

SALES CONTRACT

Sellers: ________________	Contract No.: ________________
Address: ________________	Date: ________________
Buyers: ________________	Signed at: ________________
Address: ________________	Telex: ________________

Fax: ______________________

This Sales Contract is made by and/between the Sellers and the Buyers, whereby the Sellers agree to sell and the Buyers agree to buy the under – mentioned goods according to the terms and conditions stipulated below:

(1) 货号、品名及规格 NAME OF COMMODITY AND SPECIFICATIONS	(2) 数量 QUANTITY	(3) 单价 UNIT PRICE	(4) 金额 AMOUNT
% more or less both in amount and quantity allowed			
	Total Amount		

(5) Packing: to be packed in __________ suitable for transportation.

(6) Delivery from __________ to __________.

(7) Shipping Marks: to be supplied by the seller.

(8) Latest Shipment Date: __________.

Transshipment __________ and partial shipment __________.

(9) Terms of Payment: By 100% Irrevocable Letter of Credit payable at __________ sight in favor of the Sellers to be opened and to reach China before __________ and to remain valid for negotiation in China until __________ days after the foresaid Time of Shipment.

(10) Insurance: To be effected by Sellers for 110% of full invoice value against __________ and __________ as per __________.

(11) Quality/Quantity Discrepancy and Claim:

In case the quality and/or quantity/weight are found by the Buyers to be not in conformity with the Contract after arrival of the goods at the port of destination, the Buyers may lodge claim with the Sellers supported by survey report issued by an inspection organization agreed upon by both parties, with the exception, however, of those claims for which the insurance company and or the shipping company are to be held responsible, claim for quality discrepancy should be filed by the Buyers within __________ days after arrival of the goods at the port of destination. The Sellers shall, within __________ days after receipt of the notification of the claim, send reply to the Buyers.

(12) Force Majeure: In case of Force Majeure, the Sellers shall not be held responsible for late delivery or non – delivery of the goods but shall notify the Buyers by cable. The Sellers shall deliver to the Buyers by registered mail, if so requested by the Buyers, a certificate issued by the China Council for the Promotion of International Trade or/and competent authorities.

(13) Arbitration: All dispute arising from the execution of or in connectionwith this contract shall be settled amicably by negotiation. In case no settlement can be reached through negotiation the case shall then be submitted to China International Economic & Trade Arbitration Commission. In Qingdao (or in Beijing) for arbitration in act with it's sure of procedures. The arbitral award is

final and binding upon both parties for setting the Dispute. The fee for arbitration shall be borne by the losing party unless otherwise awarded.

(14) Contract shall take effect after countersign on fax by two parties' authorized representatives.

SELLERS: BUYERS:

二、认知合同的主要条款

销售合同样章的主要条款如下：

（一）品名条款

品名（Commodity Name）条款一般列明买卖双方成交商品的名称即可。

注意事项：

（1）具体明确，切实反映商品的情况，如可进一步列明商品的品种、规格、型号、等级或商标等。

（2）尽可能使用国际上通用的名称。

（二）品质条款

品质（Quality Of Goods），是商品的内在素质（包括物理、化学、生物的构造、成分和性能）和外观形态的综合。

品质条款的基本内容是通过一定的方法对商品品质进行描述。表示品质的方法主要分为两大类：以实物表示商品的品质和以说明表示商品品质。前者包括看货买卖和凭样品买卖；后者包括凭规格、凭等级、凭标准、凭说明书及图样、凭商标或牌号、凭产地名称买卖。

注意事项：

（1）对于某些品质不稳定或易出现误差的商品可规定一定的品质机动幅度或品质公差。

（2）视商品特性采用不同的表示商品品质的方法，凡能用一种方法表示的不宜用两种或两种以上的方法。

【例 1-1-1】

东北大米，良好平均品质，杂质最高 0.2%，碎粒最高 18%，水分最高 10%。

Dongbei Rice, F. A. Q., Admixture (Max.) 0.2%, Broken Grains (Max.) 18%, Moisture (Max.) 10%.

（三）数量条款

数量（Quantity of Goods），是指以一定的度量衡单位表示商品的重量、数量、长度、面积、体积、容积等。

数量条款是买卖双方交接货物和处理争议的根据，在买卖合同的数量条款中，一般需订明数量和计量单位，以重量计量的，还须明确计量的方法。

注意事项：

（1）必须正确掌握进出口商品的数量。

（2）合理地规定数量机动幅度，即溢短装条款。

【例 1-1-2】

中国大豆，5000 公吨，允许 5% 溢短装，由卖方决定。

Chinese Soybean, 5000 M/T, 5% more or less allowed, at seller's option.

资料卡

《联合国国际货物销售合同公约》规定，按约定的数量交付货物是卖方的一项基本义务，如卖方交货数量大于约定的数量，买方可以拒收多交的部分，也可以收取多交部分中的一部分或全部，但应按合同价格付款。如卖方交货数量少于约定的数量，卖方应在规定的交货期届满前补交，但不得使买方遭受不合理的不便或承担不合理的开支，即使如此，买方也有保留要求损害赔偿的权利。

（四）价格条款

价格条款一般包括商品单价（Unit Price）和总值（Total Amount）两部分。单价包括计价货币、单位价格金额、计价单位和贸易术语。总值是单价和数量的乘积。

签订价格条款应注意：如果合同价格中包含支付给中间商的佣金（Commission），则应在条款中表明。

【例 1-1-3】

每纸箱 750 美元，成本加运费、保险费运至伦敦，含 2% 的佣金。

USD750.00 PER CARTON, CIF C2 LONDON.

资料卡

《2010 年国际贸易术语解释通则》（INCOTERMS® 2010），是国际商会（ICC）根据国际货物贸易的发展，对 2000 通则的修订，于 2011 年 1 月 1 日开始全球实施（见表 1-1-1）。

表 1-1-1

国际代码	中英文名称	运输	保险	运输方式
EXW	Ex Works (named place of delivery) 工厂交货（指定交货地点）	买方	买方	任何
FAS	Free Alongside Ship (named port of shipment) 船边交货（指定装运港）	买方	买方	水运
FOB	Free on Board (named port of shipment) 船上交货（指定装运港）	买方	买方	水运
FCA	Free Carrier (named place of delivery) 货交承运人（指定交货地点）	买方	买方	任何
CFR	Cost and Freight (named port of destination) 成本加运费（指定目的港）	卖方	买方	水运
CPT	Carriage Paid To (insert named place of destination) 运费付至（指定目的地）	卖方	买方	任何
CIF	Cost Insurance and Freight (named port of destination) 成本加保险费、运费（指定目的港）	卖方	卖方	水运

续表

国际代码	中英文名称	运　输	保　险	运输方式
CIP	Carriage and Insurance Paid To（named place of destination）运费保险费付至（指定目的地）	卖方	卖方	任何
DAP	Delivered At Place（named place of destination）目的地交货（指定目的地）	卖方	卖方	任何
DAT	Delivered At Terminal（named terminal at port or place of destination）运输终端交货（指定港口或目的地的运输终端）	卖方	卖方	任何
DDP	Delivered Duty Paid（named place of destination）完税后交货（指定目的地）	卖方	卖方	任何

（五）包装条款

包装（Packing）是货物说明中的重要内容之一。包装条款一般包括包装方式、包装材料、包装规格以及包装标志、包装费用的负担等内容。

【例 1－1－4】

货物包装应为适合海运出口的标准纸箱，1 件装 1 个塑料包，20 包装 1 个纸箱。包装费用由卖方承担。唛头由卖方提供。

Packing should be seaworthy exportable standard carton. One piece in a plastic bag, 10 bags in a carton. The cost of packing is for seller's account. Shipping Marks are supplied by the seller.

资料卡

常见包装种类

纸箱——Carton　　木箱——Wooden case
桶——Drum　　袋——Bag
包——Bale　　捆——Bundle
卷——Coil/Roll　　托盘——Pallet

包装标志包括运输标志、指示性标志和警告性标志。其中运输标志即唛头（Shipping Marks），一般需要在包装条款中列明，有利于货物顺利运输至目的地，也方便进口方清点货物。

根据国际标准化组织的推荐，运输标志（唛头）一般由四部分构成：收货人或买方名称的英文缩写字母或简称；参考号；目的港名称；货物件数。

【例 1－1－5】

F. I. C——进口商公司缩写
MSR719——参考号（合同号）
ROTTERDAM——目的港
NO. 1－2450——货物总包装数

（六）装运条款

装运（Shipment）条款一般包括装运期、装运港（地）、目的港（地）、运输方式、是否允许分批装运和转运等。

【例1-1-6】

货物通过海运从中国青岛港运至日本名古屋，最迟装运期2013年5月4日，不允许分批装运和转运。

Shipment from Shanghai China to Nagoya Japan by sea at latest May 4, 2013. Partial shipment and transshipment are not allowed.

（七）支付条款

支付（Payment）条款一般包括支付工具、支付方式、支付时间和地点等。

国际贸易中，主要的支付工具包括三种：汇票（Bill of Exchange）、本票（Promissory note）、支票（Cheque）。其中最常用的金融票据是汇票。

国际贸易货款的支付方式也包括三种：汇付（Remittance）、托收（Collection）、信用证（Letter of Credit）。

1. 汇付

使用汇付支付方式，应在条款中列明是电汇（T/T）、信汇（M/T）还是票汇（D/D）。

2. 托收

使用托收支付方式，应在条款中列明是跟单托收还是光票托收。如果跟单托收条件下，是付款交单（D/P）还是承兑交单（D/A）。

3. 信用证

使用信用证支付方式，应在条款中列明信用证种类、开证行、开证时间、有效期及地点等。

【例1-1-7】

付款条件：买方应通过卖方可接受的银行（中国银行青岛分行）向卖方开出以卖方为受益人的不可撤销即期信用证。信用证必须在装船日前30天开到卖方，信用证有效期至装运日期后21天在中国到期。

Terms of payment: The buyer shall open through a bank acceptable to the seller a irrevocable Letter of Credit payable at sight in favor of the seller to reach Bank of China Qingdao branch 30 days before the day of shipment, valid for negotiation in China until the 21st day after the date of shipment.

（八）保险条款

保险（Insurance）条款可以根据贸易术语来确定：

（1）使用FOB/FCA/CFR/CPT术语出口时，由买方负责办理保险。

【例1-1-8】

保险由买方负责。

Insurance: To be covered by the buyers.

(2) 使用CIF/CIP术语出口时，由卖方负责办理保险，合同需写明投保险别、投保金额。

【例1-1-9】

保险条款：卖方按发票金额的110%投保CIC条款的一切险和战争险。

Insurance: To be covered by sellers for 110% of full invoice value covering All Risks and War Risks as per CIC clause.

(九) 其他条款

其他条款一般包括检验 (inspection)、索赔 (claim)、不可抗力 (force majeure)、仲裁 (arbitration) 条款等。

【工作指导】

张丽的师傅李华根据青岛海富贸易有限公司与荷兰FUTURO公司交易磋商的往来函电和买卖双方的要求，起草了青岛春卷的出口销售合同。

资料：

(1) 买方：FUTURO INDUSTRIAL CO. LTD.,
ROTTERDAM NETHERLANDS
业务代表：JOHN SMITH

(2) 卖方：QINGDAO HAIFU TRADING CO. LTD.,
NO. 1HONGKONG ROAD, QINGDAO CHINA
业务代表：李华

(3) 合同号：MSR719
合同日期：2013年4月12日

(4) 货物名称：QINGDAO SPRING ROLLS 青岛春卷
数量：2450纸箱
单价：每纸箱15.50美元 CIF ROTTERDAM

(5) 运输方式：通过海运从中国青岛运至荷兰鹿特丹，不迟于2013年7月10日。

(6) 包装：20克/个，50个/盒，9盒/纸箱

(7) 唛头：F. I. C.
MSR719
ROTTERDAM
NO. 1-2450

(8) 付款方式：远期信用证，提单日期后60天付款。

(9) 保险：由卖方按发票金额的110%投保协会货物中的A险和战争条款，根据1982年1月1日的协会货物保险条款办理。

师傅李华起草的销售合同如下：

销 售 合 同
SALES CONTRACT

Sellers：QINGDAO HAIFU TRADING CO. LTD.　　Contract No.：MSR719
Address：NO. 1 HONGKONG ROAD，QINGDAO CHINA　　Date：APR. 12，2013
Buyers：FUTURO INDUSTRIAL CO. LTD.　　Signed at：QINGDAO，CHINA
Address：ROTTERDAM NETHERLANDS　　Telex：86－0532－85896210
Fax：86－0532－85896211

This Sales Contract is made by and between the Sellers and the Buyers，whereby the Sellers agree to sell and the Buyers agree to buy the under－mentioned goods according to the terms and conditions stipulated below：

（1）货号、品名及规格 NAME OF COMMODITY AND SPECIFICATIONS	（2）数量 QUANTITY	（3）单价 UNIT PRICE	（4）金额 AMOUNT
QINGDAO SPRING ROLLS 20G PER PC，50PCS IN A BOX，9 BOXES IN A CARTON 5% more or less both in amount and quantity allowed	2450CARTONS	CIF ROTTERDAM USD15. 50PER CTN	USD37975. 00
	Total Amount		USD37975. 00

（5）Packing：to be packed in CARTONS suitable for transportation.

（6）Delivery from QINGDAO CHINA to ROTTERDAM，NETHERLANDS

（7）Shipping Marks：to be supplied by the seller.

（8）Latest Shipment Date：JUL. 10，2013.

Transshipment ALLOWED and partial shipment ALLOWED

（9）Terms of Payment：By 100% Irrevocable Letter of Credit payable at 60 DAYS AFTER B/L SHIPMENT DATE sight in favor of the Sellers to be opened and to reach China before JUN. 10，2013 and to remain valid for negotiation in China until 21 days after the foresaid Time of Shipment.

（10）Insurance：To be effected by Sellers for 110% of full invoice value against ICC（A）and ICC WAR CLAUSE as per INSTITUTE CARGO CLAUSE DATED 1/1/1982.

（11）Quality/Quantity Discrepancy and Claim：

In case the quality and/or quantity/weight are found by the Buyers to be not in conformity with the Contract after arrival of the goods at the port of destination，the Buyers may lodge claim with the Sellers supported by survey report issued by an inspection organization agreed upon by both parties，with the exception，however，of those claims for which the insurance company and or the shipping company are to be held responsible，claim for quality discrepancy should be filed by the Buyers within 60 days after arrival of the goods at the port of destination. The Sellers shall，within 30 days after receipt of the notification of the claim，send reply to the Buyers.

（12）Force Majeure：In case of Force Majeure，the Sellers shall not be held responsible for late delivery or non - delivery of the goods but shall notify the Buyers by cable. The Sellers shall deliver to the Buyers by registered mail, if so requested by the Buyers, a certificate issued by the China Council for the Promotion of International Trade or/and competent authorities.

(13) Arbitration: All dispute arising from the execution of or in connection with this contract shall be settled amicably by negotiation. In case no settlement can be reached through negotiation the case shall then be submitted to China International Economic & Trade Arbitration Commission. In Qingdao (or in Beijing) for arbitration in act with it's sure of procedures. The arbitral award is final and binding upon both parties for setting the Dispute. The fee for arbitration shall be borne by the losing party unless otherwise awarded.

(14) Contract shall take effect after countersign on fax by two parties' authorized representatives.

SELLERS:	BUYERS:
QINGDAO HAIFU TRADING CO. LTD.,	FUTURO INDUSTRIAL CO. LTD.,
LIHUA	JOHN SMITH
APR. 12, 2013	APR. 12, 2013

【工作演练】

张丽在师傅李华的指导下，已经基本掌握了缮制外贸合同的基本技能。下面请你和张丽一起根据相关资料起草一份出口销售合同。

资料1：

(1) 买方：KINGDOM CO. LTD.,
　　NO. 12 QUEEN ROAD SEOUL KOREA
　　业务代表：DAVID LI

(2) 卖方：QINGDAO HAIFU TRADING CO. LTD.,
　　NO. 1 HONGKONG ROAD, QINGDAO CHINA
　　业务代表：李华

(3) 合同号：CW12031
　　合同日期：2013 年 1 月 5 日

(4) 货物名称：DRIED CHINESE WOLFBERRY 脱水中国枸杞
　　商品编码：12119031
　　型号：160 - 180 PCS/KG　　190 - 210 PCS/KG
　　数量：1.3MTS　　1.5MTS
　　单价：USD18500.00/MT FOB QINGDAO
　　USD17600.00/MT FOB QINGDAO

(5) 运输方式：通过海运从中国青岛运至韩国釜山，不迟于 2013 年 3 月 30 日。

(6) 包装：20 千克/ 纸箱

（7）唛头：K. C. L.
CW12031
BUSAN
NO. 1－140

（8）付款方式：即期信用证

资料2：销售合同

销售合同书
SALES CONTRACT

卖方：
The Seller:
买方：
The buyer:

编号 No:
日期 Date:
签订地 Signed at

买卖双方同意成交下列产品，订立条款如下：

The undersigned Seller and Buyer have agreed to conclude the following transaction on terms and conditions as specified below:

（1）货号、货物名称、规格 ARTICLE NUMBER, NAME OF COMMODITY AND SPECIFICATION	（2）数量 QUANTITY	（3）单价 UNIT PRICE	（4）总值 TOTAL VALUE
TTL:			
TOTAL AMOUNT:			

（5）装运时间、装运港和目的港
TIME OF SHIPMENT: ________________
SHIPMENT FROM ____________ TO ________________ BY SEA.

（6）包装、装运标识：
PACKING
SHIPPING MARKS:

（7）溢短装条款：TOLERENCE:
数量及总值均有____%的增减，由卖方决定。
With ____% more or less both in amount and quantity allowed at Seller's option.

（8）付款条件：
Payment by 100% Irrevocable Letter of Credit payable at _____ sight in favor of the Sellers to be opened and to reach China before ____ and to remain valid for negotiation in China until ____ days after the foresaid Time of Shipment.

(9) 保险：INSURANCE：

□由卖方按发票金额的 ______ 保一切险及战争险。买方如要求增加保额或保险范围，须承担因此增加的保险费。

To be covered by the Seller for ______ of the invoice value against All Risks and War Risks. If additional insurance amount or coverage is required, the additional premium is to be borne by the Buyer.

□由买方自理 To be effected by the Buyer.

(10) 数量/品质异议，如出现数量或品质不符，买方须分别于货物抵港后____天内提出索赔，品质索赔买方需提供国际公证机构或其他代表性或代理签发的检验证书。检验费及证书费由买方承担。QUANTITY/QUALITY DISCREPANCY：In case of quantity and quality discrepancy, the claim shall be issued by the Buyer within ____ days respectively after the arrival of the goods at port of destination. In case of quality discrepancy the inspection certificate issued by an international surveyor or its agent (or representative) is requested together with the claim by the buyer. All charges and costs of such inspection and certificate shall be borne by the Buyer.

(11) 凡因执行本合同所发生的或与本合同有关的一切争议，应由双方通过友好协商解决，如果协商不能解决，应提交中国国际经济贸易仲裁委员会进行仲裁，仲裁裁决是终局的，对双方都有约束力。All disputes arising from the execution or in connection with this Sales Contract shall be settled amicably through friendly negotiation. In case no settlement can be reached through negotiation, the case shall be submitted China International Economic and Trade Arbitration Commission for arbitration. The arbitral award is final and binding upon both parties.

(12) 备注：

Remarks：

买方（签章）	卖方（签章）
Buyer's Signature	Seller's Signature

提示：

(1) 认真填写数量，单价，准确计算货物金额。

(2) 不要遗漏重要信息，注意单词拼写正确。

(3) 认真审核合同条款，确认无误后方可签字。

【工作评价】

1. 评价标准

销 售 合 同 书

SALES CONTRACT

卖方：QINGDAO HAIFU TRADING CO. LTD.,	编号 No：CW12031
NO. 1 HONGKONG ROAD, QINGDAO CHINA	日期 Date：JAN. 5, 2013
买方：KINGDOM CO. LTD.,	签订地 Signed at:
The buyer：NO. 12 QUEEN ROAD SEOUL KOREA	QINGDAO, CHINA

买卖双方同意成交下列产品，订立条款如下：The undersigned Seller and Buyer have agreed to conclude the following transaction on terms and conditions as specified below：

（1）货号、货物名称、规格 ARTICLE NUMBER，NAME OF COMMODITY AND SPECIFICATION	（2）数量 QUANTITY	（3）单价 UNIT PRICE	（4）总值 TOTAL VALUE
DRIED CHINESE WOLFBERRY 160－180 PCS/KG 190－210 PCS/KG	 1. 3MTS 1. 5MTS	FOB QINGDAO USD18500. 00/MT USD17600. 00/MT	 USD24050. 00 USD26400. 00
TTL：	2. 8MTS		USD50450. 00
TOTAL AMOUNT：SAY U. S. DOLLARS FIFTY THOUSAND FOUR HUNDRED AND FIFTY ONLY.			

（5）装运时间、装运港和目的港

LATEST DATE OF SHIPMENT：MAR. 30，2013

SHIPMENT FROM QINGDAO CHINA TO BUSAN KOREA BY SEA.

（6）包装、装运标识：

PACKING：20KGS/ CARTON

SHIPPING MARK：K. C. L.
CW12031
BUSAN
NO. 1－140

（7）溢短装条款：TOLERENCE：

数量及总值均有 5 %的增减，由卖方决定。

With 5 % more or less both in amount and quantity allowed at Seller's option.

（8）付款条件：

Payment by 100% Irrevocable Letter of Credit payable at / sight in favor of the Sellers to be opened and to reach China before THE END OF JAN. 2013 and to remain valid for negotiation in China until 21 days after the foresaid Time of Shipment.

（9）保险：INSURANCE：

□由卖方按发票金额的110%保一切险及战争险。买方如要求增加保额或保险范围，须承担因此增加的保险费。

To be covered by the Seller for 110% of the invoice value against All Risks and War Risks. If additional insurance amount or coverage is required，the additional premium is to be borne by the Buyer.

☑由买方自理 To be effected by the Buyer.

（10）数量/品质异议，如出现数量或品质不符，买方须分别于货物抵港后 60 天内提出索赔，品质索赔买方需提供国际公证机构或其他代表性或代理签发的检验证书。检验费及证书费由买方承担。QUANTITY/QUALITY DISCREPANCY：In case of quantity and quality discrepancy, the claim shall be issued by the Buyer within 60 days respectively after the arrival of the goods at port of destination. In case of quality discrepancy the inspection certificate issued by an international surveyor or its agent (or representative) is requested together with the claim by the buyer. All charges and costs of such inspection and certificate shall be borne by the Buyer.

(11) 凡因执行本合同所发生的或与本合同有关的一切争议，应由双方通过友好协商解决，如果协商不能解决，应提交中国国际经济贸易仲裁委员会进行仲裁，仲裁裁决是终局的，对双方都有约束力。All disputes arising from the execution or in connection with this Sales Contract shall be settled amicably through friendly negotiation. In case no settlement can be reached through negotiation, the case shall be submitted China International Economic and Trade Arbitration Commission for arbitration. The arbitral award is final and binding upon both parties.

(12) 备注：

Remarks:

买方（签章）	卖方（签章）
KINGDOM CO. LTD.,	QINGDAO HAIFU TRADING CO. LTD.,
Buyer's Signature	Seller's Signature
DAVID LI	**LIHUA**

2. 评价表（见表1-1-2）

表1-1-2

评价人 / 评价指标	自　评	互　评	师　评
独立完成情况（20分）			
格式规范性（20分）			
内容完整性、正确性（50分）			
内容简明性、整洁性（10分）			
合计总分			

任务二　开立、审核、修改信用证

【工作认知】

在进出口单证业务的汇付和托收支付方式下，单据流程简单，且单据制作要求相对较低。因此，本书将重点阐述信用证支付方式下单证的制作。

一、认知信用证的基本内容

（一）信用证的定义及特点

信用证（Letter of Credit，L/C）是指由银行（开证行）依照（申请人）的要求和指示或自己主动，在符合信用证条款的条件下，凭规定单据向第三者（受益人）或其指定方进行付款的书面文件。即信用证是一种银行开立的有条件的承诺付款的书面文件。

信用证的特点：

（1）信用证是一种银行信用。开证行处于第一付款人的地位。

（2）信用证是一种独立文件。信用证的开立以买卖合同为依据，但一经开出，就成为独立于买卖合同以外的另一种契约，不受买卖合同的约束。

（3）信用证业务是单据业务。信用证项下，实行凭单付款，只要“单证一致、单单一致”，开证行就承担付款或承兑的责任，银行处理的是单据而不是货物。

资料卡

信用证按其开立方式不同，可分为电开信用证和信开信用证。目前，前者更常用。

电开信用证，是指开证行以电子文本的形式开立信用证的有效文本，并用电信方式（电报、电传或 SWIFT 系统）传递给通知行的信用证。

SWIFT 是“环球同业银行金融电讯协会”的英文缩写，是一个国际银行同业间的国际合作组织，成立于 1973 年。目前全球大多数国家大多数银行已使用 SWIFT 系统。该系统支持通过安全、可靠、快捷、标准化、自动化的通讯业务，大大提高了银行的结算速度。目前信用证的格式主要采用 SWIFT 电文。

（二）信用证的种类（见表 1-2-1）

表 1-2-1　信用证的分类

划分依据	种类	定义
汇票是否附有货运单据	跟单信用证	凭跟单汇票或仅凭单据（如海运提单）付款的信用证
	光票信用证	凭不随附货运单据的光票付款的信用证
信用证的性质	不可撤销信用证	信用证一经开出，在有效期内，未经受益人及有关当事人的同意，开证行不能片面修改和撤销，只要受益人提供的单据符合信用证规定，开证行必须履行付款义务
	可撤销信用证	开证行不必征得受益人或有关当事人同意有权随时撤销的信用证，应在信用证上注明“可撤销”字样。 < <UCP600> >规定银行不可开立可撤销信用证
有无另一银行加以保证兑付	保兑信用证	开证行开出的信用证，由另一银行保证对符合信用证条款规定的单据履行付款义务。对信用证加以保兑的银行，称为保兑行
	不保兑信用证	开证行开出的信用证没有经另一家银行保兑

续表

划分依据	种　类	定　义
付款时间	即期信用证	开证行或付款行收到符合信用证条款的跟单汇票或装运单据后，立即履行付款义务的信用证
	远期信用证	开证行或付款行收到信用证的单据时，在规定期限内履行付款义务的信用证
受益人对信用证的权利可否转让	可转让信用证	开证行授权通知行在信用证的受益人（第一受益人）要求时，将信用证全部或部分转让给一个或数个受益人（第二受益人）使用的信用证。在信用证中要明确注明“可转让”（transferable），且只能转让一次
	不可转让信用证	受益人不能将信用证的权利转让给他人的信用证
其　他	循环信用证	信用证被全部或部分使用后，其金额又恢复到原金额，可再次使用，直至达到规定的次数或规定的总金额为止
	对开信用证	两张信用证申请人互以对方为受益人而开立的信用证
	对背信用证	受益人要求原证的通知行或其他银行以原证为基础，另开一张内容相似的新信用证

（三）信用证的当事人

（1）开证申请人（Applicant），是指向银行申请开立信用证的人，一般是进口方，即买卖合同的买方。

（2）开证行（Issuing Bank），是指接受开证申请人的申请，开立信用证的银行，一般是进口方所在地的银行。

（3）通知行（Advising Bank），是指受开证银行委托，将信用证转交给出口方的银行，一般是出口方所在地的银行。

（4）受益人（Beneficiary），是指信用证上所指定的有权使用该证的人，一般是出口方，即买卖合同的卖方。

（5）议付行（Negotiating Bank），是指愿意买入受益人交来的跟单汇票并垫付资金的银行。

（6）付款行（Paying Bank），是指信用证上指定的付款银行。一般是开证行。

（四）信用证的单据业务流程

信用证的单据业务流程如图 1－2－1 所示。

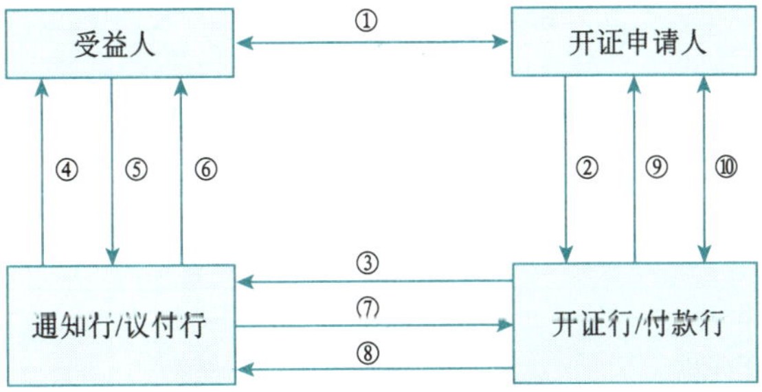

图 1－2－1　跟单信用证业务流程图

说明：

①买卖双方签订合同，约定信用证支付方式。

②买方填写开证申请书，向开证行申请开立信用证。

③开证行开出信用证，并电传给卖方所在地通知行。

④通知行核对，并通知受益人。

⑤受益人审证无误后发货，制作全套结汇单据，交单议付。

⑥议付行审单无误后，议付。

⑦议付行将全套结汇单据寄开证行或付款行索偿。

⑧开证行或付款行审单无误后，偿付货款。

⑨开证行通知开证申请人即买方付款赎单。

⑩买方验单无误后付款，开证行向买方交单，买方凭单提货。

二、认知信用证的主要条款

（一）信用证的基本内容

信用证的基本内容如表 1－2－2 所示。

表 1－2－2 信用证的基本内容

代 号	英文含义	中文解释
*27	SEQUENCE OF TOTAL	页 次
*40A	FORM OF DOCUMENTARY CREDIT	跟单信用证类别
*20	DOCUMENTARY CREDIT NUMBER	跟单信用证号码
31C	DATE OF ISSUE	开证日期
*31D	DATE AND PLACE OF EXPIRY	信用证有效期及有效地
51A	APPLICANT BANK	开证行
*50	APPLICANT	开证申请人
*59	BENEFICIARY	受益人
*32B	CURRENCY CODE AMOUNT	货币代号，金额
*41A	AVAILABLE WITH…	由……银行议付汇票收款人
42C	DRAFT AT	汇票付款期限
42A	DRAWEE	汇票付款人
43P	PARTIAL SHIPMENT	分批装运
43T	TRANSSHIPMENT	转 运
44E	PORT OF LOADING	装运港
44F	PORT OF DISCHARGE	目的港
44C	LATEST DATE OF SHIPMENT	最迟装运期
45A	DESCRIPTION GOODS AND/OR SERVICES	货物/服务描述
46A	DOCUMENTS REQUIRED	单据要求
47A	ADDITIONAL CONDITIONS	附加条件
71B	CHARGES	费 用
48	PERIOD FOR PRESENTATION	交单期限

续表

代 号	英文含义	中文解释
*49	CONFIRMATION INSTRUCTION	保兑指示
53A	REIMBURSEMENT BANK	偿付行
78	PAY / ACCOUNT / NEGOTIATION BANK	付款/议付行
57A	ADVISING BANK	通知行

（二）信用证的单据条款

1. 商业发票条款

+SIGNED COMMERCIAL INVOICE IN TRIPLICATE CERTIFYING MERCHANDISE COUNTRY OF ORIGIN AND SHOWING FREIGHT CHARGE.

已签字的商业发票一式三份，证明货物原产国并显示运费。

2. 提单条款

+FULL SET ORIGINAL CLEAN ON BOARD OCEAN BILLS OF LADING MADE OUT TO ORDER OF SHIPPER AND MARKED FREIGHT PREPAID AND NOTIFY APPLICANT AND ISSUING BANK.

全套正本清洁已装船海运提单，抬头填写凭托运人指示，注明运费预付，并通知开证申请人和开证行。

3. 装箱单条款

+PACKING LIST IN DUPLICATE MUST SHOW GROSS WEIGHT, NET WEIGHT AND MEASUREMENT PER CARTON SEPARATELY.

装箱单一式两份必须分别表明每纸箱的毛重、净重和尺码。

4. 保险单条款

+MARINE INSURANCE POLICY OR CERTIFICATE ENDORSED IN BLANK BY THE INSURED FOR AT LEAST 110% OF THE CIF VALUE COVERING ALL RISKS AS PER OCEAN MARINE CARGO CLAUSE (1/1/1981) OF PICC.

海运保险单或保险凭证由投保人空白背书，保险金额不少于 CIF 价值的 110%，投保中国人民保险公司海洋运输货物保险条款（1981 年 1 月 1 日）的一切险。

5. 产地证条款

+ORIGINAL CERTIFICATE OF ORIGIN SIGNED AND STAMPED BY CHAMBER OF COMMERCE.

正本一般原产地证由商会盖章签字。

6. 其他条款

+BENEFICIARY'S CERTIFICATE CERTIFYING THAT ONE SET OF COPIES OF SHIPPING DOCUMENTS HAS BEEN SENT TO APPLICANT WHTHIN 5 DAYS AFTER SHIPMENT.

受益人证明需要证明一套装运单据的副本已经在装运后 5 天内寄给了开证申请人。

+A COPY OF SHIPPING ADVICE INDICATING SHIPPING MARKS, INVOICE VALUE, BILL OF LADING NO., DATE OF SHIPMENT, NAME OF VESSEL, VOYAGE NUMBER AND ETA DATE AT THE PORT OF DESTINATION SENT TO APPLICANT WITHIN FIVE DAYS OF SHIPMENT.

装船通知的副本显示：唛头、发票价值、提单号、装运日期、船名航次号和预计到港日期，并在装运后五天内寄给开证申请人。

三、申请开立信用证

当进出口双方在贸易合同中确立以信用证方式结算后，进口方即可按贸易合同的规定向当地银行申请开立信用证，填写开证申请书（Application For Irrevocable Documentary Credit）。这样，进口商即成为开证申请人，开证申请书是银行开具信用证的依据。进口商填写信用证申请书，以书面的形式向开证行提出申请，银行按照开证申请书开立信用证后，在法律上就与进口商构成了开立信用证的权利与义务关系，两者之间的契约就是开证申请书。

买方按约定的时间开证，是卖方履行合同的前提条件。

（一）申请开立信用证的手续

（1）递交有关合同的副本及附件：进口商向银行申请开证时，要向银行递交进口合同的副本以及所需附件，如进口许可证、进口配额证、某些部门审批文件等。

（2）填写开证申请书：进口商根据银行规定的统一开证申请书格式填写。填写开证申请书，必须按合同条款的具体规定，写明信用证的各项要求，内容要明确、完整。

（3）缴纳保证金：按照国际贸易的习惯做法，进口商向银行开立信用证，应向银行缴付一定比例的保证金。保证金的比例一般根据进口商的资信情况而定。

（二）申请开立信用证的流程

（1）进口商向银行提出开证申请，填写“开证申请书”。

（2）开证行收到进口商的申请及进口商提供的各种材料，经审核无误后，开出信用证给通知行。

（3）通知行收到信用证，审核信用证的真伪及开证行的资信等内容后，通知受益人。

（三）开立信用证应注意的问题

进口商向银行提出开证之前，对以下几点必须予以充分注意，以使国际结算顺利进行，并减少双方纠纷：

（1）申请开证前，要落实进口批准手续及资金情况，符合国家的法律法规。

（2）开证时间的掌握应以卖方在收到信用证后能按合同规定的装运时间内为原则。

（3）开证时，注意信用证与合同要完全一致，要以对外签订的买卖合同为依据，不能违背合同上的有关条款。

（4）要明确付款期限，注意按规定填写装运日期、交单日期及信用证的有效日期等，价格条款必须与相应的合同要求相吻合。

（5）信用证内容必须明确无误，明确规定各单据要表述的内容，只要单据表面与信用证条款相符合，开证行就必须按规定付款。

（6）进口商对卖方的要求：在申请开证时，应按合同有关规定转化成单据的具体规定在信用证中。

（7）一般信用证都应明确表示可撤销或不可撤销。如无此规定，根据“UCP600”的规定，应视为不可撤销的信用证。

（8）所开出的信用证在单据处理和国家惯例的执行方面不应有困难。

（四）开证申请书样章

开证申请书样章如下所示。

IRREVOCABLE DOCUMENTARY CREDIT APPLICATION

TO： 1 2 Date：

<table>
<tr><td colspan="2">( ) Issue by airmail ( ) With brief advice by teletransmission
( ) Issue by express delivery 3
( ) Issue by teletransmission (which shall be the operative instrument)</td><td>Irrevocable Documentary Credit</td><td>Number 4</td></tr>
<tr><td colspan="2" rowspan="2">Applicant 6</td><td colspan="2">Date and place of expiry 5</td></tr>
<tr><td colspan="2">Beneficiary 7</td></tr>
<tr><td colspan="2">Advising Bank 8 Ref. nr</td><td colspan="2">Amount 9</td></tr>
<tr><td>Partial shipments 10
( ) allowed
( ) not allowed</td><td>Transhipment 11
( ) allowed
( ) not allowed</td><td colspan="2" rowspan="3">Credit available with 13
( ) by sight payment ( ) by acceptance
( ) by negotiation
( ) by deferred payment at
against the documents detailed herein
( ) and beneficiary's draft for % of invoice value
at
on</td></tr>
<tr><td colspan="2">Loading on board/dispatch/taking charge at/from 12
Not later than
For transportation to：</td></tr>
<tr><td colspan="2">( ) FOB ( ) CFR ( ) GIF
( ) or other terms 14</td></tr>
</table>

Documents required：(marked with x) 15

1) ( ) Manually Signed Commercial Invoice in copies indicating this L/C No. and Contract No. (Photo copy and carbon copy not acceptable as original).

2) ( ) Full set (included original and non – negotiable copies) of Clean On Board "Freight " Ocean Bills of Lading made out to order and blank endorsed, marked "Notifying ".

3) ( ) Air Waybills showing "Freight " and consigned to

4) ( ) Rail Way Bills showing "Freight " and consigned to

5) ( ) Memorandum issued by consigned to

6) ( ) Full set (included original and copies) of Insurance Policy/Certificate for 110% of the invoice value, showing claims payable in China, in currency of the draft, blank endorsed, covering (< > ocean marine transportation/ < > air transportation/ < > over, land transportation) All Risks and War Risks.

7) ( ) Weight Memo/Packing List in copies issued by indicating quantity/gross and net weights of each package.

8) ( ) Certificate of Quantity/Weight in copies issued by indicating the actual surveyed quantity/weight of shipped goods.

9) ( ) Certificate of Quality in copies issued by

10) ( ) Beneficiary's certified copy of Fax dispatched to the applicant within hours after shipment advising < >name of vessel/< >flight No. ? < >wagon No. date, quantity, /weight and value of shipment.

11) ( ) Beneficiary's Certificate certifying that extra copies of documents have been dispatched according to the contract terms.

12) ( ) Shipping Co's Certificate attesting that the carrying vessel is chartered or booked by Applicant or their shipping agents.

13) ( ) 1/3 set of Original B/L and must be sent to The Applicant by courier within hours after shipment.

14) ( ) Other documents, if any:

Covering:: 16

Additional instructions: 17

1. ( ) all banking charges outside the opening bank are for beneficiary's account.
2. ( ) Documents must be presented within days after the date of issuance of the transport documents but within the validity of this credit.
3. ( ) Third party as shipper is not acceptable. Short Form/Blank Back B/L is not acceptable.
4. ( ) Both quantity and amount % more or less are allowed.
5. ( ) Prepaid freight drawn in excess of L/C amount is acceptable against presentation of original charges voucher issued by shipping co. /Air Line/or it's agent.
6. ( ) all documents to be forwarded in one cover, unless otherwise stated above.
7. ( ) Other terms, if any:

Account No. ; 18 with ______________________ (name of bank)

Transacted by: (Applicant: name, signature of authorized person)

Telephone No. : (with seal)

(五) 开证申请书的填制说明

(1) TO (致)。银行印制的申请书上事先都会印就开证银行的名称、地址，银行的SWIFT CODE、TELEX NO 等也可同时显示。

(2) DATE (申请开证日期)。在申请书右上角填写实际申请日期。

(3) 开证的格式。开证方式多为电开 (BY TELEX)，也可以是信开、快递或简电开立。

(4) L/C NUMBER (信用证号码)。此栏由银行填写。

(5) 信用证的有效期和有效地。

(6) APPLICANT (申请人)。填写申请人的全称及详细地址，有的要求注明联系电话、传真号码等。

（7）BENEFICIARY（受益人）。填写受益人的全称及详细地址。

（8）ADVISING BANK（通知行）。由开证行填写。

（9）AMOUNT（信用证金额）。分别用数字和文字两种形式表示，并且表明币制。如果允许有一定比率的上下浮动，要在信用证中明确表示出来。

（10）PARTIAL SHIPMENT（分批装运）。根据合同的实际规定打“×”进行选择。

（11）TRANSHIPMENT（转运）。根据合同的实际规定打“×”进行选择。

（12）LOADING IN CHARGE、FOR TRANSPORT TO、LATEST DATE OF SHIPMENT（装运地/港、目的地/港的名称，最迟装运日期）。按实际填写，如允许有转运地/港，也应清楚标明。

（13）CREDIT AVAILABLE WITH/BY（付款方式）。在所提供的即期、承兑、议付和延期付款四种信用证有效兑付方式中选择与合同要求一致的类型。

BENEFICIARY'S DRAFT（汇票要求）。金额应根据合同规定填写为：发票金额的一定百分比；发票金额的100%（全部货款都用信用证支付）；如部分信用证，部分托收时按信用证下的金额比例填写。付款期限可根据实际填写即期或远期，如属后者必须填写具体的天数。

（14）价格术语。根据对外签署的合同填制。

（15）DOCUMENTS REQUIRED（单据条款）。各银行提供的申请书中已印就的单据条款通常为十几条，从上至下一般为发票、运输单据（提单、空运单、铁路运输单据及运输备忘录等）、保险单、装箱单、质量证书、装运通知和受益人证明等，最后一条是OTHER DOCUMENTS，IF ANY（其他单据），如要求提交超过上述所列范围的单据就可以在此栏填写，比如有的合同要求CERTIFICATE OF NO SOLID WOOD PACKING MATERIAL（无实木包装材料证明）、CERTIFICATE OF FREE SALE（自由销售证明书）、CERTIFICATE OF CONFORMITY（合格证明书）等。申请人填制这部分内容时应依据合同规定，不能随意增加或减少。选中某单据后对该单据的具体要求（如一式几份、要否签字、正副本的份数、单据中应标明的内容等）也应如实填写，如申请书印制好的要求不完整应在其后予以补足。

（16）COVERING/EVIDENCING SHIPMENT OF（商品描述）。所有内容（品名、规格、包装、单价、唛头）都必须与合同内容相一致，价格条款里附带“AS PER INCOTERMS 2010”、数量条款中规定“MORE OR LESS”或“ABOUT”、使用某种特定包装物等特殊要求必须清楚列明。

（17）ADDITIONAL INSTRUCTIONS（附加指示）。该栏通常体现为以下一些条款：

+ALL DOCUMENTS MUST INDICATE CONTRACT NUMBER（所有单据加列合同号码）。

+ALL BANKING CHARGES OUTSIDE THE OPENING BANK ARE FOR BENEFICIARY'S ACCOUNT（所有开证行以外的银行费用由受益人承担）。

+BOTH QUANTITY AND AMOUNT FOR EACH ITEM % MORE OR LESS ALLOWED（每项数量与金额允许百分比的增减）。

+THIRD PARTY AS SHIPPER IS NOT ACCEPTABLE（第三方作为托运人是不能接受的）。

+DOCUMENTS MUST BE PRESNTED WITHIN ××× DAYS AFTER THE DATE OF ISSUANCE OF THE TRANSPORT DOCUMENTS BUT WITHIN THE VALIDITY OF THIS CREDIT（单据必须在提单日后×××天送达银行并且不超过信用证有效期）。

+SHORT FORM/BLANK BACK/CLAUSED/CHARTER PARTY B/L IS UNACCEPTABLE（银行不接受略式/不清洁/租船提单）。

+ALL DOCMENTS TO BE FORWARDED IN ONE COVER，UNLESS OTHERWISE STAT-

ED ABOVE（除非有相反规定，所有单据应一次提交）。

+PREPAID FREIGHT DRAWN IN EXCESS OF L/C AMOUNT IS ACCEPTABLE AGAINST PRESENTATION OF ORIGINAL CHARGES VOUCHER ISSUED BY SHIPPING CO. /AIR LINE OR ITS AGENT（银行接受凭船公司/航空公司或其代理人签发的正本运费收据索要超过信用证金额的预付运费）。

+DOCUMENT ISSUED PRIOR TO THE DATE OF ISSUANCE OF CREDIT NOT ACCEPTABLE（不接受早于开证日出具的单据）。

如需要已印就的上述条款，可在条款前打“×”，对合同涉及但未印就的条款还可以做补充填写。

（18） NAME，SIGNATURE OF AUTHORISED PERSON. TEL NO.，FAX，A CCOUNT NO.（授权人名称、签字、电话、传真、账号等内容）。

四、审核与修改信用证

（一）审核信用证

1. 审证依据

（1）销售合同。

（2）跟单信用证统一惯例（《UCP600》）。

2. 审证步骤

第一步：熟悉外贸合同各条款内容。

第二步：对照外贸合同条款，按照可操作性原则，逐条审核信用证各条款。

第三步：审核信用证中是否存在一些“软”条款。

第四步：列出信用证中的不符条款（见表1－2－3）。

表1－2－3 信用证中的不符条款与修改

序号	信用证不符之处	应改为
1		
2		
3		
4		
5		

3. 审核要点

（1）审核信用证受益人和开证申请人的名称和地址，以利于顺利完成收汇。

（2）审核信用证最迟装运期，判断信用证有效期和交单期的合理性。

（3）审核信用证的金额与货币币种，做到信用证金额和币种与合同相符、单价和总值填写正确、大小写金额一致。

（4）审核信用证的到期地点，一般要求到期地点在我国境内，以方便我方合理控制交单时间。

（5）审核信用证上注明的商品名称、品质、规格、数量、包装等条款，并注意溢短装条款。

（6）审核信用证的“软条款”。例如，信用证规定“货物到达目的港之后，需通过我方检验方可付款”。在这种情况下，卖方不能明确对方的检验方法及指标，对方可以以此为借口拒绝付款。

（7）审核信用证规定的单据能否提供，提前确认单据可否及时办理以及办理费用是否过高。

（8）运输条款。信用证运输条款中的装运港（地）和目的港（地）应与外贸合同相符，交货地点也必须与价格条款一致。若信用证中未注明可否转运及/或分批，则视为允许转运及/或分批。

（9）保险条款。若来证要求的投保险别或投保金额超出了外贸合同的规定，除非信用证上表明由此而产生的超保费由开证申请人承担并允许在信用证项下支取，否则应予修改。

（二）修改信用证

出口方审证后发现信用证与合同或《UCP600》不相符，须立即向开证申请人提出修改要求，并发出“要求修改的函电”。进口方收到函电后，会向开证行提出改正申请，开证行同意后即向原通知行发出“修改通知书”。原通知行再将“修改通知书”转给出口方改证。

需要注意的是，“修改通知书”的内容，要么全部接受，要么全部拒绝，部分接受修改中的内容是无效的。

【工作指导】

青岛海富贸易有限公司与荷兰的 FUTURO 公司在签订贸易合同 15 天后，收到了荷兰银行开来的信用证。张丽的师傅李华根据合同内容来审核荷兰银行开来的信用证，找出信用证中与合同的不符条款并进行修改。

资料 1：销售合同

销售合同

SALES CONTRACT

Sellers: QINGDAO HAIFU TRADING CO. LTD.,　　Contract No. : MSR719

Address: NO. 1 HONGKONG ROAD, QINGDAO CHINA　　Date : APR. 12, 2013

Buyers: FUTURO INDUSTRIAL CO. LTD.,　　Signed at : QINGDAO, CHINA

Address: ROTTERDAM NETHERLANDS　　Telex: 86－0532－85896210

Fax: 86－0532－85896211

This Sales Contract is made by and between the Sellers and the Buyers, whereby the Sellers agree to sell and the Buyers agree to buy the under－mentioned goods according to the terms and conditions stipulated below:

（1）货号、品名及规格 NAME OF COMMODITY AND SPECIFICATIONS	（2）数量 QUANTITY	（3）单价 UNIT PRICE	（4）金额 AMOUNT
QINGDAO SPRING ROLLS 20G PER PC, 50PCS IN A BOX, 9 BOXES IN A CARTON 5 % more or less both in amount and quantity allowed	2450CARTONS	CIF ROTTERDAM USD15. 50PER CTN	USD37975. 00
	Total Amount		USD37975. 00

(5) Packing: to be packed in CARTONS suitable for transportation.

(6) Delivery from QINGDAO CHINA to ROTTERDAM, NETHERLANDS

(7) Shipping Marks: to be supplied by the seller.

(8) Latest Shipment Date: JUL. 10, 2013.

Transshipment ALLOWED and partial shipment ALLOWED

(9) Terms of Payment: By 100% Irrevocable Letter of Credit payable at 60 DAYS AFTER B/L SHIPMENT DATE sight in favor of the Sellers to be opened and to reach China before THE END OF MAY 2013 and to remain valid for negotiation in China until 21 days after the foresaid Time of Shipment.

(10) Insurance: To be effected by Sellers for 110% of full invoice value against ICC (A) and ICC WAR CLAUSE as per INSTITUTE CARGO CLAUSE DATED 1/1/1982.

(11) Quality/Quantity Discrepancy and Claim:

In case the quality and/or quantity/weight are found by the Buyers to be not in conformity with the Contract after arrival of the goods at the port of destination, the Buyers may lodge claim with the Sellers supported by survey report issued by an inspection organization agreed upon by both parties, with the exception, however, of those claims for which the insurance company and or the shipping company are to be held responsible, claim for quality discrepancy should be filed by the Buyers within 60 days after arrival of the goods at the port of destination. The Sellers shall, within 30 days after receipt of the notification of the claim, send reply to the Buyers.

(12) Force Majeure: In case of Force Majeure, the Sellers shall not be held responsible for late delivery or non - delivery of the goods but shall notify the Buyers by cable. The Sellers shall deliver to the Buyers by registered mail, if so requested by the Buyers, a certificate issued by the China Council for the Promotion of International Trade or/and competent authorities.

(13) Arbitration: All dispute arising from the execution of or in connection with this contract shall be settled amicably by negotiation. In case no settlement can be reached through negotiation the case shall then be submitted to China International Economic& Trade Arbitration Commission. In Qingdao (or in Beijing) for arbitration in act with it's sure of procedures. The arbitral award is final and binding upon both parties for setting the Dispute. The fee for arbitration shall be borne by the losing party unless otherwise awarded.

(14) Contract shall take effect after countersign on fax by two parties' authorized representatives.

SELLERS:	BUYERS:
QINGDAO HAIFU TRADING CO. LTD.,	FUTURO INDUSTRIAL CO. LTD.,
LIHUA	JACKSON
APR. 12, 2013	APR. 12, 2013

资料2：信用证

LETTER OF CREDIT

MT：700	ISSUE OF A DOCUMENTARY CREDIT	
SEQUENCE OF TOTAL	*27：	1/1
FORM OF DOC. CREDIT	*40A：	IRREVOCABLE
DOC. CREDIT NUMBER	*20：	IC01925U
DATE OF ISSUE	31C：	20130525
EXPRIRY	*31D：	DATE 20130725 IN QINGDAO
ISSUING BANK	51A：	WACHOVIA BANK, NO. 3K STREET，RM 504 FUNGLEE COMM. BLDG. ROTTERDAM NETHERLANDS
APPLICANT	*50：	FUTURO INDUSTRIAL CO. LTD.， ROTTERDAM　NETHERLANDS TEL：031 431 7295
BENEFICIARY	*59：	QINGDAO HAOFU TRADING CO. LTD.， NO. 1HONGKONG ROAD， QINGDAO　CHINA
AMOUNT	*32B：	CURRENCY USD AMOUNT USD40000. 00
AVAILABLE WITH /BY	*41D：	ANY BANK BY DEF PAYMENT
DRAFT AT…	42C：	AT SIGHT
DRAWEE	42A：	ISSUING BANK
PARTIAL SHIPMENT	43P：	ALLOWED
TRANSHIPMENT	43T：	ALLOWED
LOADING IN CHARGE	44A：	QINGDAO，CHINA
FOR TRANSPORT TO	44B：	ROTTERDAM PORT，NETHERLANDS
LATEST SHIPMENT DATE	44C：	20130610
DESCRIPTION OF GOODS	45A：	

2450CARTONS（ONE CONTAINER）OF QINGDAO SPRING ROLLS AT CNY15. 50PER CTN CIF ROTTERDAM

PACKING：20G PER PC，50PCS IN A BOX，9 BOXES IN A CARTON

PACKED IN PLANT OF QINGDAO BANMU FOODS PRODUCTS CO. LTD.，QINGDAO INDUSTRIAL ZONE QINGDAO.

AS PER CONTRACT NO. MSR719　DATE：20130412

DOCUMENTS REQUIRED 46A：

\+ SIGNED COMMERCIAL INVOICE IN THREE COPIES CERTIFYING COUNTRY OF ORIGIN.

+FULL SET OF ORIGINAL CLEAN ON BAORD OCEAN BILLS OF LADING CONSIGNED TO ORDER OF SHIPPER MARKED FREIGHT PREPAID NOTIFY APPLICANT AND ISSUING BANK.

+PACKING LIST IN THREE COPIES.

+ MARINE INSURANCE POLICY OR CERTIFICATE IN DUPLICATE ENDORSED IN BLANK, WITH CLAIM PAYABLE IN NETHLANDS IN THE CURRENCY OF THE DRAFT, COVERING 110 PERCENT OF INVOICE VALUE, INCLUDING ALL RISKS AND WAR RISKS AS PER INSTITUTE CARGO CLAUSE DATED 1/1/1982.

+ SHIPPING ADVICE HAS BEEN SENT TO APPLICANT WITHIN 3 DAYS FROM DATE OF SHIPMENT INDICATING L/C NO., INVOICE NO., AMOUNT, DETAILS OF GOODS, NAME OF VESSEL, VOYAGE NO., DATE OF SHIPMENT, PORT OF LOADING, B/L NO., CONTAINER NO., SEAL NO., ESTIMATED TIME OF ARRIVAL.

+ CERTIFICATE OF ORIGINAND GSP FORM A SIGNED BY C. I. Q.

+ COPY OF BENEFICIARY CERTIFICATE CERTIFY THAT ONE COMPLETE SET OF N/N DOCUMENTS HAS BEEN SENT TO APPLICANT BY COURIER WITHIN FIVE DAYS OF THE B/L DATE.

ADDITIONAL COND. 47A:

+SHIPMENT DOCUMENTS EVIDENCE THIS L/C NO.

+THE INVOICE SEPARATELY MENTION FOB VALUE, FREIGHT CHARGE.

+B/L MUST MARK THAT THE GOODS SHIPPED IN 40' HR CONTAINER AND SET AT -18 DEGREES CENTIGRADE OR LOWER

DETAILS OF CHARGES: 71B:

ALL BANK CHARGES OUTSIDEROTTERDAM ARE FOR ACCOUNT OF BENEFICIARY.

CONFIRMATION INSTRUCTIONS *49: WITHOUT

"ADVISE THROUGH" BANK 57A: BANK OF CHINA LTD., SHANDONG BRANCH

师傅李华找出的信用证中的不符条款与修改（见表1-2-4）。

表1-2-4 信用证中的不符条款与修改

序号	信用证不符之处	应改为
1	*59 "QINGDAO HAOFU TRADING CO. LTD., NO. 1 HONGKONG ROAD, QINGDAO CHINA" 受益人公司名称不符	QINGDAO HAIFU TRADING CO. LTD., NO. 1 HONGKONG ROAD, QINGDAO CHINA
2	42C "AT SIGHT" 汇票的付款期限不符	AT 60 DAYS AFTER B/L SHIPMENT DATE SIGHT
3	44C "20130610" 最迟装运期不符	20130710
4	45A "CNY15. 50 PER CTN" 商品单价货币单位不符	USD15. 50 PER CTN
5	46A "ALL RISKS AND WAR RISKS" 保险条款的保险险种不符	ICC (A) AND ICC WAR CLAUSE AS PER INSTITUTE CARGO CLAUSE DATED 1/1/1982.

修改好的信用证如下所示：

LETTER OF CREDIT

MT：700	ISSUE OF A DOCUMENTARY CREDIT	
SEQUENCE OF TOTAL	*27：	1/1
FORM OF DOC. CREDIT	*40A：	IRREVOCABLE
DOC. CREDIT NUMBER	*20：	IC01925U
DATE OF ISSUE	31C：	20130525
EXPRIRY	*31D：	DATE 20130725 PLACE AT YOUR COUNTRY IN QINGDAO
ISSUING BANK	51A：	WACHOVIA BANK, NO. 3K STREET，RM 504 FUNGLEE COMM. BLDG. ROTTERDAM NETHERLANDS
APPLICANT	*50：	FUTURO INDUSTRIAL CO. LTD.， ROTTERDAM NETHERLANDS TEL：031 431 7295
BENEFICIARY	*59：	QINGDAO HAIFU TRADINC CO. LTD.， NO. 1HONGKONG ROAD, QINGDAO CHINA
AMOUNT	*32B：	CURRENCY USD AMOUNT USD40000. 00
AVAILABLE WITH /BY	*41D：	ANY BANK BY DEF PAYMENT
DRAFT AT···	42C：	AT 60 DAYS AFTER B/L SHIPMENT DATE
DRAWEE	42A：	ISSUING BANK
PARTIAL SHIPMENT	43P：	ALLOWED
TRANSHIPMENT	43T：	ALLOWED
LOADING IN CHARGE	44A：	QINGDAO，CHINA
FOR TRANSPORT TO	44B：	ROTTERDAM PORT，NETHERLANDS
LATEST SHIPMENT DATE	44C：	20130710
DESCRIPTION OF GOODS	45A：	

2450CARTONS (ONE CONTAINER) OF QINGDAO SPRING ROLLS AT USD15. 50PER CTN CIF ROTTERDAM

PACKING：20G PER PC，50PCS IN A BOX，9 BOXES IN A CARTON

PACKED IN PLANT OF QINGDAO BANMU FOODS PRODUCTS CO. LTD.，QINGDAO INDUSTRIAL ZONE QINGDAO.

AS PER CONTRACT NO. MSR719 DATE：20130412

DOCUMENTS REQUIRED 46A：

+ SIGNED COMMERCIAL INVOICE IN THREE COPIES CERTIFYING COUNTRY OF ORIGIN.

+ FULL SET OF ORIGINAL CLEAN ON BAORD OCEAN BILLS OF LADING CONSIGNED TO ORDER OF SHIPPER MARKED FREIGHT PREPAID NOTIFY APPLICANT AND ISSUING BANK.

+ PACKING LIST IN THREE COPIES.

+ MARINE INSURANCE POLICY OR CERTIFICATE IN DUPLICATE ENDORSED IN BLANK, WITH CLAIM PAYABLE IN NETHLANDS IN THE CURRENCY OF THE DRAFT, COVERING 110 PERCENT OF INVOICE VALUE, INCLUDING ICC (A) AND ICC WAR CLAUSE AS PER INSTITUTE CARGO CLAUSE DATED 1/1/1982.

+ SHIPPING ADVICE HAS BEEN SENT TO APPLICANT WITHIN 3 DAYS FROM DATE OF SHIPMENT INDICATING L/C NO., INVOICE NO., AMOUNT, DETAILS OF GOODS, NAME OF VESSEL, VOYAGE NO., DATE OF SHIPMENT, PORT OF LOADING, B/L NO., CONTAINER NO., SEAL NO., ESTIMATED TIME OF ARRIVAL.

+ CERTIFICATE OF ORIGIN AND GSP FORM A SIGNED BY C. I. Q.

+ COPY OF BENEFICIARY CERTIFICATE CERTIFY THAT ONE COMPLETE SET OF N/N DOCUMENTS HAS BEEN SENT TO APPLICANT BY COURIER WITHIN FIVE DAYS OF THE B/L DATE.

ADDITIONAL COND.　　47A:

+SHIPMENT DOCUMENTS EVIDENCE THIS L/C NO.

+THE INVOICE SEPARATELY MENTION FOB VALUE, FREIGHT CHARGE.

+B/L MUST MARK THAT THE GOODS SHIPPED IN 40' HR CONTAINER AND SET AT -18 DEGREES CENTIGRADE OR LOWER

DETAILS OF CHARGES:　　71B:

ALL BANK CHARGES OUTSIDE ROTTERDAM ARE FOR ACCOUNT OF BENEFICIARY.

CONFIRMATION INSTRUCTIONS *49:　　WITHOUT

"ADVISE THROUGH" BANK 57A:　BANK OF CHINA LTD., SHANDONG BRANCH

【工作演练】

张丽在师傅李华的指导下，已经能够熟练解读合同和信用证的相关条款。下面请你和张丽一起根据所提供的合同审核并修改信用证。

资料1：销售合同

SALES CONTRACT

NO: 205

001

DATE: JAN. 9, 2013

THE BUYERS: SAGIR AND COMBO CO.

38 ASADGONI CHITTAGONG BANGLADESH

THE SELLERS: QINGDAO HAIFU TRADING CO. LTD.,
NO. 1HONGKONG ROAD, QINGDAO CHINA

This Contract is made by and between the Buyers and the Sellers, in JAN. 9, 2013, whereby the Buyers agree to buy and the Sellers agree to sell the under mentioned commodity according to the terms and condition s stipulated below:

COMMODITY, SPECIFICATION	QUANTITY	UNIT PRICE	TOTAL AMOUNT
X - RAY APPARATUS SPECIFICTION: AG - 1409A	16 SETS	USD4600. 00	USD73600. 00
SUB TOTAL CIF CHITTAGONG USD73600. 00	SAYU. S. DOLLARS SEVENTY - THREE THOUSAND SIX HUNDRED ONLY		

1. COUNTRY OF ORIGIN AND MANUFACTURERS: CHINA

2. PACKING: To be packed in WOODEN CASES, suitable for the shipment.
One set in acase, total 16 wooden cases.

3. SHIPPING MARKS: The Sellers shall mark on each package with fadeless paint the package number, gross weight, measurements.

S&C
205001
CHITTAGONG
NO. 1 - UP

4. TIME OF SHIPMENT: Before MAR. 10, 2013

5. PORT OF SHIPMENT: ANY PORT IN CHINA

6. PORT OF DESTINATION: CHITTAGONG BANGLADESH

7. INSURANCE: To be covered by the Seller for 110% of the invoice value against All Risks and War Risks. If additional insurance amount or coverage is required, the additional premium is to be borne by the Buyer.

8. PAYMENT:

Paymentby 100% Irrevocable Letter of Credit payable at __/__ sight in favor of the Sellers to be opened and to reach China before __THE END OF FEB. 2013__ and to remain valid for negotiation in China until __21__ days after the foresaid Time of Shipment.

9. SHIPPING ADVICE: The Sellers shall, immediately upon the completion of the loading of the goods, advise by cable/letter the transportation department of Buyers of the Contract No., Commodity, quantity, invoice No., ocean bill No., gross weight, name of vessel and date of sailing etc.

10. CLAIMS: Within 90 days after the arrival of the goods at destination, should the quality, specification or quantity be found not in conformity with the stipulations of the Contract except those claims for which the insurance company or the owners of the vessel are liable, the Buyers on the

strength of the Inspection Certificate issued by the China Commodity Inspection Bureau, have the right to claim for replacement with new goods, or for compensation, and all the expenses (such as inspection charges, freight for returning the goods and for sending the replacement, insurance premium, storage and loading and unloading charge etc.) shall be borne by the Sellers. As regards quality, the Sellers guarantee that if, within 12 months from the date of arrival of the goods at destination, damages occur in the course of operation by reason of inferior quality, bad workmanship or the use of inferior materials, the Buyers shall immediately notify the Sellers in writing and put forward a claim supported by Inspection Certificate issued by the China Commodity Inspection Bureau. The Certificate so issued shall be accepted as the base of a claim. The sellers, in accordance with the Buyers claim shall be responsible for the immediate elimination of the defect (s), complete or partial replacement of the commodity or shall devaluate the commodity according to the state of defect (s) . Where necessary, the Buyers shall be at liberty to eliminate the defect (s) themselves at the Sellers expenses. If the Sellers fail to answer the Buyers within one month after receipt of the aforesaid claim, the claim shall be reckoned as having been accepted by the Sellers.

11. FORCE MAJEURE: The Sellers shall not be held responsible for the delay shipment or non – delivery of the goods due to Fore Major, which might occur during the process of manufacturing or in the course of loading or transit. The Sellers shall advise the Buyers immediately of the occurrence mentioned above and within fourteen days thereafter, the Sellers shall send by airmail to the Buyers a certificate of the accident issued by the competent government authorities, Chamber of Commerce or registered notary public of the place where the accident occurs as evidence thereof. Under such circumstances the Sellers, however, are still under the obligation to take all necessity measures to hasten the delivery of the good. In case the accident lasts for more than 10 weeks, the Buyers shall have the right to cancel the Contract.

12. ARBITRATION: All disputes in connection with this contract or the execution thereof shall be settled friendly through negotiations. Incase no settlement can be reached, the case shall be submitted for arbitration to the China International Economic and Trade Arbitration Commission Beijing in accordance with the Provisional Rules of Procedures by the said Arbitration Committee. The Arbitration shall take place in Beijing and the decision of the Arbitration Committee shall be final and binding upon both parties, neither party shall seek recourse to a law court nor other authorities to appeal for revision of the decision. Arbitration fee shall be borne by the losing party.

13. All appendixes to the Contract shall form an integral part of the Contract and have the same effectiveness as the contract . IN WITNESS THERFOF, both parties in two original copies sign this Contract. Each party holds one copy.

THE BUYERS	THE SELLERS
SAGIR AND COMBO CO.	QINGDAO HAIFU TRADING CO. LTD. ,
BILL WOODS	**LIHUA**

资料2：信用证

FORM OF DOC. CERDIT	*40A:	IRREVOCABLE
DOC. CREDIT NUMBER	*20:	3409010097
DATE OF ISSUE	31C:	FEB. 15, 2013
APPLICABLE RULES	*40E:	UCP LATEST VERSION
EXPIRY	31D:	DATE APR. 20, 2013 PLACE IN CHINA
APPLICANT BANK	51A:	NATIONAL BANK LTD., CHITTAGONG
APPLICANT	*50:	SAGIR AND COMBO CO. 38 ASADGONI CHITTAGONG BANGLADESH
BENEFICIARY	*59:	QINGDAO HAIFU TRADING CO. LTD., NO. 1HONGKONG ROAD, QINGDAO CHINA
AMOUNT	*32B:	CURRENCY USD AMOUNT 73600. 00
AVAILABLE WITH /BY	*41D:	ANY BANK BY PAYMENT
DRAFTS	42C:	45 OAYS AFTER SIGHT
DRAWEE	42A:	NATIONAL BANK LTD., CHITTAGONG
PARTIAL SHIPMENTS	43P:	ALLOWED
TRANSHIPMENT	43T:	ALLOWED BUT SHIPMENT BY CONTAINER
PORT OF LOADING	44E:	CHITTAGONG BANGLADESH
PORT OF DISCHARGE	44F:	ANY PORT OF CHINA
ALATEST DATE OF SHIP	44C:	MAR. 10, 2013
DESCRIPT. OF GOODS	45A:	

X-RAY APPARATUS　CIF CHITTAGONG BANGLADESH

AS PER SALES CONTRACT NO. 205001 OF JAN. 9, 2013

SPECIFICTION	UNIT PRICE	QUANTITY
AG-1409A	USD4600. 00/SET	16 SETS

PACKING: ONE SET IN ONE CARTON WHICH MUST BE SUITABLE FOR SHIPMENT.

DOCUMENTS REQUIRED 46A:

+MANUALLY SIGNED　COMMERCIAL INVOICE IN 1 ORIGINAL 2 COPIES INDICATING L/C NO. AND CONTRACT NO. CERTIFYING THE CONTENTS IN THIS INVOICE ARE TURE AND CORRECT.

+FULL SET OF OCEAN B/L MADE OUT TO ORDER OF SHIPPER MARKED FREIGHT PREPAID AND NOTIFY APPLICANT.

+PACKING LIST IN THREE COPIES SHOWING EACH NET WEIGHT GROSS WEIGHT

ADDITIONAL COND. 47A:

+SHIPMENT MUST BE EFFECTED BY 40HR’ CONTAINER

+THE K INTERNATIONA LINE AS CARRIER

+ON BOARD VESSEL NOTATION INDICATING THE DATE DISPLAY ON B/L

+ALL DOCUMENTS EVIDENCE SHIPPING MARKS: S&C/205001/CHITTAGONG/NO. 1-UP

找出信用证中的不符条款并修改（见表1－2－5）。

表1－2－5 信用证中的不符条款与修改

序号	信用证不符之处	应改为
1		
2		
3		
4		
5		

提示：

（1）首先读懂合同，然后对应合同内容，逐条审核L/C。

（2）尤其注意买卖双方名称拼写、日期、价格等内容。

（3）认真审核信用证条款，防止软条款出现。

【工作评价】

1. 评价标准（见表1－2－6）

表1－2－6 信用证的不符条款与修改

序号	信用证不符之处	应改为
1	31C：“DATE OF ISSUE FEB. 15，2013” 开证日期不符	合同要求信用证应在2013年2月之前开到受益人处
2	42C：“DRAFTS：45 DAYS AFTER SIGHT” 汇票的付款期限不符	DRAFTS：SIGHT
3	44E：PORT OF LOADING：CHITTAGONG BANGLADESH 44F：PORT OF DISCHARGE：ANY PORT OF CHINA 装运港与目的港颠倒	PORT OF LOADING：ANY PORT OF CHINA PORT OF DISCHARGE：CHITTAGONG BANGLADESH
4	46A：“PACKING：ONE SET IN ONE CARTON WHICH MUST BE SUITABLE FOR SHIPMENT” 包装种类不符	PACKING：ONE SET IN ONE WOODEN CASE WHICH MUST BE SUITABLE FOR SHIPMENT
5	合同要求提交SHIPPING ADVICE，信用证未注明	46A ＋SHIPPING ADVICE SHOULD BE IMMEDIATELY SENT TO APPLICANT BY CABLE AFTER SHIPMENT ADVISING THE CONTRACT NO.，COMMODITY，QUANTITY，INVOICE NO.，OCEAN BILL NO.，GROSS WEIGHT，NAME OF VESSEL AND DATE OF SAILING ETC

修改好的信用证如下所示：

FORM OF DOC. CERDIT	*40A:	IRREVOCABLE
DOC. CREDIT NUMBER	*20:	3409010097
DATE OF ISSUE	31C:	JAN. 15, 2013
APPLICABLE RULES	*40E:	UCP LATEST VERSION
EXPIRY	31D:	DATE APR. 20, 2013 PLACE IN CHINA
APPLICANT BANK	51A:	NATIONAL BANK LTD., CHITTAGONG
APPLICANT	*50:	SAGIR AND COMBO CO. 38 ASADGONI CHITTAGONG BANGLADESH
BENEFICIARY	*59:	QINGDAO HAIFU TRADING CO. LTD., NO. 1 HONGKONG ROAD, QINGDAO CHINA
AMOUNT	*32B:	CURRENCY USD AMOUNT 73600.00
AVAILABLE WITH /BY	*41D:	ANY BANK BY PAYMENT
DRAFTS	42C:	AT SIGHT
DRAWEE	42A:	NATIONAL BANK LTD., CHITTAGONG
PARTIAL SHIPMENTS	43P:	ALLOWED
TRANSHIPMENT	43T:	ALLOWED BUT SHIPMENT BY CONTAINER
PORT OF LOADING	44E:	ANY PORT OF CHINA
PORT OF DISCHARGE	44F:	CHITTAGONG BANGLADESH
ALATEST DATE OF SHIP	44C:	MAR. 10, 2013
DESCRIPT. OF GOODS	45A:	

X-RAY APPARATUS　CIFCHITTAGONG BANGLADESH

AS PER SALES CONTRACT NO. 205001 OF JAN. 9, 2013

SPECIFICTION	UNIT PRICE	QUANTITY
AG-1409A	USD4600.00/SET	16 SETS

PACKING: ONE SET IN ONEWOODEN CASE WHICH MUST BE SUITABLE FOR SHIPMENT.

DOCUMENTS REQUIRED 46A:

+MANUALLY SIGNED　COMMERCIAL INVOICE IN 1 ORIGINAL 2 COPIES INDICATING L/C NO. AND CONTRACT NO. CERTIFYING THE CONTENTS IN THIS INVOICE ARE TURE AND CORRECT

+FULL SET OF OCEAN B/L MADE OUT TO ORDER OF SHIPPER MARKED FREIGHT PREPAID AND NOTIFY APPLICANT.

+PACKING LIST IN THREE COPIES SHOWING EACH NET WEIGHT GROSS WEIGHT

+SHIPPING ADVICE SHOULD BE IMMEDIATELY SENT TO APPLICANT BY CABLE AFTER SHIPMENT ADVISING THE CONTRACT NO., COMMODITY, QUANTITY, INVOICE NO., OCEAN BILL NO., GROSS WEIGHT, NAME OF VESSEL AND DATE OF SAILING ETC.

ADDITIONAL COND.　47A:

+SHIPMENT MUST BE EFFECTED BY 40HR' CONTAINER

+THE K INTERNATIONA LINE AS CARRIER

+ON BOARD VESSEL NOTATION INDICATING THE DATE DISPLAY ON B/L

+ALL DOCUMENTS EVIDENCE SHIPPING MARKS: S&C/205001/CHITTAGONG/NO. 1-UP

2. 评价表（见表1－2－7）

表1－2－7　　评　价　表

评价人／评价指标	自　评	互　评	师　评
独立完成情况（20分）			
格式规范性（20分）			
内容完整性、正确性（50分）			
内容简明性、整洁性（10分）			
合计总分			

项 目 实 训

资料1：

买方：

ESTA CO. , LTD.

59－C BLOCK KING STREET，HAMBURG，GERMANY

卖方：

潮州华力陶瓷制品工厂

CHAOZHOU HUALI CERAMICS FACTORY

FENGYI INDUSTRIAL DISTRICT，GUXIANG TOWN，

CHAOZHOU CITY，GUANGDONG PROVINCE，CHINA.

TEL：0086－0768－82587712

FAX：0086－0768－82587716

1. 货物信息：卫浴陶瓷制品（SANITARY WARE）

	货号	数量	单价
（1）	SY－2189	200套	115欧元
（2）	SY－2245	250套	95欧元
（3）	SV－2981	450套	72欧元

FOB深圳

2. SALES CONFIRMATION NO. HX59114

DATE：20130415

3. 装运港：深圳
目的港：汉堡
不允许分批装运
不允许转船
最迟装运期：2013. 8. 26

4. 唛头：ESTA／　HAMBURG／　NO. 1 －500

5. 付款条件：即期不可撤销信用证
（开证日期不得迟于2013年4月）

6. 出口方代表：张强
进口方代表：KINLIN　GREEN

资料2：

FROM：　BANK OF CYPRUS LTD
40A：FORM OF DOCUMENTARY CREDIT：　IRREVOCABLE
20：CUMENTARY CREDIT NUMBER ：　00143 －01 －0053557
31C：DATE OF ISSUE ：　130501
31：DATE AND PLACE OF EXPIRY 130920 IN CHINA
50：APPLICANT：ESTA CO. , LTD.
59 －C BLOCK KING STREET，NICOSIA，CYPRUS
59：BENEFICIARY：CHAOZHOU HUALI CERAMICS FACTORY
FENGYI INDUSTRIAL DISTRICT，GUXIANG TOWN，
CHAOZHOU CITY，GUANGDONG PROVINCE，CHINA.
32B：CURRENCY CODE，AMOUNTUSD150000
41D：AVAILABLE WITH. . .
STANDARD CHARTERED BANKCHINA BY NEGOTIATION
42C：DRAFTS　AT SIGHT
42A：DRAWEE　BANK OF CYPRUS LTD
43：PARTIAL SHIPMENTS　NOT ALLOWED
43T：TRANSHIPMENT　ALLOWED
44：LOADING ON BOARD/DISPATCH/TAKING IN CHARGE AT/FROM. . . SHENZHEN PORT
44B：FOR TRANSPORTATION TOLIMASSOL PORT
44C：LATEST DATE OF SHIPMENT 130626
045A：DESCRIPTION OF GOODS AND/OR SERVICES
SANITARY WARE　F O B SHENZHEN PORT，AS PER INCOTERMS 2010
1）　SY －2189　200SETS　@USD 115/SET

2) SY－2245 250SETS @USD 95/SET
3) SV－2981 450SETS @USD 72/SET
PACKING: 2 SETS IN A CARTON
46A: DOCUMENTS REQUIRED
* FULL SET (AT LEAST THREE) ORIGINAL CLEAN SHIPPED ON BOARD BILLS OF LADING ISSUED TO THE ORDER OF BANK OF CYPRUS PUBLIC COMPANY LTD, CYPRUS, NOTIFY PARTIES APPLICANT AND OURSELVES, SHOWING FREIGHT PAYABLE AT DESTINATION AND BEARING THE NUMBER OF THIS CREDIT.
* PACKING LIST IN 3 COPIES.
* CERTIFICATE ISSUED BY THE SHIPPING COMPANY/CARRIER OR THEIR AGENT STATING THE B/L NO (S) AND THE VESSEL (S) NAME CERTIFYING THAT THE CARRYING VESSEL (S) IS/ARE HOLDING A VALID SAFETY MANAGEMENT SYSTEM CERTIFICATE AS PER TERMS OF INTERNATIONAL SAFETY MANAGEMENT CODE
* COMMERCIAL INVOICE IN 4 COPIES DULY SIGNED BY THE BENEFICIARY/IES, STATING THAT THE GOODS SHIPPED: A) ARE OFCHINA ORIGIN. B) ARE IN ACCORDANCE WITH BENEFICIARIES PROFORMA INVOICE NO. HL050307 DATED13/04/05.
47A: ADDITIONAL CONDITIONS
* THE NUMBER AND DATE OF THE CREDIT AND THE NAME OF OUR BANK MUST BE QUOTED ON ALL DRAFTS (IF REQUIRED) .
* TRANSPORT DOCUMENTS TO BE CLAUSED: VESSEL IS NOT SCHEDULED TO CALL ON ITS CURPENT VOYAGE ATFAMAGUSTA, KYRENTA OR KARAVOSTASSI, CYPRUS.
* INSURANCE WILL BE COVERED BY THE BENEFICIARY's.
* ALL DOCUMENTS TO BE ISSUED IN ENGLISH LANGUAGE.

资料3:

______________________公司
____
____
____

售货确认书

SALES CONFIRMATION

Tel: ____________________ 编号: No. __________
Fax: ____________________ 日期: Date __________
TO Messrs:
____
____

谨启者: 兹确认授予你方下列货品，其成交条款如下:
Dear Sirs: We hereby confirm having sold to you the following goods on the terms and conditions as specified below:

（1）货物名称及规格 Name of Commodity and Specification	（2）数量 Quantity	（3）单价 Unit Price	（4）总价 Amount

（5）装运期限：Time of Shipment：LATEST DATE OF SHIPMENT ________

（6）装运港：Port of Loading：________

（7）目的港：Port of Destination：________

（8）分批装运：Partial Shipment：________

（9）转船：Transshipment：________

（10）付款条件：Terms of Payment：________

（11）运输标志：Shipping Marks：____________________

（12）保险：Insurance：The Seller should cover insurance for　　　　% of the total invoice value against ________ as per Ocean Marine Cargo Clauses of PICC dated 1/1/1981.

（13）仲裁：Arbitration：All disputes arising from the execution of，or in connection with this Sales Confirmation，shall be settled amicably through friendly negotiation. In case no settlement can be reached through negotiation，the case shall then be submitted to China International Economic and Trade Arbitration Commission，Shanghai Commission for arbitration in accordance with Rules of Arbitration of China International Economic and Trade Arbitration Commission. The award made by the Commission should be accepted as final and binding upon both parties.

（14）REMARKS：买方须于____年____月____日前开出本批交易的信用证（或通知售方进口许可证号码）。否则，售方有权不经过通知取消本确认书，或向买方提出索赔。

The Buyer shall establish the covering Letter of Credit（or notify the Import License Number）before ________，falling which the Seller reserves the right to rescind without further notice，or to accept whole or any part of this Sales Confirmation non－fulfilled by the Buyer，or，to lodge claim for direct losses sustained，if any.

凡以 CIF 条件成交的业务，保额为发票价的____，投保险别以售货确认书中所开列的为限，买方如果要求增加保额或保险范围，应于装船前经卖方同意，因此而增加的保险费由买方负责。

For transactions concluded on C. I. F. basis it is understood that the insurance amount will be for ____ of the invoice value against the risks specified in the Sales Confirmation. If additional Insurance amount of coverage is required，the buyers must have the consent of the Sellers before Shipment and the additional premium is to be borne by the buyers.

本确认书内所述全部或部分商品，如因任何不可抗拒的原因，以致不能履约或延迟交货，卖方概不负责。

The Seller shall not be held liable for failure of delay in delivery of the entire lot or a portion of the goods under this Sales Confirmation in consequence of any Force Majeure incidents.

买方在开给卖方的信用证上请填注本确认书号码。

The Buyer is requested always to quote THE NUMBER OF THIS SALES CONFIRMATION in the Letter of Credit to be opened in favour of the Seller.

买方收到本售货确认书后请立即签回一份，如买方对本确认书有异议，应于收到后五天内提出，否则认为买方已同意接受本确认书所规定的各项条款。

The buyer is requested to sign and return one copy of the Sales Confirmation immediately after the receipt of same, Objection, if any, should be raised by the Buyer within five days after the receipt of this Sales Confirmation, in the absence of which it is understood that the Buyer has accepted the terms and condition of the Sales Confirmation.

买方　　　　　　　　　　　　卖方

资料 4：

信用证中的不符条款与修改填写在表 1－2－8 中。

表 1－2－8

序号	信用证不符之处	应改为
1		
2		
3		
4		
5		

实训要求：

1. 根据资料 1，填制一份售货确认书。
2. 根据填制完成的合同审核资料 2 信用证，找出不符之处，并改正。

参考答案

1. 填制的售货确认书

潮州华力陶瓷制品工厂

CHAOZHOU HUALI CERAMICS FACTORY

FENG YI INDUSTRIAL DISTRICT, GUXIANG TOWN,

CHAOZHOU CITY, GUANGDONG PROVINCE, CHINA

售货确认书

SALES CONFIRMATION

Tel：0086－0768－82587712　　　　编号：No. HX59114

Fax: 0086 - 0768 - 82587716

日期: Date APR. 15, 2013

TO Messrs:

ESTA CO., LTD.

59 - C BLOCK KING STREET, HAMBURG, GERMANY

谨启者: 兹确认授予你方下列货品, 其成交条款如下:

Dear Sirs: We hereby confirm having sold to you the following goods on the terms and conditions as specified below:

(1) 货物名称及规格 Name of Commodity and Specification	(2) 数量 Quantity	(3) 单价 Unit Price	(4) 总价 Amount
SANITARY WARE		FOB SHENZHEN	
(1) SY - 2189	200SETS	EUR115.00/SET	EUR23000.00
(2) SY - 2245	250SETS	EUR95.00/SET	EUR23750.00
(3) SV - 2981	450SETS	EUR72.00/SET	EUR32400.00
TOTAL:	900SETS		EUR79150.00

(5) 装运期限: Time of Shipment: LATEST DATE OF SHIPMENT AUG. 26, 2013

(6) 装运港: Port of Loading: SHENZHEN

(7) 目的港: Port of Destination: HAMBURG

(8) 分批装运: Partial Shipment: NOT ALLOWED

(9) 转船: Transshipment: NOT ALLOWED

(10) 付款条件: Terms of Payment: IRREVOCABLE L/C AT SIGHT

(11) 运输标志: Shipping Marks: ESTA/HAMBURG/ NO. 1 - 500

(12) 保险: Insurance: The Seller should cover insurance for 110% of the total invoice value against All Risks as per Ocean Marine Cargo Clauses of PICC dated 1/1/1981.

(13) 仲裁: Arbitration: All disputes arising from the execution of, or in connection with this Sales Confirmation, shall be settled amicably through friendly negotiation. In case no settlement can be reached through negotiation, the case shall then be submitted to China International Economic and Trade Arbitration Commission, Shanghai Commission for arbitration in accordance with Rules of Arbitration of China International Economic and Trade Arbitration Commission. The award made by the Commission should be accepted as final and binding upon both parties.

(14) REMARKS: 买方须于 2013 年 5 月 1 日前开出本批交易的信用证(或通知售方进口许可证号码)。否则, 售方有权不经过通知取消本确认书, 或向买方提出索赔。

The Buyer shall establish the covering Letter of Credit (or notify the Import License Number) before MAY 1, 2013, falling which the Seller reserves the right to rescind without further notice, or to accept whole or any part of this Sales Confirmation non ________ fulfilled by the Buyer, or, to lodge claim for direct losses sustained, if any.

凡以 CIF 条件成交的业务，保额为发票价的 110%，投保险别以售货确认书中所开列的为限，买方如果要求增加保额或保险范围，应于装船前经卖方同意，因此而增加的保险费由买方负责。

For transactions concluded on C. I. F. basis it is understood that the insurance amount will be for 110% of the invoice value against the risks specified in the Sales Confirmation. If additional Insurance amount of coverage is required, the buyers must have the consent of the Sellers before Shipment and the additional premium is to be borne by the buyers.

本确认书内所述全部或部分商品，如因人力不可抗拒的原因，以致不能履约或延迟交货，卖方概不负责。

The Seller shall not be held liable for failure of delay in delivery of the entire lot or a portion of the goods under this Sales Confirmation in consequence of any Force Majeure incidents.

买方在开给卖方的信用证上请填注本确认书号码。

The Buyer is requested always to quote THE NUMBER OF THIS SALES CONFIRMATION in the Letter of Credit to be opened in favour of the Seller.

买方收到本售货确认书后请立即签回一份，如买方对本确认书有异议，应于收到后五天内提出，否则认为买方已同意接受本确认书所规定的各项条款。

The buyer is requested to sign and return one copy of the Sales Confirmation immediately after the receipt of same, Objection, if any, should be raised by the Buyer within five days after the receipt of this Sales Confirmation, in the absence of which it is understood that the Buyer has accepted the terms and condition of the Sales Confirmation.

买方	卖方
THE BUYER	THE SELLER
KINLIN GREEN	张强
ESTA CO. , LTD.	CHAOZHOU HUALI CERAMICS FACTORY

2. 根据合同审核信用证（见表 1-2-9）

表 1-2-9　信用证中的不符条款与修改

序号	信用证不符之处	应改为
1	合同要求：信用证开证日期不得迟于 2013 年 4 月，信用证为：31C：DATE OF ISSUE 130501，信用证不符	信用证应改为：31C：DATE OF ISSUE ：130430
2	合同要求：不允许转船。信用证为：43T：TRANSHIPMENT ALLOWED ，信用证不符	信用证应改为：43T：TRANSHIPMENT：NOT ALLOWED

续表

序号	信用证不符之处	应改为
3	合同规定的货币为欧元，信用证为 USD，信用证不符	信用证应改为： 32B：CURRENCY CODE，AMOUNT EUR150000 45A：@ EUR 115/SET @ EUR 95/SET @ EUR 72/SET
4	合同要求：最迟装运期：2013. 8. 26，信用证为：44C：LATEST DATE OF SHIPMENT 130626　信用证不符	信用证应改为：44C：LATEST DATE OF SHIPMENT 130826
5	合同规定贸易术语为 FOB 深圳，信用证为：47A * INSURANCE WILL BE COVERED BY THE BENEFICIARY'S. 信用证不符	信用证应改为：47A * INSURANCE WILL BE COVERED BY THE APPLICANT'S

项目二

结 汇 单 据

项目介绍

在进出口业务中，出口方在货物装船后，将准备好相关单据，在信用证有效期及交单期内向议付银行交单议付。只要出口方提交的单据符合信用证的要求，做到“单证一致、单单一致”，就可以顺利结汇，收回货款。因此要求单证员必须能够准确、熟练地制作结汇单据。

学习目标

知识目标

- □ 掌握商业发票、装箱单、汇票的缮制要求。
- □ 了解产地证和其他结汇单据的缮制要求。

能力目标

能够根据信用证条款或合同条款，准确填写商业发票、装箱单、汇票等结汇单据的相关项目。

德育目标

培养学生认真仔细、严谨负责的学习和工作态度。

项目情境

张丽实习的青岛海富贸易有限公司与荷兰 FUTURO 公司签订了一份出口合同。合同中规定采用信用证方式支付货款，师傅李华带领张丽按照制单要求，完成出口青岛春卷这一合同的商业发票、装箱单、汇票、产地证和其他结汇单据制作。

英文储备

Commercial Invoice	商业发票
Packing List	装箱单
Bill of Exchange / Draft	汇　票
Certificate of Origin	一般产地证
GSP Certificate of Origin form A	普惠制原产地证
Shipping Advise	装船通知
Beneficiary's Certificate	受益人证明

任务分解

为了完成结汇单据项目的学习，具体可分解为以下五个任务：

(1) 缮制商业发票。

(2) 缮制装箱单。

(3) 缮制汇票。

(4) 缮制产地证。

(5) 缮制其他结汇单据。

任务一　缮制商业发票

【工作认知】

一、认知商业发票

(一) 商业发票的含义

商业发票（Commercial Invoice），简称“发票”。它是出口方向进口方开列的发货价目清单，是买卖双方记账的依据，也是进出口报关交税的总说明。

（二）商业发票的作用

商业发票是全套出口单据的核心，是进出口结汇单证中最重要的单据之一，是出口方缮制其他单据的依据。

（1）商业发票是买卖双方交易的证明文件。

（2）商业发票是买卖双方收付货款和记账的凭证。

（3）商业发票是进出口双方办理进出口报关并缴纳税款的依据。

（4）在不需要卖方出具汇票的情况下，发票可替代汇票作为付款的依据。

（5）发票还是托运、投保、理赔、出口核销、出口退税等业务的重要凭证。

（三）商业发票样章

商业发票样章如下所示：

COMMERCIAL INVOICE

Original

To: 5. 收货人/抬头人

Invoice No.: 1. 发票编号

Date: 2. 出票日期

L/C No.: 3. 信用证号

Contract No.: 4. 合同号

From: 6. 装运港 To 目的港

Shipping Marks	Quantities & Descpription	Unit Price	Amount
7. 唛头	8. 数量及货物描述 11. 声明文句	9. 单价	10. 总值 12. 出票人签名或盖章

二、缮制商业发票

（一）商业发票的格式

商业发票无统一格式，一般都由出口商自行设计，但基本栏目大致相同，内容必须要符合信用证或合同要求。一般来说，商业发票应该具备以下三部分：

1. 首文部分

首文部分应该列明发票的名称、发票号码、合同号码、发票的出票日期和地点，以及装运港、卸货港、发货人、收货人等。这部分一般都是已印刷的项目，后面留有的空格须填写。

2. 文本部分

发票的文本主要包括唛头、商品名称、货物数量、规格、单价、总价毛重/净重等内容。

3. 结文部分

发票的结文一般包括信用证中加注的特别条款或文句。

发票的结文还包括发票的出票人签字。发票的出票人签字一般在发票的右下角，通常包括两部分内容：一是出口商的名称（信用证的受益人）；二是出口公司经理或其他授权人手签，有时也用手签图章代替手签。

（二）商业发票的缮制规范

商业发票的主要内容如下：

1. 发票编号（Invoice No.）

由各公司统一编号。发票作为中心票据，其他票据的号码均可与此号码相一致，如汇票号码、装箱单号码等一般均与发票号码一致。

2. 出票日期（Date）

在全套单据中，发票是签发日最早的单据。它应该不早于合同的签订日期，不迟于提单的签发日期。

3. 信用证号（L/C No.）

当采用信用证支付货款时，填写信用证号码。当采用其他支付方式时，此项不填。

4. 合同号（Contract No.）

合同号码应与信用证上列明的一致，一笔交易牵涉几个合同的，应在发票上表示出来。

5. 收货人/抬头人（To）

抬头人即买方名称，应与信用证中所规定的严格一致。如果信用证中没有特别的规定，则将信用证的开证申请人或收货人的名称、地址填入此栏。

【例2-1-1】 信用证开证申请人为"ABC Co. Ltd., New York"，但又规定"Invoice to be made out in the name of XYZ Co. Ltd., New York"，则发票的抬头应为XYZ CO. LTD., NEW YORK。

6. 装运及目的港（From…To…）

本栏要填上货物自装运地（港）至目的地（港）的地名，有转运情况应予以表示。这些内容应与提单上的相关部分一致。如果货物需要转运则注明转运地。

【例2-1-2】 信用证规定货物从青岛港启运，运至纽约，转运至波士顿。则发票应填写 From QINGDAO, CHINA To NEW YORK, USA W/T BOSTON。

7. 唛头（Shipping Marks）

运输标志，又称"唛头"，一般由四部分组成：（1）收货人或买方名称的英文缩写字母或简称；（2）合同号/参考号；（3）目的港名称；（4）货物件数。

注意事项：

（1）如果无唛头，可以打上 N/M（No mark）；

（2）发票中的唛头应与全套单据的唛头相一致；

（3）如果来证规定唛头，可按照来证缮制。

【例2-1-3】 信用证要求自制唛头。已知开证申请人为 Golden Garden Co. Ltd.，合同号为 JM8015，目的港为 London，货物总包装数为 500Cartons，则唛头应制作为：

G. G. C.
JM8015
LONDON
NO. 1-500

8. 数量及货物描述（Quantity and Description）

信用证支付方式下的发票对货物描述应严格与信用证的描述一致。货物描述内容一般包括合同的四个主要条款：数量条款、品质条款、包装条款、详见合约。

【例2-1-4】 2500 Dozen Gloves，Article No. FS23，Packed in 12 Bags，as per contract No. 331 .

资料卡

信用证引导货物内容的词或词组主要有：

（1）Description of Goods；
（2）Covering Shipment of；
（3）Description of Merchandise；
（4）Covering the following Goods by；
（5）Covering Value of；
（6）Shipment of goods.

有时候来证在有关货物内容引导词的引导下，还包括其他不属于这一类的内容，如有关价格、装运等条款。在制单时，应把这些内容分别填写在合适的单据和栏目中。

注意事项：

（1）缮制发票时，数量必须反映货物的实际装运数量，做到单证一致。尤其当信用证只给定界限时，如“Not Exceed20000M/T，Minus 5% Quantity Allowance”，在这样的条件下需要注明实际装运数量。

（2）如果信用证规定或者实际业务需要，一批货物要分制几套单据，则每套单据应缮制一份发票，各发票的货物数量之和应等于该批货物的总货物数量。

（3）如果信用证允许分批装运，又规定了一定的增减幅度，则每批货物应该按照相同的增减幅度掌握。

（4）《UCP600》规定：“about”、“circa”、“approximate”等字样，允许增减10%。

（5）对成交商品规格较多的，信用证常规定“AS PER S/C NO. …”，制单时须分别详列各种规格和单价。

9. 单价（Unit Price）

单价包括计价货币、计价单位、单位价格金额和贸易术语四部分，如“USD60.00 PER CTN CIF LONDON”。

如果信用证有具体规定，则应与信用证一致。发票金额一般应与汇票金额相同，且不能超过信用证总金额。

注意事项：

（1）发票的单价必须与信用证上的单价完全一致；

（2）一定要写明货币名称、计量单位；

（3）贸易术语是关系到买卖双方的风险划分、费用负担问题，同时也是海关征税的依据，应正确缮制。

10. 总值（Amount）

除非信用证上另有规定，货物总值不能超过信用证金额。

实际制单时，来证要求在发票中扣除佣金或折扣的，则必须扣除。折扣与佣金的处理方法相同。

【例 2－1－5】 来证要求“THE AMOUNT OF 2% COMMISSION SHOULD BE DEDUCTED FROM INVOICE”，且总额为“USD20000.00 FOBC2 OSLO”，则填在价格栏中的金额的计算如下：

	USD20000.00
LESS COMMISSION OF 2%：	USD400.00
TOTAL：	USD19600.00

11. 声明文句

信用证要求在发票内特别加列船名、原产地、进口许可证号码等声明文句，制单时必须一一详列。常用的声明字句有：

（1）证明所到货物与合同或订单所列货物相符。

如：We hereby certify that the goods named have been supplied in conformity with Order No. 123. 兹证明本发票所列货物与第 123 号合同相符。

（2）证明原产地。

如：We hereby certify that the above mentioned goods are of China Origin. 兹证明所列货物是中国原产。

（3）证明货真价实。

如：We certify that this invoice is in all respects true and correct both as regards to the price and description of the goods referred herein. 兹证明本发票所列货物在价格和品质规格各方面均真实无误。

12. 出票人签名或盖章

商业发票只能由信用证中规定的受益人出具。除非信用证另有规定，如果用影印、电脑处理或者复写方法制作出来的发票，应该在作为正本的发票上注明“正本”（ORIGINAL）的字样，并且由出单人签字。

资料卡

《UCP600》规定商业发票可不必签字，但有时来证规定发票需要手签的，则不能盖胶皮签字章，必须手签。向墨西哥、阿根廷出口商品，即使信用证没有规定，也必须手签。

【工作指导】

青岛海富贸易有限公司收到的来自荷兰 FUTURO 公司申请开出的信用证，张丽的师傅李华根据信用证所给内容及相关资料制作了一份商业发票。

资料 1：信用证

MT：700		ISSUE OF A DOCUMENTARY CREDIT
SEQUENCE OF TOTAL	*27：	1/1
FORM OF DOC. CREDIT	*40A：	IRREVOCABLE
DOC. CREDIT NUMBER	*20：	IC01925U
DATE OF ISSUE	31C：	20130525
EXPRIRY	*31D：	DATE 20130725 PLACE AT YOUR COUNTRY INQINGDAO
ISSUING BANK	51A：	WACHOVIA BANK, NO. 3 K STREET，RM 504 FUNGLEE COMM. BLDG. ROTTERDAM NETHERLANDS
APPLICANT	*50：	FUTURO INDUSTRIAL CO. LTD.， ROTTERDAM NETHERLANDS TEL：031 431 7295
BENEFICIARY	*59：	QINGDAO HAIFU TRADING CO. LTD.， NO. 1HONGKONG ROAD， QINGDAO CHINA
AMOUNT	*32B：	CURRENCY USD AMOUNT USD40000. 00
AVAILABLE WITH /BY	*41D：	ANY BANK BY DEF PAYMENT
DRAFT AT…	42C：	AT 60 DAYS AFTER B/L SHIPMENT DATE
DRAWEE	42A：	ISSUING BANK
PARTIAL SHIPMENT	43P：	ALLOWED
TRANSHIPMENT：	43T：	ALLOWED
LOADING IN CHARGE	44A：	QINGDAO，CHINA
FOR TRANSPORT TO	44B：	ROTTERDAM PORT，NETHERLANDS
LATEST SHIPMENT DATE	44C：	20130710
DESCRIPTION OF GOODS	45A：	

2450CARTONS (ONE CONTAINER) OF QINGDAO SPRING ROLLS AT USD15. 50PER CTN CIFROTTERDAM

PACKING：20G PER PC，50PCS IN A BOX，9 BOXES IN A CARTON

PACKED IN PLANT OF QINGDAO BANMU FOODS PRODUCTS CO. LTD.，QINGDAO INDUSTRIAL ZONE QINGDAO.

AS PER CONTRACT NO. MSR719 DATE: 20130412
DOCUMENTS REQUIRED 46A:

+ SIGNED COMMERCIAL INVOICE IN THREE COPIES CERTIFYING COUNTRY OF ORIGIN.
+ FULL SET OF ORIGINAL CLEAN ON BAORD OCEAN BILLS OF LADING CONSIGNED TO ORDER OF SHIPPER MARKED FREIGHT PREPAID NOTIFY APPLICANT AND ISSUING BANK.
+ PACKING LIST IN THREE COPIES.
+ MARINE INSURANCE POLICY OR CERTIFICATE IN DUPLICATE ENDORSED IN BLANK, WITH CLAIM PAYABLE IN NETHLANDS IN THE CURRENCY OF THE DRAFT, COVERING 110 PERCENT OF INVOICE VALUE, INCLUDING ICC (A) AND ICC WAR CLAUSE AS PER INSTITUTE CARGO CLAUSE DATED 1/1/1982.
+ SHIPPING ADVICE HAS BEEN SENT TO APPLICANT WITHIN 3 DAYS FROM DATE OF SHIPMENT INDICATING L/C NO., INVOICE NO., AMOUNT, DETAILS OF GOODS, NAME OF VESSEL, VOYAGE NO., DATE OF SHIPMENT, PORT OF LOADING, B/L NO., CONTAINER NO., SEAL NO., ESTIMATED TIME OF ARRIVAL.
+ CERTIFICATE OF ORIGINAND GSP FORM A SIGNED BY C. I. Q.
+ COPY OF BENEFICIARY CERTIFICATE CERTIFY THAT ONE COMPLETE SET OF N/N DOCUMENTS HAS BEEN SENT TO APPLICANT BY COURIER WITHIN FIVE DAYS OF THE B/L DATE.

ADDITIONAL COND.　　47A:

+ SHIPMENT DOCUMENTS EVIDENCE THIS L/C NO.
+ THE INVOICE SEPARATELY MENTION FOB VALUE, FREIGHT CHARGE.
+ B/L MUST MARK THAT THE GOODS SHIPPED IN 40 HR CONTAINER AND SET AT -18 DEGREES CENTIGRADE OR LOWER

DETAILS OF CHARGES:　　71B:
ALL BANK CHARGES OUTSIDE ROTTERDAM ARE FOR ACCOUNT OF BENEFICIARY.
CONFIRMATION INSTRUCTIONS *49:　　WITHOUT
"ADVISE THROUGH" BANK 57A:　BANK OF CHINA LTD., SHANDONG BRANCH

资料2:

INVOICE NO.: QD528
C/O. NO. G370213070203
H. S. CODE: 19022200
VESSEL NAME: SITCQINGDAO V. 23　　B/L NO. SITC229173
CONTAINER NO. SITC1292748　SEAL NO. 006265
FREIGHT CHARGE: USD3150.00
PACKING PER CTN: N. W. 9.00KGS / G. W. 10.00KGS / MEASUREMENT 0.0195CBM

THE CARRIER AS NYK LING SHIPPING CO.,
MARKS: MAKE A STANDARD MARK BY SELF
师傅李华制作的商业发票：

QINGDAO HAIFU TRADING CO. LTD.
NO. 1 HONGKONG ROAD, QINGDAO CHINA
TEL: 86－0532－85896210 FAX: 86－0532－85896211

COMMERCIAL INVOICE

Original

To: FUTURO INDUSTRIAL CO. LTD.,
ROTTERDAM NETHERLANDS
TEL: 031－431 7295

No. QD528
Date: JUN. 25, 2013
L/C No.: IC01925U
Contract: MSR719

From: QINGDAO, CHINA **To** ROTTERDAM PORT, NETHERLANDS

Shipping Marks	Quantities & Descpription	Unit Price	Amount
F. I. C. MSR719 ROTTERDAM NO. 1－2450	2450CARTONS (ONE CONTAINER) OF QINGDAO SPRING ROLLS	CIF ROTTERDAM @USD15.50/CTN	USD37975.00 =======

H. S. CODE: 19022200
PACKING: 20G PER PC, 50PCS IN A BOX, 9 BOXES IN A CARTON
AS PER CONTRACT NO. MSR719 DATE: APR. 12, 2013
PACKED IN PLANT OF QINGDAO BANMU FOODS PRODUCTS CO. LTD.,
QINGDAO INDUSTRIAL ZONE QINGDAO
FREIGHT CHARGE: USD3150.00
FOB VALUE: USD34825.00
WE HEREBY CERTIFY THAT THE GOODS ARE OF CHINA ORIGIN

QINGDAO HAIFU TRADING CO. LTD.,
LIHUA

【工作演练】

张丽在师傅李华的指导下，已经基本掌握了制作商业发票的技能。下面请你和张丽一起根据青岛海富贸易有限公司收到的来自美国的 PRADA 公司的信用证及相关资料独立制作一份商业发票。

资料1：信用证

LETTER OF CREDIT

FORM OF DOC. CREDIT	*40A:	IRREVOCABLE
DOC. CREDIT NUMBER	*20:	KL21909
DATE OF ISSUE	31C:	20130310
APPLICABLE RULES	*40E:	UCP LATEST VERSION
EXPIRY	*31D:	DATE 20130510 PLACE IN CHINA
ISSUING BANK	51A:	HSBC BANK CANADA
APPLICANT	*50:	PRADA LTD., CO. 627 EAST LAMEN STREET, TORONTO CANADA
BENEFICIARY	*59:	QINGDAO HAIFU TRADING CO. LTD., NO. 1 HONGKONG ROAD, QINGDAO CHINA
AMOUNT:	*32B:	CURRENCY USD AMOUNT 50000.00
AVAILABLE WITH/BY	*41D:	ANY BANK IN CHINA BY DRAFT
DRAFTS AT	42C:	30 DAYS AFTER B/L DATE
DRAWEE	*42A:	HSBC BANK CANADA
PARTIAL SHIPMENTS	43P:	ALLOWED
TRANSHIPMENT	43T:	ALLOWED
PORT OF LOADING:	44E:	ANY PORT IN CHINA
PORT OF DISCHARGE	44F:	TORONTO CANADA
LATEST DATE OF SHIPMENT	44C:	20130420
DESCRIPT. OF GOODS	45A:	

SILK FABRIC CIFTORONTO

SIZE	QUANTITY	PACKAGE	UNIT PRICE
GRADE I	24000 YDS	120BALES	USD26.00/YD
GRADE II	16000 YDS	80BALES	USD19.00/YD
GRADE III	12000YDS	60BALES	USD15.00/YD

PACKING: 200 YARDS IN A BALE AS PER CONTRACT NO. KS3761 DATED FEB. 27, 2011

DOCUMENTS REQUIRED 46A:

+SIGNED COMMMERCIAL INVOICE IN ONE ORIGINAL AND TWO COPIES CERTIFYING COUNTRY OF ORIGIN.

+ FULL SET OF CLEAN ON BOARD OCEAN BILLS OF LADING MADE OUT TO ORDER OF SHIPPER AND MARKED FREIGHT PREPAID AND NOTIFY ISSUING BANK AND APPLICANT.

+ PACKING LIST IN TWO COPIES .

ADDITIONAL COND. 47A:

+ALL DOCUMENTS TO BE IN ENGLISH LANGUAGE AND MUST BEAR L/C NO. AND DATE.

+ B/L SHOWING CARRIER AS : COSCO CONTAINER LINE

+ THE WORDS "ONE PART OF SAMPLE HAS BEEN SENT TO APPLICANT" MUST BE GIVEN ON THE INVOICE.
+ SHIPPING MARK: PRADA/TORONTO/NO. 1 – UP APPEAR ON ALL DOCUMENTS
+ B/L INDICATED THAT THE PACKAGE HAS BEEN SEAWORTHY EXPORT STANDARD PACKING.

资料 2：

1. INVOICE NO. TD51921
2. B/L NO. COSCO48935　　VESSEL NAME: BLUE BIRD V. 72E
CONTAINER NO. PL5610　　SEAL NO. 20457
3. MEAS. 1.350CBM /BALE　　N. W. 100KGS/BALE　　G. W. 110KGS /BALE

资料 3：

QINGDAO HAIFU TRADING CO. LTD.
NO. 1 HONGKONG ROAD, QINGDAO CHINA
TEL: 86 – 0532 – 85896210　FAX86 – 0532 – 85896211

COMMERCIAL INVOICE

Original

To:

Invoice No.:
Date:
L/C No.:
Contract No.:

From:　　　　**To**

Shipping Marks	Quantities & Descpription	Unit Price	Amount

提示：

（1）按照实际情况，注意发票日期的填写应在信用证开证之后。

（2）制作时，注意信用证发票条款对加注内容的要求。

【工作评价】

1. 评价标准

QINGDAO HAIFU TRADING CO. LTD.

NO. 1HONGKONG ROAD，QINGDAO CHINA

TEL：86－0532－85896210 FAX86－0532－85896211

COMMERCIAL INVOICE

Original

To: PRADA LTD.，CO.
627 EAST LAMEN STREET，TORONTO
CANADA

Invoice No.：TD51921
Date：MAR. 17，2013
L/C No.：KL21909
Contract No.：KS3761

From：QINGDAO，CHINA To TORONTO，CANADA

Shipping Marks	Quantities & Descpription			Unit Price	Amount
PRADA	SILK FABRIC			CIFTORONTO	
KS3761	SIZE	QUANTITY	PACKAGE		
TORONTO	GRADE I	24000 YDS	120BALES	USD26.00/YD	USD624000.00
NO. 1－260	GRADE II	16000 YDS	80 BALES	USD19.00/YD	USD304000.00
	GRADE III	12000 YDS	60 BALES	USD15.00/YD	USD180000.00
	TOTAL：	52000YDS	260BALES		USD1108000.00

PACKED IN 260 BALES OF 200 YARDS EACH.
AS PER CONTRACT NO. KS3761 DATED FEB. 27，2011
WE HEREBY CERTIFY THAT THE GOODS ARE OF CHINA ORIGIN.
L/C NO. KL21909 DATED MAR. 10，2011
ONE PART OF SAMPLE HAS BEEN SENT TO APPLICANT.

QINGDAO HAIFU TRADING CO. LTD.，

ZHANG LI

2. 评价表（见表 2－1－1）

表 2－1－1

评价指标 \ 评价人	自　评	互　评	师　评
独立完成情况（20 分）			
格式规范性（20 分）			
内容完整性、正确性（50 分）			
内容简明性、整洁性（10 分）			
合计总分			

任务二　缮制装箱单

【工作认知】

包装单据是记载和描述商品包装情况的单据，是商业发票的补充。常用的包装单据有装箱单、包装明细单、重量单、磅码单、尺码单等。

一、认知装箱单

（一）装箱单的含义

装箱单（Packing List），又称包装单，是信用证要求的主要单据之一，是表明装箱货物的名称、规格、数量、重量、唛头、箱号、件数以及包装形式、包装内容的单据，通常与发票同时缮制。

（二）包装的作用

（1）包装单据是出口商缮制商业发票及其他单据时计量、计价的基础资料。

（2）包装单据是进口商清点数量或重量的依据。

（3）包装单据是海关查验货物的凭证。

（4）包装单是公证或商检机构查验货物的参考资料。

（三）装箱单样章

装箱单样章如下所示：

PACKING LIST

Original

To:	5. 收货人/抬头人	**No.**	1. 编号
		Date:	2. 出票日期
		L/C No.:	3. 信用证号
		Contract:	4. 合同号
From:	6. 装运港	To	6. 目的港

Shipping Marks	NO. & kind of pkgs: Description of the Goods	Net Weight	Gross Weight	Measurement
7. 唛头	8. 数量及货物描述	9. 净重	10. 毛重	11. 体积

声明文句

12. 出票人签名或盖章

二、缮制装箱单

（一）装箱单的格式

装箱单没有统一格式，一般都由出口商自行设计，内容必须符合合同和信用证要求。

（二）装箱单的缮制规范

装箱单样章见图2-2-1，其主要内容如下：

1. 编号（No.）

本栏填写应与发票号码一致。

2. 出票日期（Date）

装箱单一般与商业发票同时制作。因此装箱单日期通常与发票日期相同或晚于发票日期，但不能晚于提单日期。

3. 信用证号（L/C No.）

本栏填写要求同商业发票。

4. 合同号（Contract No.）

本栏填写要求同商业发票。

5. 收货人/抬头人（To）

本栏填写要求同商业发票。抬头人即买方、信用证的开证申请人或收货人。

6. 装运及目的港（From…To…）

本栏填写要求同商业发票。填写货物自装运地（港）至目的地（港）的地名，如果货物需要转运则注明转运地。

7. 唛头（Shipping Marks）

本栏填写要求同商业发票。

8. 数量及货物描述（Quantity & Description）

本栏填写要求同商业发票。商品规格和包装规格按货物情况和信用证要求详细列明。

9. 净重（Net Weight）

本栏应注明每个包装的净重，并合计所有货物的总净重。常用计重单位为千克（Kg）。

10. 毛重（Gross Weight）

本栏应注明每个包装的毛重，并合计所有货物的总毛重。常用计重单位为千克（Kg）。

11. 尺码（Measurement）

本栏应根据实际每个包装的体积来填写，即每包装的长 * 宽 * 高，并合计所有货物的总体积。常用尺码单位为立方米（CBM/M^3），且一般保留 3 位小数。

【例 2-2-1】

Mearsurement per carton：40cm * 50cm * 60cm

Total package：400cartons

每纸箱的尺码：0.120CBM　总尺码：48.000CBM

12. 出票人签名或盖章

本栏签章与商业发票一致。如要求中性装箱单，则不能签章。

【工作指导】

青岛海富贸易有限公司收到的来自荷兰 FUTURO 公司申请开出的信用证，张丽的师傅李华经根据信用证所给内容及相关资料制作了一份装箱单。

资料 1：信用证

MT：700	ISSUE OF A DOCUMENTARY CREDIT	
SEQUENCE OF TOTAL	*27：	1/1
FORM OF DOC. CREDIT	*40A：	IRREVOCABLE
DOC. CREDIT NUMBER	*20：	IC01925U
DATE OF ISSUE	31C：	20130525
EXPRIRY	*31D：	DATE 20130725 IN QINGDAO
ISSUING BANK：	51A	WACHOVIA BANK, NO. 3K STREET，RM 504 FUNGLEE COMM. BLDG. ROTTERDAM NETHERLANDS
APPLICANT.	*50：	FUTURO INDUSTRIAL CO. LTD.， ROTTERDAM NETHERLANDS TEL：031 431 7295
BENEFICIARY	*59：	QINGDAO HAIFU TRADING CO. LTD.，

		NO. 1HONGKONG ROAD,
		QINGDAO CHINA
AMOUNT	*32B:	CURRENCY USD AMOUNT USD40000. 00
AVAILABLE WITH /BY	*41D:	ANY BANK BY DEF PAYMENT
DRAFT AT···	42C:	AT 60 DAYS AFTER B/L SHIPMENT DATE
DRAWEE	42A:	ISSUING BANK
PARTIAL SHIPMENT	43P:	ALLOWED
TRANSHIPMENT:	43T:	ALLOWED
LOADING IN CHARGE	44A:	QINGDAO, CHINA
FOR TRANSPORT TO	44B:	ROTTERDAM PORT, NETHERLANDS
LATEST SHIPMENT DATE	44C:	20130710

DESCRIPTION OF GOODS 45A:

2450CARTONS (ONE CONTAINER) OF QINGDAO SPRING ROLLS AT USD15. 50PER CTN CIF ROTTERDAM

PACKING: 20G PER PC, 50PCS IN A BOX, 9 BOXES IN A CARTON

PACKED IN PLANT OF QINGDAO BANMU FOODS PRODUCTS CO. LTD., QINGDAO INDUSTRIAL ZONE QINGDAO.

AS PER CONTRACT NO. MSR719 DATE: 20130412

DOCUMENTS REQUIRED 46A:

+ SIGNED COMMERCIAL INVOICE IN THREE COPIES CERTIFYING COUNTRY OF ORIGIN.

+ FULL SET OF ORIGINAL CLEAN ON BOARD OCEAN BILLS OF LADING CONSIGNED TO ORDER OF SHIPPER MARKED FREIGHT PREPAID NOTIFY APPLICANT AND ISSUING BANK.

+ PACKING LIST IN THREE COPIES.

+ MARINE INSURANCE POLICY OR CERTIFICATE IN DUPLICATE ENDORSED IN BLANK, WITH CLAIM PAYABLE IN NETHLANDS IN THE CURRENCY OF THE DRAFT, COVERING 110 PERCENT OF INVOICE VALUE, INCLUDING ICC (A) AND ICC WAR CLAUSE AS PER INSTITUTE CARGO CLAUSE DATED 1/1/1982.

+ SHIPPING ADVICE HAS BEEN SENT TO APPLICANT WITHIN 3 DAYS FROM DATE OF SHIPMENT INDICATING L/C NO., INVOICE NO., AMOUNT, DETAILS OF GOODS, NAME OF VESSEL, VOYAGE NO., DATE OF SHIPMENT, PORT OF LOADING, B/L NO., CONTAINER NO., SEAL NO., ESTIMATED TIME OF ARRIVAL.

+ CERTIFICATE OF ORIGINAND GSP FORM A SIGNED BY C. I. Q.

+ COPY OF BENEFICIARY CERTIFICATE CERTIFY THAT ONE COMPLETE SET OF N/N DOCUMENTS HAS BEEN SENT TO APPLICANT BY COURIER WITHIN FIVE DAYS OF THE B/L DATE.

ADDITIONAL COND. 47A:

+SHIPMENT DOCUMENTS EVIDENCE TIIIS L/C NO.

+THE INVOICE SEPARATELY MENTION FOB VALUE, FREIGHT CHARGE.

+B/L MUST MARK THAT THE GOODS SHIPPED IN 40'HR CONTAINER AND SET AT -18 DEGREES CENTIGRADE OR LOWER

DETAILS OF CHARGES：71B：
ALL BANK CHARGES OUTSIDE ROTTERDAM ARE FOR ACCOUNT OF BENEFICIARY.
CONFIRMATION INSTRUCTIONS ＊49： WITHOUT
"ADVISE THROUGH" BANK 57A： BANK OF CHINA LTD.，SHANDONG BRANCH

资料2：

INVOICE NO.：QD528
C/O. NO. G370213070203
H. S. CODE：19022200
VESSEL NAME：SITC QINGDAO V. 23 B/L NO. SITC229173
CONTAINER NO. SITC1292748 SEAL NO. 006265
FREIGHT CHARGE：USD3150. 00
PACKING PER CTN：N. W. 9. 00KGS / G. W. 10. 00KGS / MEASUREMENT 0. 0195CBM
THE CARRIER AS NYK LING SHIPPING CO.，
MARK：MAKE A STANDARD MARK BY SELF

师傅李华制作的装箱单：

PACKING LIST

Original

To：FUTURO INDUSTRIAL CO. LTD.，
ROTTERDAM NETHERLANDS
TEL：031 431 7295

No. QD528
Date：JUN. 25，2013
L/C No.：IC01925U
Contract：MSR719

From：QINGDAO，CHINA **To** ROTTERDAM PORT，NETHERLANDS

Shipping Marks	NO. & kind of pkgs：Description of the Goods	Net Weight	Gross Weight	Measurement
F. I. C.	2450CARTONS（ONE CONTAINER）			
MSR719	OF QINGDAO SPRING ROLLS	@9. 00KGS/CTN	@10. 00KGS/CTN	@0. 0195CBM/CTN
ROTTERDAM	TOTAL：	22050. 00KGS	24500. 00KGS	47. 775CBM
NO. 1－2450				

PACKING：20G PER PC，50PCS IN A BOX，9 BOXES IN A CARTON

QINGDAO HAIFU TRADING CO. LTD.，
LIHUA

【工作演练】

张丽在师傅李华的指导下，已经掌握了制作装箱单的技能。下面请你和张丽一起根据所提供的信用证制作一份装箱单。

资料1：信用证

APPLICATION HEADER	*0 700:	
	KOOKMIN BANK SEOUL, KOREA	
MSG UESR REF.	*108:	: 0274000
FORM OF DOC. CREDIT	*40A:	IRREVOCABLE
DOC. CREDIT NUMBER	*20:	M0912NS19
DATE OF ISSUE	31C:	DEC. 20, 2012
APPLICABLE RULES	*40E:	UCP LATEST VERSION
EXPIRY	*31D:	FEB. 28, 2013
APPLICANT BANK	51A:	KOOKMIN BANK SEOUL KOREA (HEAD OFFICE)
APPLICANT	*50:	GEO ENTERPRISE CO., LTD. 104 – 2 E – MOY – DONG JANGAN – KU KOREA
BENEFICIARY	*59:	QINGDAO SUNNY BRIGHT TRADING CO. 36 DONGHAI ROAD QINGDAO CHINA
AMOUNT:	*32B:	CURRENCY AMOUNT USD8500.00
AVAILABLE WITH/BY	*41D:	ANY BANK OF CHINA BY DRAFT
DRAFTS AT	42C:	30 DAYS SIGHT
DRAWEE	42A:	KOOKMIN BANK SEOUL KOREA (HEAD OFFICE)
PARTIAL SHIPMENTS	43P:	ALLOWED
TRANSHIPMENT	43T:	ALLOWED BUT SHIPMENT BY CONTAINER
PORT OF LOADING	44E:	ANY PORT OF CHINA
PORT OF DISCHARGE	44F:	BUSAN KOREA
LATEST DATE OF SHIP.	44C:	JAN. 10, 2013
DESCRIPT. OF GOODS	45A:	

BABY TOY

ART. NO.	QUANTITY	UNIT PRICE
WWP – 2A	350 PCS	USD3.20 PER PC
WWB – 2A	200 PCS	USD4.15 PER PC
WGF – 1F	520 PCS	USD4.50 PER PC

PACKING: ONE PC IN ONE PLASTIC BAG, TEN BAGS IN ONE CARTON

CFR BUSAN AS PER CONTRACT NO. 0112T DATED NOV. 15, 2012

DOCUMENTS REQUIRED 46A:

+SIGNED INVOICE IN THREE COPIES.

+FULL SET OF CLEAN SHIPPED ON BOARD B/L TO THE ORDER OF SHIPPER MARKED FREIGHT PREPAID SHOWING CONTAINER NO. AND FCL/FCL SHIPMENT AND NOTIFY APPLICANT.

+PACKING LIST IN TWO COPIES MENTIONING DETAILS OF EACH PACKAGE.

ADDITIONAL COND.: 47A:
+COSCO OCEAN LINE AS CARRIER
+SHIPMENT IN 20 CONTAINER
+P/L CERTIFY THAT THE OUTER CARTONS HAVE BEEN MARKED WITH THE SHIPPING MARKS.

资料2:

INVOICE NO. SDT2105
VESSEL NAME: YANGMING HEQD V. 025E
B/L NO. SITT9321022
SHIPPING MARKS: GEC
TD453
BUSAN
NO. 1-107
CONTAINER NO. COLU3922101 SEAL NO. 003121
PER CARTONS: 5KGS N. W. 6KGS G. W. 0. 35CBM MEARS.

资料3:装箱单

PACKING LIST

Original

To:

No.

Date:

L/C No.:

Contract:

From: ________ To ________

Shipping Marks	NO. & kind of pkgs: Description of the Goods	Net Weight	Gross Weight	Measurement

提示:

(1) 填制装箱单时,凡是信用证中出现与包装相关的条款和内容,均应体现在装箱单上。

(2) 不同货物或同一种货物不同型号,均应分别计算出净重、毛重和尺码,再合计算出总量。

【工作评价】

1. 评价标准

PACKING LIST

ORIGINAL

To: GEO ENTERPRISE CO. , LTD.
104 – 2 E – MOY – DONG JANGAN – KU KOREA

No. SDT2105
Date: DEC. 27, 2012
L/C No.: M0912NS19
Contract: 0112T

From: QINGDAO, CHINA　　To BUSAN, KOREA

Shipping Marks	NO. & kind of pkgs: Description of the Goods			Net Weight	Gross Weight	Measurement
	BABY TOY					
GEC	ART. NO.	QUANTITY	PACKAGE	@5.00KGS/PKG	@6.00KGS/PKG	@0.350CBM/PKG
TD453	WWP – 2A	350PCS	35PKGS	175.00KGS	210.00KGS	12.250CBM
BUSAN	WWB – 2A	200PCS	20PKGS	100.00KGS	120.00KGS	7.000CBM
NO. 1 – 107	WGF – 1F	520PCS	52PKGS	260.00KGS	312.00KGS	18.200CBM
	TOTAL	1070PCS	107PKGS	535.00KGS	642.00KGS	37.450CBM

PACKED IN 107 CARTONS AND ONE PC IN ONE PLASTIC BAG, TEN BAGS IN ONECARTON.

WE HEREBY CERTIFY THAT THE OUTER CARTONS HAVE BEEN MARKED WITH THE SHIPPING MARKS

QINGDAO SUNNY BRIGHT TRADING CO.
ZHANGLI

2. 评价表（见表 2 – 2 – 1）

表 2 – 2 – 1

评价指标＼评价人	自　评	互　评	师　评
独立完成情况（20 分）			
格式规范性（20 分）			
内容完整性、正确性（50 分）			
内容简明性、整洁性（10 分）			
合计总分			

任务三 缮制汇票

【工作认知】

一、认知汇票

（一）汇票的含义

汇票（Bill of Exchange / Draft），是由出票人签发的，要求付款人在见票时或在一定期限内，无条件支付确定的金额给某人或其指定的人或持票人的书面命令。汇票是国际结算中使用最广泛的一种支付工具。

（二）汇票的种类

（1）按照出票人的不同，汇票分为银行汇票和商业汇票。

银行汇票（Bankers Draft）的出票人和付款人都是银行。银行汇票由银行签发后，交汇款人，由汇款人寄交国外收款人向付款行取款。银行汇票多为光票，不附单据。

商业汇票（Trade Draft）的出票人是商号或个人，付款人可以是商号、个人，也可以是银行。在国际贸易结算中，商业汇票通常由出口商开立，向国外进口商或银行收取货款。商业汇票大多附有货运单据。

（2）按照付款期限的不同，汇票分为即期汇票和远期汇票。

即期汇票（Sight Draft）是在提示或见票时立即付款的汇票。

远期汇票（Usance Draft）是在一定期限或特定日期付款的汇票。

（3）按照有无附属单据的不同，汇票分为光票和跟单汇票。

光票（Clean Draft）是不附带货运单据的汇票。银行汇票多是光票。

跟单汇票（Documentary Draft）是附带货运单据的汇票。商业汇票一般多为跟单汇票。在国际贸易货款结算中，绝大多数使用跟单汇票作为结算工具。

（三）汇票样章

汇票样章如下所示：

No. 1. 汇票号码 **Qingdao,** 2. 出票日期

EXCHANGE FOR 3. 汇票小写金额

At 5. 付款期限 **sight of this First of EXCHANGE（SECOND OF THE SAME TENOR AND DATE UNPAID）** **Pay to the order of** 6. 收款人

the sum of 4. 汇票大写金额

Drawn under	7. 出票依据	
To 8. 付款人		9. Authorized Signature 出票人签章

二、缮制汇票

（一）汇票的格式

汇票一般为一式两份，第一联、第二联在法律上无区别。其中一联生效则另一联自动作废。

（二）汇票的缮制规范

汇票的主要内容如下：

1. 汇票号码（No.）

本栏由出票人自行编号填入，一般使用商业发票的号码作为汇票的编号。

2. 出票日期（Dated）

本栏填写汇票出具的日期。一般由银行填写，应在提单日期后信用证有效期或规定交单期前。

3. 汇票小写金额（Exchange for）

本栏填写汇票的小写金额。一般要求汇票金额使用货币缩写和用阿拉伯数字表示的金额小写数字。

4. 汇票大写金额（the sum of）

本栏填写汇票大写金额。格式为"SAY U. S. DOLLARS + 大写的金额 + ONLY."

【例 2-3-1】

USD1234. 00

SAY U. S. DOLLARS ONE THOUSAND TWO HUNDRED AND THIRTY - FOUR ONLY.

注意事项：

（1）大小写金额均应端正地填写在虚线格内，不得涂改。

（2）汇票的大小写金额必须一致。

（3）除非信用证另有规定，汇票金额不得超过信用证金额，而且汇票金额应与发票金额一致，汇票币别必须与信用证规定和发票所使用的币别一致。

5. 付款期限（At ________ sight）

汇票按照付款期限不同，可分为即期付款和远期付款两类。

即期付款只需在汇票固定格式栏at ______ sight 中间，打上×××即可。

远期付款一般有以下四种情况：

（1）见票后××天付款，At ×× days sight，即以付款人见票承兑日为起算日，××天后到期付款。

（2）出票后××天付款，At ×× days after sight，即以汇票出票日为起算日，××天后到期付款。

（3）提单日后××天付款，At ×× days after B/L date sight，即付款人以提单签发日为起算日，××天后到期付款。

（4）某指定日期付款，指定×年×月××日为付款日，如“JUL. 9，2013”。

6. 收款人（Pay to the order of）

本栏也称汇票的“抬头”。在信用证方式下通常为出口地银行。

汇票的抬头通常有以下三种写法：

（1）指示性抬头（To order/To order of …），这种抬头的汇票须持票人背书方可转让。在我国对外贸易中，指示性抬头使用较多。

【例2-3-2】

“付××公司或其指定人”

Pay ×× Co.，或者 order / pay to the order of ×× Co.

（2）限制性抬头，这种抬头的汇票不可转让。

【例2-3-3】

“仅付××公司”

Pay ×× Co. only.

（3）持票人或来票人抬头（To bearer），这种抬头的汇票无须持票人背书即可转让。

【例2-3-4】

“付给来人”

Pay to bearer.

注意事项：

在信用证业务中，汇票要按照信用证规定填写。

（1）若来证规定“由中国银行指定”或来证对汇票收款人未规定，此应填上“pay to the order of Bank of China（由中国银行指定）”。

（2）若来证规定“由开证行指定”，此栏应填上“Pay to the order of ×× Bank（开证行名称）”。

7. 出票依据（Drawn Under）

本栏填写三项内容：开证行名称（Issuing Bank）、信用证号码（L/C No.）和开证日期（Dated）。

【例2-3-5】

Drawn under HSBC BANK HONGKONG BRANCH，L/C NO. 96KW513 DATED APR. 20，2013.

本汇票根据汇丰银行香港分行2013年4月20日的第96KW513号信用证开立。

8. 付款人（To）

本栏应填写付款行，一般为开证行。根据 UCP600 规定，信用证方式的汇票以开证行或其指定银行为付款人。如果信用证未规定付款人的名称，汇票付款人亦应填开证行名称。

在信用证业务中，汇票付款人是按信用证“draw on ××”或“drawee”确定。如果出现“drawn on ourselves/us ”条款，表明以开证行为付款人。

【例 2-3-6】

Available with any bank in China by draft(s) drawn on us.

本汇票可由中国任何银行议付，并以开证行为付款人。

9. 出票人签章（右下方空白栏 Authorized Signature）

出票人签章，即出口商签字，填写受益人公司名称。该项填写与发票相同。

【工作指导】

青岛海富贸易有限公司收到的来自荷兰 FUTURO 公司申请开出的信用证，张丽的师傅李华根据信用证所给内容及相关资料制作了一份汇票。

资料 1：信用证

MT：700 ISSUE OF A DOCUMENTARY CREDIT

SEQUENCE OF TOTAL	*27：	1/1
FORM OF DOC. CREDIT	*40A：	IRREVOCABLE
DOC. CREDIT NUMBER	*20：	IC01925U
DATE OF ISSUE	31C：	20130525
EXPRIRY	*31D：	DATE 20130725 PLACE AT YOUR COUNTRY IN QINGDAO
ISSUING BANK	51A：	WACHOVIA BANK, NO. 3K STREET, RM 504 FUNGLEE COMM. BLDG. ROTTERDAM NETHERLANDS
APPLICANT	*50：	FUTURO INDUSTRIAL CO. LTD. , ROTTERDAM NETHERLANDS TEL：031 431 7295
BENEFICIARY	*59：	QINGDAO HAIFU TRADING CO. LTD. , NO. 1HONGKONG ROAD, QINGDAO CHINA
AMOUNT	*32B：	CURRENCY USD AMOUNT USD40000. 00
AVAILABLE WITH /BY	*41D：	ANY BANK BY DEF PAYMENT
DRAFT AT…	42C：	AT 60 DAYS AFTER B/L SHIPMENT DATE
DRAWEE	42A：	ISSUING BANK

资料2：商业发票

QINGDAO HAIFU TRADING CO. LTD.
NO. 1HONGKONG ROAD, QINGDAO CHINA
TEL: 86-0532-85896210 FAX86-0532-85896211

COMMERCIAL INVOICE

Original

To: FUTURO INDUSTRIAL CO. LTD.,
ROTTERDAM NETHERLANDS

TEL: 031 431 7295

No. QD528
Date: JUN. 25, 2013
L/C No.: IC01925U
Contract: MSR719

From: QINGDAO, CHINA To ROTTERDAM PORT, NETHERLANDS

Shipping Marks	**Quantities & Description**	**Unit Price**	**Amount**
F. I. C. MSR719 ROTTERDAM NO. 1-2450	2450CARTONS (ONE CONTAINER) OF QINGDAO SPRING ROLLS	CIF ROTTERDAM @USD15. 50/CTN	USD37975. 00 ===========

H. S. CODE: 19022200
PACKING: 20G PER PC, 50PCS IN A BOX, 9 BOXES IN A CARTON
AS PER CONTRACT NO. MSR719 DATE: APR. 12, 2013
PACKED IN PLANT OF QINGDAO BANMU FOODS PRODUCTS CO. LTD.,
QINGDAO INDUSTRIAL ZONE QINGDAO
FREIGHT CHARGE: USD3150. 00
FOB VALUE: USD34825. 00
WE HEREBY CERTIFY THAT THE GOODS ARE OFCHINA ORIGIN

QINGDAO HAIFU TRADING CO. LTD.,
LIHUA

师傅李华制作的汇票如下所示：

No. QD528 **Qingdao,** JUL. 12, 2013

EXCHANGE FOR USD37975. 00

At 60 **DAYS sight of this First of EXCHANGE** (**SECOND OF THE SAME TENOR** AFTER B/L DATE (JUL. 9, 2013)

AND DATE UNPAID) **pay to the order of** BANK OF CHINA, QINGDAO CHINA

the sum of SAY U. S. DOLLARS THIRTY-SEVEN THOUSAND NINE HUNDRED AND SEVENTY-FIVE ONLY

Drawn under WACHOVIA BANK, NO. 3 K STREET, RM 504 FUNGLEE COMM. BLDG.
ROTTERDAM NETHERLANDS L/C NO. IC01925U DATED 20130525

To WACHOVIA BANK,
NO. 3 K STREET, RM 504 FUNGLEE COMM. BLDG.
ROTTERDAM NETHERLANDS

QINGDAO HAIFU TRADING CO. LTD.,
LIHUA

【工作演练】

张丽在师傅李华的指导下，已经基本掌握了制作汇票的技能。下面请你和张丽一起根据青岛海富贸易有限公司收到的来自孟加拉国 NEPUTUNE 公司的信用证和已经制作完成的商业发票，制作一份汇票。

资料1：信用证

DEAR SIRS,

IN ACCORDANCE WITH THE TERMS OF ARTICLE 7 (A) OF UCP 600 WE ADVISE HAVING RECEIVED THE FOLLOWING TELETRANSMISSION

FROM: SOUTHEAST BANK LIMITED, PRINCIPAL BRANCH

40A	FORM OF DC:	IRREVOCABLE
20	CREDIT NO:	1335-06-06-0207
31C	DATE OF ISSUE:	11 JUN 13
31D	EXPIRY DATE AND PLACE:	25 JUL13 IN CHINA
50	APPLICANT:	NEPUTUNE GARMENTS LTD. HOUSE NO. 79, 3RD FLOOR, BLOCK-H ZIA INT'L AIR PORT ROAD, DHAKA-1213, BANGLADESH
59	BENEFICIARY:	QINGDAO HAIFU CO. LTD. NO. 1 HONGKONG ROAD, QINGDAO, CHINA
32B	AMOUNT:	GBP56900.00
41D	AVAILABLE WITH/BY:	ANY BANK IN CHINA BY NEGOTIATION
42C	DRAFTS AT:	120 DAYS SIGHT
42D	DRAWEE:	SOUTHEAST BANK LIMITED PRINCIPAL BRANCH DHAKA-1000, BANGLADESH

资料2：商业发票

COMMERCIAL INVOICE

ORIGINAL

To:	NEPUTUNE GARMENTS LTD.	No.	I06/QD 000117
	HOUSE NO. 79, 3RD FLOOR, BLOCK-H	Date:	JUN. 27, 2013
	ZIA INT'L AIR PORT ROAD,	L/Cno.:	1335-06-06-0207
	DHAKA-1213, BANGLADESH	Contract:	QDBJ07115

From: QINGDAO, CHINA To CHITTAGONG, BANGLADESH

Shipping Marks	Quantities & Descpription			Unit Price	Amount
NPT	PRINTED FABRIC			CIFCHITTAGONG	
QDBJ07115	SIZE	QUANTITY	PACKING		
CHITTAGONG	DSN#1 WHITE/BLUE	30300YDS	101BALES	@ GBP1. 00/YD	GBP30300. 00
NO. 1 - 160	DSN#2 WHITE/RED	17700YDS	59BALES	@ GBP1. 50/YD	GBP26550. 00
	TOTAL	48000YDS	160BALES		GBP56850. 00

PACKED IN 160BALES AND 300YARDS PER BALES

AS PER S/C NO. QDBJ07115

WE HEREBY CERTIFY THAT THE GOODS ARE OF CHINA ORIGIN

H. S. CODE NO. 5209. 4200. 00

LCS NO. 3180

APPLICANT'S IRC NO. BA - 131610

EXPORT L/C NO. DCTST115056 DATED 06/06/2013

WE HEREBY CERTIFY THAT THE QUOTED INVOICE PRICE IS NET AND DOES NOT INCLUDE ANY COMMISSION FOR ANY AGENT IN BANGLADESH

L/C NO.: 1335 - 06 - 06 - 0207 DATED JUN. 7, 2013

QINGDAO HAIFU CO. LTD.

ZHANGLI

资料3：汇票

No. **Qingdao,**

EXCHANGE FOR

At **sight of this First of EXCHANGE (SECOND OF THE SAME TENOR AND DATE UNPAID) pay to the order of** ____________

the sum of

Drawn under ____________

To ____________

____

提示：

（1）填制汇票时，特别需要注意的是大小写金额是否一致，拼写是否正确。

（2）注意汇票付款期限，应严格按照信用证要求。

【工作评价】

1. 评价标准

No. I06/QD 000117	Qingdao,	AUG. 17, 2007
EXCHANGE FOR	GPB56850. 00	
At 120 DAYS	sight of this First of EXCHANGE (SECOND OF THE SAME TENOR	
AND DATE UNPAID)	pay to the order of	BANK OF CHINA, QINGDAO BRANCH
the sum of	SAY GREAT BRITAIN POUNDS FIFTY - SIX THOUSAND EIGHT HUNDRED	
AND FIFTY ONLY		
Drawn under	SOUTHEAST BANK LIMITED, PRINCIPAL BRANCH	
	L/C NO.: 1335 - 06 - 06 - 0207 DATED JUN. 7, 2011	
To	SOUTHEAST BANK LIMITED PRINCIPAL	
	BRANCH DHAKA - 1000, BANGLADESH	
		QINGDAO HAIFU CO. LTD.
		ZHANGLI

2. 评价表（见表 2-3-1）

表 2-3-1

评价指标＼评价人	自　评	互　评	师　评
独立完成情况（20 分）			
格式规范性（20 分）			
内容完整性、正确性（50 分）			
内容简明性、整洁性（10 分）			
合计总分			

任务四　缮制产地证

【工作认知】

一、认知原产地证

（一）原产地证的含义

原产地证书（Certificate of Origin，简称 C/O），是出口商应进口商的要求而提供的，由公证机构或出口商等出具的证明货物原产地和制造地的一种证明文件。

（二）原产地证的作用

在国际贸易中，世界各国根据各自的对外贸易政策，普遍实行进口贸易管制，对进口商品实施差别关税和数量限制，并由海关执行统计。进口国要求出口国出具货物的原产地证明，已成为国际惯例，因此原产地证书是进行国际贸易的一项重要证明文件，归纳起来，具有以下几个方面的作用：

（1）原产地证书用于订有互惠条约国家间的贸易，凭原产地证书可以享受优惠关税。

（2）原产地证书还起到证明商品内在品质、提高商品竞争力的作用。例如，在国际市场上持有中国原产地证书的丝绸比持有其他不产丝绸国家产地证的丝绸更能卖好价。

（3）原产地证书是进口国进行贸易统计的重要依据。

（4）原产地证书有时还是贸易双方进行交接、结汇的必备单据。

（5）对于实行普遍优惠制的国家，进口商凭普惠制产地证书享受进口关税优惠。

（三）原产地证的种类

原产地证书一般可分为一般原产地证、普惠制原产地证、区域性经济集团互惠原产地证、专用原产地证四大类。

1. 一般原产地证

一般原产地证，即我们常说的 C/O（CERTIFICATE OF ORIGIN），是用以证明有关出口货物生产地、制造地的一种证明文件，是在国际贸易行为中证明货物“原籍”的证书。在特定情况下进口国据此对进口货物给予不同的关税待遇。

根据签发者不同，一般原产地证可分为以下三类：

（1）官方机构出具的原产地证；

（2）民间机构出具的原产地证，如中国国际贸易促进委员会（CCPIT）出具的一般原产地证，简称贸促会产地证书（CCPIT CEERTIFICATE OF ORIGIN）；

（3）出口商出具的原产地证。

2. 普惠制原产地证

普惠制原产地证（Generalized System of Preference Certificate of Origin Form A，简称 G. S. P. FORM A）是依据给惠国要求而出具的能证明出口货物原产自受惠国的证明文件，并能使货物在给惠国享受普遍优惠关税待遇的官方凭证。

资料卡

> 普惠制，全称“普遍优惠制”，是发达国家给予发展中国家出口制成品和半制成品（包括某些初级产品）普遍的、非歧视的、非互惠的一种关税优惠制度。为使普惠制所给予的优惠落实到原产于受惠国的商品，享受普惠制待遇的产品，必须原产于受惠国，由受惠国直接运输至给惠国（直运规则），在向给惠国海关报关时提供普惠制产地证。

在国际贸易实务中，应该提供哪种产地证明书，主要依据合同或信用证的要求。一般对于实行普惠制国家出口货物，都要求出具普惠制产地证。如果信用证并未明确规定原产地证的出具者，那么银行应该接受任何一种产地证。

（四）原产地证样章

1. 一般原产地证样章

一般原产地证样章如下所示：

<table>
<tr><td colspan="2">1. Exporter</td><td colspan="3" rowspan="3">Certificate No.

CERTIFICATE OF ORIGIN
OF
THE PEOPLE'S REPUBLIC OF CHINA</td></tr>
<tr><td colspan="2">2. Consignee</td></tr>
<tr><td colspan="2">3. Means of Transport and Route</td></tr>
<tr><td colspan="2">4. Country/Region of Destination</td><td colspan="3">5. Certifying Authority Use Only</td></tr>
<tr><td>6. Marks and Numbers</td><td>7. Number and Kind of Packages; Description of Goods</td><td>8. H. S. Code</td><td>9. Quantity</td><td>10. Number and Date of Invoices</td></tr>
<tr><td></td><td></td><td></td><td></td><td></td></tr>
<tr><td colspan="2">11. Declaration by the Exporter
The undersigned declares that the above details and statements are correct; that all the goods were produced in China and that they comply with the Rules of Origin of the People's Republic of China.</td><td colspan="3">12. Cetification
It is hereby certified that the declaration by the exporter is correct.</td></tr>
<tr><td colspan="2">Place and date, signature and stamp of authorized signatory</td><td colspan="3">Place and date, signature and stamp of certifying authority</td></tr>
</table>

2. 普惠制原产地证样章

普惠制原产地证样章如下所示：

<table>
<tr><td colspan="3">1. Goods Consigned from (Exporter's business name, address, country)</td><td colspan="3" rowspan="2">Reference No.
CENERALIZES SYSTEM OF PREFERENCES
CERTIFICATE OF ORIGIN
(Combined declaration and certificate)
FORM A
issued in --------
See Notes Overleaf</td></tr>
<tr><td colspan="3">2. Goods Consigned to (Consignee's name, address, country)</td></tr>
<tr><td colspan="3">3. Means of Transport and Route (as far as known)</td><td colspan="3">4. For official use</td></tr>
<tr><td>5. Item Number</td><td>6. Marks and Numbers of Packages</td><td>7. Number and Kind of Packages; Description of Goods</td><td>8. Origin criterion (see Notes Overleaf)</td><td>9. Gross Weight or other Quantity</td><td>10. Number and Date of Invoices</td></tr>
<tr><td colspan="3">12. Certification
it is hereby certified that the declaration by the exporter is correct</td><td colspan="3">11. Declaration by the Exporter
The undersigned hereby declares that the above details and statements are correct; that all the goods were produced in
and that they comply with origin requirements specified for those goods in the Generalized System of Preferences for goods exported to
--</td></tr>
<tr><td colspan="3">Place and date, signature and stamp of certifying authority</td><td colspan="3">Place and date, signature and authorized signatory</td></tr>
</table>

二、缮制原产地证

（一）原产地证的格式

一般原产地证与普惠制原产地证有多项内容相同，本书中将合并讲解。

（二）原产地证的缮制规范

一般原产地证和普惠制原产地证的主要内容如下：

产地证申报人员应按照证书中各栏要求，将本批货物的有关情况如实填制，保证所填的证书真实、准确。证书一律不得涂改，不得加盖更正章，具体各栏填制要求如下：

1. 产地证标题栏（右上角）

此栏包括“Reference No.”（证书号）和“Issued in ________”（签发国别）两项内容。

其中，“Reference No.”填写检验检疫机构编定的证书号；“Issued in ________”填写THE PEOPLE'S REPUBLIC OF CHINA，国名必须填写英文全称，不得简化。国内印制的证书，多数已将此栏印妥，缮制时无须再填写。

2. 发货人（Goods Consigned from 或 Exporter）

此栏的填写带有强制性。应填写出口商的名称、详细地址（包括街道名、门牌号）和国别。如果信用证无特别规定时，一般填写信用证中指定的受益人的名称、地址和国别。

3. 收货人（Goods Consigned to 或 Consignee）

此栏一般应填写给惠国的最终收货人名称、详细地址和国别，不得填写中间商名称。如果信用证无特别规定时，一般填写商业发票的抬头人。

【例2－4－1】

信用证申请人是法国ABC公司，货物实际目的地为瑞士XYZ公司，此栏应填制瑞士XYZ公司。

4. 运输方式和路线（Means of Transport and Route）

运输方式的填写分下列几种情况：

（1）如果是海运，可填“by sea”或“by steamer”；

（2）如果是陆运，可填“by train”或“railway”；

（3）如果是空运，可填“by air”。

运输路线填写信用证规定的装运地和到货地，如果运输中途转运也要标明在本栏目中。

【例2－4－2】

“From Shanghai To Hamburg Via Hong Kong”.

5. 国家或最终目的地（Country/ Region of Destination）

货物的最终目的地国家或地区。

6. 商品顺序号（Item Number）

同批出口货物如有不同品种，则按不同品种、发票号等分列“1”、“2”、“3”……如果是单项商品，此栏一般填“1”。

7. 唛头及包装号码（Marks and Numbers of Packages）

此栏填写的唛头应与商业发票上的唛头完全一致。

如果本批货物无唛头，此栏填写“N/M”，不能留空。

如果本批货物唛头过多，此栏不够用，可加附页。

8. 包装的数量和种类；商品名称（Numbers and Kind of Packages；Description of Goods）

注意事项：

（1）包装的数量必须用英文和阿拉伯数字同时表示。

【例2-4-3】 One Hundred and Twenty（120）Cartons of Shoes.

（2）如果是散装货，应该在商品名称后面加“In Bulk”。

（3）填写在此栏的商品名称要明确具体，不能用“Machine（机器）”、“Garments（服装）”等统称。

（4）填写完此栏内容后在下一行加上“＊＊＊＊＊＊＊＊＊”，表示内容已填完，防止加填伪造内容。

（5）如果信用证中有些特殊条款，如信用证规定“All Documents Must Be Indicated This Credit No. 1234”，可填在此栏结束符号下面的空白处。

9. 商品编码（H. S. Code）

H. S. 分类是以商品原料来源为主，结合加工程度和用途等来划分。缮制产地证此栏时，按照出口商品编码的前4位数填写。

10. 发票号码及日期（Number and Date of Invoices）

此栏不得留空。填写实际的发票号码和发票日期，其中日期中的月份要用英文来写。

【例2-4-4】
QD860
DATE：MAR. 5，2013

11. 签证当局证明（Certification）

此栏填写签证机构的签证地点和日期，签证日期不得早于商业发票日期（第十栏）和申请日期（第十二栏）但不能晚于货物的装运日期。

出入境检验检疫局签证人审核后在此栏（正本）盖章并手签。

12. 出口商声明（Declaration by the Exporter）

（1）生产国别：填写“China”。

（2）进口国别：填写最终进口国的名称。

（3）出口商申请日期、地点及签章：填写申请日期和地点，申请日期不得早于商业发票的日期。再由已在签证机构注册的人员签名并加盖申请单位中英文的印章，签字和盖章不得重叠。

下面特别讲解普惠制原产地证与一般原产地证不同的项目：

13. 供官方使用（For Official Use）

申请签证的单位应将此栏留空，由签证机构在必要时填写。

14. 原产地标准（Origin Criterion）：

资料卡

普惠制原产地标准：

- 完全是中国原产的商品，不论出口至哪个给惠国，均填“P”。
- 含有进口成分的商品，出口至欧盟15国、瑞士、挪威、波兰和日本的，符合上述有关给惠国的加工标准的，填“W”，并在“W”的下方加注该商品的四位数字级的HS税目号，如“W”62.03。
- 含有进口成分的商品，出口至加拿大的，进口成分的价值不超过该商品出厂价的40%的，填“F”。
- 出口至澳大利亚、新西兰的商品，此栏可留空。
- 出口至俄罗斯、白俄罗斯、哈萨克斯坦、乌克兰、捷克、斯洛伐克的，进口成分的价值不超过商品离岸价50%的，填“Y”，并在“Y”下方加注该商品进口成分的价值占商品离岸价的百分比。

此栏用字最少，但却是给惠国海关审证的核心项目。对含有进口成分的商品，因情况复杂，国外要求严格，极易弄错而造成退证。

此栏是国外海关审核的核心栏目。对含有进口成分的商品，因情况复杂，国外要求严格而极易退证查询。因此应认真审核，慎重填写“P”。

15. 毛重或其他数量（Gross Weight or Other Quantity）

此栏以商品的正常计量单位填写，如“只”、“件”、“双”、“套”、“打”等。填写时数量和计量单位都要填写，如“500 SETS”。以重量计算的填毛重，如“5030KGS”；只有净重的，填净重，但要标上“N. W.”。

16. 其他

证书编号（Certificate No.）由15位数字组成，前2位是年份，3~7位是签署证书所在地局，8~12为出口企业注册号，13~15位是出口企业单据流水号。

一般产地证证书编号首位前加字母“C”，普惠制产地证前加“G”。

【工作指导】

青岛海富贸易有限公司收到的来自荷兰FUTURO公司申请开出的信用证，张丽的师傅李华根据信用证所给内容及相关资料制作了一般原产地证和普惠制原产地证。

资料1：信用证

LETTER OF CREDIT

MT：700　　　　ISSUE OF A DOCUMENTARY CREDIT

SEQUENCE OF TOTAL　　*27：　1/1

FORM OF DOC. CREDIT	*40A:	IRREVOCABLE
DOC. CREDIT NUMBER	*20:	IC01925U
DATE OF ISSUE	31C:	20130525
EXPRIRY	*31D:	DATE 20130725 IN QINGDAO
ISSUING BANK	51A:	WACHOVIA BANK, NO. 3K STREET, RM 504 FUNGLEE COMM. BLDG. ROTTERDAM NETHERLANDS
APPLICANT	*50:	FUTURO INDUSTRIAL CO. LTD., ROTTERDAM NETHERLANDS TEL: 031 431 7295
BENEFICIARY	*59:	QINGDAO HAIFU TRADING CO. LTD., NO. 1HONGKONG ROAD, QINGDAO CHINA
AMOUNT	*32B:	CURRENCY USD AMOUNT USD40000. 00
AVAILABLE WITH /BY	*41D:	ANY BANK BY DEF PAYMENT
DRAFT AT…	42C:	AT 60 DAYS AFTER B/L SHIPMENT DATE
DRAWEE	42A:	ISSUING BANK
PARTIAL SHIPMENT	43P:	ALLOWED
TRANSHIPMENT:	43T:	ALLOWED
LOADING IN CHARGE	44A:	QINGDAO, CHINA
FOR TRANSPORT TO	44B:	ROTTERDAM PORT, NETHERLANDS
LATEST SHIPMENT DATE	44C:	20130710
DESCRIPTION OF GOODS	45A:	

2450CARTONS (ONE CONTAINER) OF QINGDAO SPRING ROLLS AT USD15. 50PER CTN CIF ROTTERDAM

PACKING: 20G PER PC, 50PCS IN A BOX, 9 BOXES IN A CARTON

PACKED IN PLANT OF QINGDAO BANMU FOODS PRODUCTS CO. LTD., QINGDAO INDUSTRIAL ZONE QINGDAO

AS PER CONTRACT NO. MSR719 DATE: 20130412

DOCUMENTS REQUIRED 46A:

+ SIGNED COMMERCIAL INVOICE IN THREE COPIES CERTIFYING COUNTRY OF ORIGIN.
+ FULL SET OF ORIGINAL CLEAN ON BOARD OCEAN BILLS OF LADING CONSIGNED TO ORDER OF SHIPPER MARKED FREIGHT PREPAID NOTIFY APPLICANT AND ISSUING BANK.

+ PACKING LIST IN THREE COPIES.
+ MARINE INSURANCE POLICY OR CERTIFICATE IN DUPLICATE ENDORSED IN BLANK, WITH CLAIM PAYABLE IN NETHLANDS IN THE CURRENCY OF THE DRAFT, COVERING 110 PERCENT OF INVOICE VALUE, INCLUDING ICC (A) AND ICC WAR CLAUSE AS PER INSTITUTE CARGO CLAUSE DATED 1/1/1982.
+ SHIPPING ADVICE HAS BEEN SENT TO APPLICANT WITHIN 3 DAYS FROM DATE OF SHIPMENT INDICATING L/C NO., INVOICE NO., AMOUNT, DETAILS OF GOODS, NAME OF VESSEL, VOYAGE NO., DATE OF SHIPMENT, PORT OF LOADING, B/L NO., CONTAINER NO., SEAL NO., ESTIMATED TIME OF AR RIVAL.
+ CERTIFICATE OF ORIGINAND GSP FORM A SIGNED BY C. I. Q.
+ COPY OF BENEFICIARY CERTIFICATE CERTIFY THAT ONE COMPLETE SET OF N/N DOCUMENTS HAS BEEN SENT TO APPLICANT BY COURIER WITHIN FIVE DAYS OF THE B/L DATE.

ADDITIONAL COND.　　47A：

+SHIPMENT DOCUMENTS EVIDENCE THIS L/C NO.
+THE INVOICE SEPARATELY MENTION FOB VALUE, FREIGHT CHARGE.
+B/L MUST MARK THAT THE GOODS SHIPPED IN 40 HR CONTAINER AND SET AT -18 DEGREES CENTIGRADE OR LOWER

DETAILS OF CHARGES：　　71B：

ALL BANK CHARGES OUTSIDE ROTTERDAM ARE FOR ACCOUNT OF BENEFICIARY.

CONFIRMATION INSTRUCTIONS *49：　　WITHOUT

"ADVISE THROUGH" BANK 57A：　BANK OF CHINA LTD., SHANDONG BRANCH

资料2：

INVOICE NO.: QD582

C/O. NO. C133701100160276

H. S.: 19022200

FORM A NO. G13370110160203

师傅李华制作的一般原产地证如下所示：

<table>
<tr><td colspan="3">1. Exporter
QINGDAO HAIFU TRADING CO. LTD. ,
NO. 1 HONGKONG ROAD, QINGDAO CHINA</td><td colspan="3" rowspan="2">Certificate No.
C133701100160276
CERTIFICATE OF ORIGIN
OF
THE PEOPLE'S REPUBLIC OF CHINA</td></tr>
<tr><td colspan="3">2. Consignee
FUTURO INDUSTRIAL CO. LTD. , ROTTERDAM NETHERLANDS
TEL: 031 431 7295</td></tr>
<tr><td colspan="3">3. Means of Transport and Routo
FROM QINGDAO TO ROTTERDAM
BY SEA FREIGHT</td><td colspan="3" rowspan="2">5. For Certllying Authorlty Use Only</td></tr>
<tr><td colspan="3">4. Country/Reglon of Destination
ROTTERDAM NETHERLANDS</td></tr>
<tr><td>6. Marks and Numbers</td><td>7. Number and Kind of Packages; Description of Goods</td><td>8. H. S. Code</td><td>9. Quantity</td><td colspan="2">10. Number and Date of Involces</td></tr>
<tr><td>F. I. C.
QD582
ROTTERDAM
NO. 1 -2450</td><td>TWO THOUSAND FOUR HUNDRED AND FIFTY (2450) CARTONS OF QINGDAO SPRING ROLLS
× × × × × × ×</td><td>19. 02</td><td>G. W.
26950. 00KGS</td><td colspan="2">QD528
DATE: JUNE 25, 2013</td></tr>
<tr><td colspan="2">11. Declaration by th Exporter
The undersigned hereby declaras that the above detalls and statements are correct, that all the goods wore produced in China and that they comply with the Rules of Orlgin of the People's Republic of China.

QINGDAO HAIFU TRADING CO. LTD. ,
LIHUA
JUNE 27, 2013 QINGDAO CHINA</td><td colspan="4">12. Certification
It is hereby certified that the doclaration by the exporter is correct.

QINGDAO C. I. Q. CHINA
ZHONGLI
JUNE 27, 2013</td></tr>
<tr><td colspan="2">Place and date, signature and stamp of authorized signatory</td><td colspan="4">Place and date signature and stamp of certifying authority</td></tr>
</table>

师傅李华制作的普惠制原产地证如下所示：

1. Goods Consigned from (Exporter's business name, address, country) QINGDAO HAIFU TRADING CO. LTD., NO. 1 HONGKONG ROAD, QINGDAO　CHINA	Reference No. G13370110160203 GENERALIZES SYSTEM OF PREFERENCES CERTIFICATE OF ORIGIN (Combined declaration and certificate) FORM A issued in P. R. OF CHINA See Notes Overleaf
2. Goods Consigned to (Consignee's name, address, country) FUTURO INDUSTRIAL CO. LTD., ROTTERDAM NETHERLANDS TEL: 031 431 7295	
3. Means of Transport and Route (as far as known) FROM QINGDAO CHINA TO ROTTERDAM NETHERLANDS BY SEA	4. For Official Use

5. Item Number	6. Marks and Numbers of Packages	7. Number and Kind of Packages: Description of Goods	8. Origin Certerion (see Notes Overleaf)	9. Gross Weight or Other Quantity	10. Number and Date of Invoices
1	F. I. C. QD582 ROTTERDAM NO. 1 - 2450	TWO THOUSAND FOUR HUNDRED AND FIFTY (2450) CARTONS QINGDAO SPRING ROLLS * * * * * * * *	"P"	26950.00KGS	QD528 DATE: JUN. 25, 2013

12. Certification It is hereby certified that the declaration by the exporter is correct. QINGDAO CIQ MUSHANBAI QINGDAO, CHINA JUN. 28, 2013 -- Place and date, signature and stamp of certifying authority	11. Declaration by the Exporter The undersigned hereby declares that the above details and statements are correct; that all the goods were produced in CHINA ------------ and that they comply with origin requirements specified for those goods in the Generalized System of Preferences for goods exported to EEG. -- QINGDAO HAIFU TRADING CO. LTD., QINGDAO, CHINA JUN. 25, 2013　LIHUA -- Place and date, signature and authorized signatory

【工作演练】

张丽在师傅李华的指导下，已经基本掌握了制作一般原产地证和普惠制原产地证的技能。下面请你和张丽一起根据青岛海富贸易有限公司收到来自日本 HANG SENG BANK 的信用证及相关资料，独立制作一份一般原产地证和普惠制原产地证。

资料 1：信用证

LETTER OF CREDIT		
DOC. CREDIT NUMBER	*20:	S-9007NU-30
DATE OF ISSUE	*31C:	2013-3-19
EXPIRY	*31D:	DATE APR. 30, 2013 PLACE IN CHINA
ISSUE BANK	*51A:	HANG SENG BANK, TOKYO BRANCH
APPLICANT	*50:	NISSAN KAISHA LTD., CHUO-KU 1-4 TOKYO JAPAN
BENEFICIARY	*59:	QINGDAO HAIFU TRADING CO. LTD., NO. 1HONGKONG ROAD, QINGDAO CHINA
AMOUNT	*32B:	CURRENCY USD AMOUNT 50000.00
AVAILABLE WITH/BY	*41D:	ANY BANK INCHINA BY DRAFT
DRAFTS AT	*42C:	AT SIGHT
DRAWEE	*42A:	HANG SENG BANK, TOKYO BRANCH, TOKYO JAPAN
PARTIAL SHIPMENTS	*43P:	ALLOWED
TRANSHIPMENT	*43T:	ALLOWED
PORT OF LOADING:	*44E:	QINGDAO CHINA
PORT OF DISCHARGE	*44F:	TOKYO JAPAN
LATEST DATE OF SHIP.	*44C:	APR. 15, 2013
DESCRIPT. OF GOODS	*45A:	

42MTS OF SHANDONG FROZEN PEELED SHRIMPS

AS PER CONTRACT NO. NK9012 DATED FEB. 12, 2013 CFR TOKYO

DOCUMENTS REQUIRED *46A:

+ COMMMERCIAL INVOICE IN ONE ORIGINAL AND TWO COPIES

+ FULL SET OF OCEAN BILLS OF LADING MADE OUT TO THE ORDER OF SHIPPER MARKED FREIGHT PREPAID NOTIFY APPLICANT

+ CERTIFICATE OF ORIGIN AND GSP FORM A BY CIQ

资料 2：

1. TOTAL SHIPMENT 42000KGS, 4200CARTONS
2. PACKING: 2KGS X5 IN ONE CARTON, EACH CARTON 10KGS IN N. W., 11KGS

IN G. W. 0.0105CBM/CTN 运输为40尺冷藏

3. INVOICE NO. FS1322 DATE：MAR. 26，2013　H. S. CODE：03061321

4. CO NO. C133701100220015　FORM A NO. G133701100220011

资料3：一般产地证

<table>
<tr><td colspan="2">1. Exporter</td><td colspan="3" rowspan="2">Certlticate NO.

CERTIFICATE OF ORIGIH
OF
THE PEOPLE'S REPUBLIC OF CHINA</td></tr>
<tr><td colspan="2">2. Consignce</td></tr>
<tr><td colspan="2">3. Means of Transport and Route</td><td colspan="3" rowspan="2">5. For Certifying Authorlty Use Only</td></tr>
<tr><td colspan="2">4. Country/Reglon of Destination</td></tr>
<tr><td>6. Marks and Numbers</td><td>7. Number and Kind of Packages; Description of Goods</td><td>8. H. S. Code</td><td>9. Quantity</td><td>10. Number and Date of Invotces</td></tr>
<tr><td colspan="2">11. Declaration by the Exporter
The undersigned hereby declares that the above detalls and statements are correct, that all the goods were produced in China and that they comply with the Rules of Origin of the People's Republic of China.

Placa and date, signature and stamp of authorized signatory</td><td colspan="3">12. Certification
It is hereby certified that the doclaration by the expoter is cor

Place and date, signature and stamp of certifying authority</td></tr>
</table>

资料4：普惠制原产地证

<table>
<tr><td colspan="3">1. Goods Consigned from (Exporter's business name, address, country)</td><td colspan="3" rowspan="2">Reference No.
CENERALIZES SYSTEM OF PREFERENCES
CERTIFICATE OF ORIGIN　　CERTIFICATE OF ORIGIN OF THE PEOPLE'S REPUBLIC OF CHINA
(Combined declaration and certificate)
FORM A
issued in
See Notes Overleaf</td></tr>
<tr><td colspan="3">2. Goods Consigned to (Consignee's name, address, country)</td></tr>
<tr><td colspan="3">3. Means of Transport and Route (as far as known)</td><td colspan="3">4. For Official Use</td></tr>
<tr><td>5. Item Number</td><td>6. Marks and Numbers of Packages</td><td>7. Number and Kind of Packages: Description of Goods</td><td>8. Origin Criterion (see Notes Overleaf)</td><td>9. Gross Weight or Other Quantity</td><td>10. Number and Date of Invoices</td></tr>
<tr><td colspan="3">12. Certification
It is hereby certified that the declaration by the exporter is correct.</td><td colspan="3">11. Declaration by the Exporter
The undersigned hereby declares that the above details and statements are correct; that all the goods were produced in
and that they comply with origin requirements specified for those goods in the Generalized System of Preferences for goods exported to
--</td></tr>
<tr><td colspan="3">Place and date, signature and stamp of certifying authority</td><td colspan="3">Place and date, signature and authorized signatory</td></tr>
</table>

提示：

（1）一般原产地证和普惠制原产地证中的出口商申报时间和签证当局签署时间的位置是互换的。

（2）关于单据日期，原则上发票日期最早，其次是出口商申报时间，然后是签证当局的签署时间，但产地证上的日期不能晚于提单日期。

【工作评价】

1. 评价标准

<table>
<tr><td colspan="3">1. Goods Consigned from (Exporter's business name, address, country)
QINGDAO HAIFU CO. LTD.,
NO. 1 HONGKONG ROAD QINGDAO CHINA</td><td colspan="3" rowspan="2">Reference No.
G133701100220011
GENERALIZES SYSTEM OF PREFERENCES
CERTIFICATE OF ORIGIN
(Combined declaration and certificate)
FORM A
issued in THE PEOPLE'S REPUBLIC OF CHINA

See Notes Overleaf</td></tr>
<tr><td colspan="3">2. Goods Consigned to (Consignee's name, address, country)
NISSAN KAISHA LTD.,
CHUO－KU 1－4 TOKYO JAPAN</td></tr>
<tr><td colspan="3">3. Means of Transport and Route (as far as known)
FROM QINGDAO, CHINA TO TOKYO JAPAN
BY SEA</td><td colspan="3">4. For Official Use</td></tr>
<tr><td>5. Item Number
1</td><td>6. Marks and Numbers of Packages
N/M</td><td>7. Number and Kind of Packages; Description of Goods

FOUR THOUSAND TWO HUNDRED (4200) CARTONS OF
FROZEN PEELED SHIRMPS
* * * * * * * *</td><td>8. Origin Certerion (see Notes Overleaf)
"P"</td><td>9. Gross Weight or Other Quantity
46200.00KGS</td><td>10. Number and Date of Invoices
FS1322
DATE:
MAR. 26
2013</td></tr>
<tr><td colspan="3">12. Certification
It is hereby certified that the declaration by the exporter is correct.
SHANDONG CIQ
QIZHIWEN
MAR. 28, 2013 QINGDAO CHINA
Place and date, signature and stamp of certifying authority</td><td colspan="3">11. Declaration by the Exporter
The undersigned hereby declares that the above details and statements are correct;
that all the goods were produced in
CHINA
----
and that they comply with origin requirements specified for those goods in the Generalized System of Preferences
for goods exported to JAPAN.

QINGDAO HAIFU CO. LTD.
QINGDAO CHINA MAR. 26, 2013 ZHANGLI

Place and date, signature and authorized signatory</td></tr>
</table>

1. Exporter
QINGDAO HAIFU CO. LTD.,
NO. 1 HONGKONG ROAD QINGDAO CHINA

Certificate No.
C133701100220015

2. Consignee
NISSAN KAISHA LTD., CHUO - KU 1 - 4 TOKYO JAPAN

3. Means of Transport and Routa
FROM QINGDAO CHINA TO TOKYO JAPAN
BY SEA

5. For Certifying Authorlty use only

4. Country/Region of Destination
TOKYO JAPAN

6. Marks and Numbers	7. Number and Kind of Packages; Description of Goods	8. H. S. Code	9. Quantity	10. Number and Date of Involces
N/M	FOUR THOUSAND TWO HUNDRED (4200) CARTONS OF FROZEN PEELED SHRIMPS * * * * * * * *	03. 06	G. W. 46200KGS	FS1322 DATE: MAR. 26, 2013

11. Declaration by the Exporter

The undersigned hereby declares that the above detalls and statements are correct, that all the goods wore produced in China and that they comply with the Rules of Orlgin of the People's Republic of China.

QINGDAO HAIFU CO. LTD.,
QINGDAO CHINA MAR. 26, 2013
LIHUA

Place and date, signature and stamp of authorized signatory

12. Certification

It is hereby certified that the doclaration by the exporter is cor

SHANDONG CIQ
QIZHIWEN
MAR. 28, 2013 QINGDAO CHINA

Place and date, signature and stamp of certirying auth thority

2. 评价表（见表2-4-1）

表2-4-1

评价人 / 评价指标	自　评	互　评	师　评
独立完成情况（20分）			
格式规范性（20分）			
内容完整性、正确性（50分）			
内容简明性、整洁性（10分）			
合计总分			

任务五　缮制其他结汇单据

【工作认知】

一、装船通知

（一）认知装船通知

装船通知（Shipping Advice）是在信用证支付方式下，若信用证有要求，则此单据就成为卖方交单议付时的单证之一。

1. 装船通知的作用

（1）让当事人及时了解货物装运情况。

（2）在FOB和CFR条件下，其是进口商办理进口货物保险的凭证之一。在卖方完成装船之后，立即通知买方，使其能够及时为货物投保，避免出现装船和投保的脱节，致使货物处于无保险的状态之中。

2. 装船通知的主要内容

装船通知主要包括所发运货物的合同号或信用证号、品名、数量、金额、运输工具名称、开航日期、启运地和目的地、提运单号码、运输标志等，并且与其他相关单据保持一致，如信用证提出具体项目要求，应严格按规定出单。此外通知中还可能出现包装说明、ETD（船舶预离港时间）、ETA（船舶预抵港时间）、ETC（预计开始装船时间）等内容。

3. 装船通知样章

装船通知样章如下所示：

QINGDAO HOPE TRADING CO. LTD.,

NO. 1HAIER ROAD, QINGDAO CHINA

INVOIE NO. QD428

L/C NO. TCS1245U

DATE: AUG. 10, 2012

SHIPPING ADVICE

TO:

TOKTAR INDUSTRIAL CO. LTD.,

DEAR SIRS:

WE SHIPPED THE GOODS 300 CARTONS OF SHANDONG PEARS TO YOU.

SHIPMENT DATE : AUG. 9, 2012

VESSEL' NAME: SITC QINGDAO V. 23

B/L NO. SITC245172

CONTAINER NO. SITC1234748

SEAL NO. 004565

AMOUNT: USD34500. 00

PORT OF LOADING : QINGDAO CHINA

PORT OF DESTINATION: TOKYO, JAPAN

ETA: AUG. 31, 2012

PLS CHECKED.

QINGDAO HOPE TRADING CO. LTD.,

LIHUA

（二）装船通知的缮制规范

装船通知的主要内容如下：

（1）日期：发送装运通知的日期。若信用证未对装运通知的出单日期做出明确规定，则需要根据贸易术语的不同及时向进口商发出装运通知。

（2）装船通知制作人名称和地址：一般情况下，装船通知的制作人就是出口公司，制作通知时标出出口公司的中英文名称。

（3）装船通知的抬头：按信用证规定填写，通常是买方，有时是买方指定的保险公司或开证行。信用证没有规定抬头，则可以填写开证申请人。

（4）提单号及船名：与提单一致。

（5）预计开船日期 ETD 和到达日期 ETA：按船期表所列的日期。

（6）商品描述部分：包括品名、数量、金额、发票总值等，可以按商业发票的内容填写。

（7）装运港、目的港、装运期：按合同或信用证的规定，一般与提单一致。

二、受益人证明

（一）认知受益人证明

1. 受益人证明的含义

受益人证明（BENEFICIARY'S CERTIFICATE）是一种由受益人自己出具的证明，以便证明自己履行了信用证规定的任务或证明自己按信用证的要求办事，如证明所交货物的品质、证明运输包装的处理、证明按要求寄单等。一般无固定格式，内容多种多样，以英文制作，通常签发一份。

2. 受益人证明样章

受益人证明样章如下所示：

QINGDAO HOPE TRADING CO. LTD.,
NO. 1HAIER ROAD, QINGDAO CHINA

INVOIE NO. QD428
L/C NO. TCS1245U
DATE: AUG. 10, 2012

BENEFICIARY CERTIFICATE

TO:
ABC INDUSTRIAL CO. LTD.,
WE HEREBY CERTIFICATE THAT ONE COMPLETE SET OF N/N DOCUMENTS HAVE BEEN SENT BY COURIER TO APPLICANT WITIIIN FIVE DAYS OF THE B/L DATE.

QINGDAO HAIFU TRADING CO. LTD.,
LIHUA

（二）缮制受益人证明

受益人证明的主要内容如下：

（1）单据名称。这种单据的名称因所证明事项不同而略异，可能是寄单证明、寄样证明（船样、样卡和码样等）、取样证明、货物产地证明、品质、唛头、包装和标签情况、电抄形式的装运通知、产品生产过程证明等。

（2）证明上通常会显示发票号、合同号或信用证号以表明与其他单据的关系。

（3）证明的内容应严格与合同或信用证规定相符。证明文件通常以“THIS IS TO CERTIFY”（或 DECLARE、STATE、EVIDENCE 等）或“WE HEREBY CERTIFY”等开始。一般的行文规则是以所提要求为准直接照搬照抄，但有时也应做必要的修改。

【例 2-5-1】

如信用证规定“BENEFICIARY'S CERTIFICATE EVIDENCING THAT TWO COPIES OF NON-NEGOTIABLE B/L WILL BE DESPATCHED TO APPLICANT WITHIN TWO DAYS AFTER SHIPMENT”，在具体制作单据时应将要求里的“WILL BE DESPATCHED”改为“HAVE BEEN DESPATCHED”。

【例2-5-2】 对“BENEFICIARY'S CERTIFICATE STATING THAT CERTIFICATE OF MANUFACTURING PROCESS AND OF INGREDIENTS ISSUED BY ABC CO SHOULD BE SENT TO SUMITOMO CORP”的要求，“SHOULD BE SENT”最好改为“HAD/HAS BEEN SENT”。

（4）因属于证明性质，按有关规定证明人（受益人）必须签字。

（5）单据一般都应在规定的时间内做出。

【工作指导】

青岛海富贸易有限公司收到的来自荷兰 FUTURO 公司申请开出的信用证，张丽的师傅李华根据信用证所给内容及相关资料制作了一份装船通知和受益人证明。

资料1：信用证

MT：700	ISSUE OF A DOCUMENTARY CREDIT	
SEQUENCE OF TOTAL	*27：	1/1
FORM OF DOC. CREDIT	*40A：	IRREVOCABLE
DOC. CREDIT NUMBER	*20：	IC01925U
DATE OF ISSUE	31C：	20130525
EXPRIRY	*31D：	DATE 20130725 PLACE IN QINGDAO
ISSUING BANK	51A：	WACHOVIA BANK, NO. 3K STREET, RM 504 FUNGLEE COMM. BLDG. ROTTERDAM NETHERLANDS
APPLICANT.	*50：	FUTURO INDUSTRIAL CO. LTD., ROTTERDAM NETHERLANDS TEL：031 431 7295
BENEFICIARY	*59：	QINGDAO HAIFU TRADING CO. LTD., NO. 1HONGKONG ROAD, QINGDAO CHINA
PARTIAL SHIPMENT	43P：	ALLOWED
TRANSHIPMENT	43T：	ALLOWED
LOADING IN CHARGE	44A：	QINGDAO, CHINA
FOR TRANSPORT TO	44B：	ROTTERDAM PORT, NETHERLANDS
LATEST SHIPMENT DATE	44C：	20130710
DESCRIPTION OF GOODS	45A：	

2450CARTONS (ONE CONTAINER) OF QINGDAO SPRING ROLLS AT USD15. 50PER CTN CIF ROTTERDAM

PACKING：20G PER PC, 50PCS IN A BOX, 9 BOXES IN A CARTON

PACKED IN PLANT OF QINGDAO BANMU FOODS PRODUCTS CO. LTD., QINGDAO INDUSTRIAL ZONE QINGDAO.

AS PER CONTRACT NO. MSR719 DATE: 20130412

DOCUMENTS REQUIRED 46A:

+ SHIPPING ADVICE HAS BEEN SENT TO APPLICANT WITHIN 3 DAYS FROM DATE OF SHIPMENT INDICATING L/C NO., INVOICE NO., AMOUNT, DETAILS OF GOODS, NAME OF VESSEL, VOYAGE NO., DATE OF SHIPMENT, PORT OF LOADING, B/L NO., CONTAINER NO., SEAL NO., ESTIMATED TIME OF ARRIVAL.
+ COPY OF BENEFICIARY CERTIFICATE CERTIFY THAT ONE COMPLETE SET OF N/N DOCUMENTS HAS BEEN SENT TO APPLICANT BY COURIER WITHIN FIVE DAYS OF THE B/L DATE.

ADDITIONAL COND. 47A:

+SHIPMENT DOCUMENTS EVIDENCE THIS L/C NO.

资料2:

INVOICE NO.: QD528

VESSEL NAME: SITC QINGDAO V. 23　　B/L NO. SITC229173

CONTAINER NO. SITC1292748　　SEAL NO. 006265

THE CARRIER AS NYK LING SHIPPING CO.,

MARK: MAKE A STANDARD MARK BY SELF

师傅李华制作的装船通知如下所示:

QINGDAO HAIFU TRADING CO. LTD.,

NO. 1HONGKONG ROAD, QINGDAO　CHINA

INVOICE NO. QD528
L/C NO. IC01925U
DATE: JUL. 10, 2013

SHIPPING ADVICE

TO:
FUTURO INDUSTRIAL CO. LTD.,
DEAR SIRS:
WE SHIPPED THE GOODS　ONE CONTAINER (2450 CARTONS) OF QINGDAO SRPING ROLLS TO YOU.
SHIPMENT DATE: JULY9, 2013
VESSEL'S NAME: SITC QINGDAO V. 23
B/L NO. SITC229173
CONTAINER NO. SITC1292748
SEAL NO. 006265
AMOUNT: USD37975. 00
PORT OF LOADING:　QINGDAO CHINA
PORT OF DESTINATION:　ROTTERDAM PORT, NETHERLANDS
ETA:　JULY31, 2013
PLS CHECKED.

QINGDAO HAIFU TRADING CO. LTD.,
LIHUA

师傅李华制作的受益人证明如下所示：

QINGDAO HAIFU TRADING CO. LTD.,

NO. 1HONGKONG ROAD, QINGDAO　CHINA

INVOICE NO. QD528

L/C NO. IC01925U

DATE：JULY 10, 2013

BENEFICIARY CERTIFICATE

TO：

FUTURO INDUSTRIAL CO. LTD.,

WE HEREBY CERTIFICATE THAT ONE COMPLETE SET OF N/N DOCUMENTS HAVE BEEN　SET BY COURIER TO APPLICANT WITHIN FIVE DAYS OF THE B/L DATE.

QINGDAO HAIFU TRADING CO. LTD.,

LIHUA

【工作演练】

张丽在师傅李华的指导下，已经基本掌握了制作装船通知和受益人证明的技能。下面请你和张丽一起根据青岛海富贸易有限公司收到国外 GOLDEN FISH CO. LTD. 开来的信用证及相关资料制作一份装船通知和受益人证明。

资料 1：信用证

+SHIPPING ADVICE SHOULD BEEN SENT TO APPLICANT WITHIN 5 DAYS FROM DATE OF SHIPMENT INDICATING L/C NO, INVOICE NO., DETAILS OF GOODS, NAME OF VESSEL, VOYAGE NO., DATE OF SHIPMENT, B/L NO., CONTAINER NO., SEAL NO., ESTIMATED TIME OF ARRIVAL.

+COPY OF BENEFICIARY CERTIFICATE TO APPLICANT EVIDENCING THAT ONE COMPLETE SET OF N/N DOCUMENTS HAVE BEEN SENT BY COURIER TO THEM WITHIN THREE DAYS OF THE B/L DATE.

资料 2：

BENEFICIARY：QINGDAO HAIFU CO. LTD.,

NO. 1 HONGKONG ROAD, QINGDAO, CHINA

DETAILS OF GOODS：5000PLASTIC BOTTLES OF ORANGE JUICE

L/C NO. TJ5219N

INVOICE NO.：SK528
B/L NO. SITC273291
B/L DATE：AUG. 25，2013
VESSEL NAME：SITC BULEBIRD V. 019
CONTAINER NO. SITC1248823
SEAL NO. 309526
ESTIMATED TIME OF ARRIVAL：SEP. 8，2013

资料3：装船通知

SHIPPING ADVISE

资料4：受益人证明

BENEFICIARY CERTIFICATE

提示：

（1）按照实际情况，注意证明信日期的填写。

（2）制作时，注意信用证条款对加注内容的要求。

【工作评价】

1. 评价标准

QINGDAO HAIFU CO. LTD.,

NO. 1HONGKONG ROAD, QINGDAO CHINA

INVOICE NO. SK528
L/C NO. TJ5219N
DATE: AUG. 25, 2013

SHIPPING ADVICE

TO:
GOLDEN FISH CO. LTD.,
DEAR SIRS:
WE SHIPPED THE GOODS 5000 PLASTIC BOTTLES OF ORANGE JUICE TO YOU.
L/C NO. TJ5219N
INVOICE NO.: SK528
B/L NO. SITC273291
DATE OF SHIPMENT: AUG. 25, 2013
VESSEL NAME: SITC BULEBIRD V. 019
CONTAINER NO. SITC1248823
SEAL NO. 309526
ESTIMATED TIME OF ARRIVAL: SEP. 8, 2013
PLS CHECKED.

QINGDAO HAIFU TRADING CO. LTD.,
ZHANGLI

QINGDAO HAIFU CO. LTD.,

NO. 1HONGKONG ROAD, QINGDAO CHINA

INVOICE NO. SK528
L/C NO. TJ5219N
DATE: AUG. 25, 2013

BENEFICIARY CERTIFICATE

TO:
GOLDEN FISH CO. LTD.,
WE HEREBY CERTIFICATE THAT ONE COMPLETE SET OF N/N DOCUMENTS HAVE BEEN SENT BY COURIER TO APPLICANT WITHIN FIVE DAYS OF THE B/L DATE.

QINGDAO HAIFU TRADING CO. LTD.,
ZHANGLI

2. 评价表（见表 2－5－1）

表 2－5－1

评价指标＼评价人	自　评	互　评	师　评
独立完成情况（20 分）			
格式规范性（20 分）			
内容完整性、正确性（50 分）			
内容简明性、整洁性（10 分）			
合计总分			

项 目 实 训

资料 1：

FORM OF DOC. CREDIT	*40A:	IRREVOCABLE
DOC. CREDIT NUMBER	*20:	66917－QX18
DATE OF ISSUE	*31C:	20130721
EXPIRYDATE	*31D:	DATE 20130930 PLACE IN CHINA
ISSUING BANK	*51A:	NATIONAL CITY BANK OF NEW YORK
APPLICANT	*50:	FLORIC TRADING CO. NO. 209 WALL STREET, NEW YORK AMERICA
BENEFICIARY	*59:	QINGDAO SUNSHINE TRADING CO. NO. 62 HAIER ROAD QINGDAO CHINA
AMOUNT	*32B:	CURRENCY USD AMOUNT83200. 00
AVAILABLE WITH/BY	*41D:	ANY BANK IN CHINA BY NEGOTIATION
DRAFTS AT	*42C:	30 DAYS SIGHT
DRAWEE	*42A:	NATIONAL CITY BANK OF NEW YORK
PARTIAL SHIPMENT	*43P:	NOT ALLOWED
TRANSHIPMENT	*43T:	NOT ALLOWED
PORT OF LOADING	*44E:	ANY CHINESE PORT
PORT OF DISCHARGE	*44F:	NEW YORK, USA
LATEST DATE OF SHIPMENT	*44C:	AUG. 20, 2013
DESCRIPT. OF GOODS	*45A:	

WOMEN'S DRESSES　　CIF NEW YORK USA

SIZE	QUANTITY	PACKAGE	UNIT PRICE
S	1560PCS	156CTNS	USD21. 00 PER PC
M	2160PCS	216CTNS	USD21. 50 PER PC
L	1080PCS	108CTNS	USD22. 50 PER PC

PACKED IN CARTON EACH OF 10PCS

AS PER CONTRACT NO. 7863JK DATE 20130701

DOCUMENTS REQUIRED *46A:

+ SIGNED COMMERCIAL INVOICE IN TRIPLICATE CERTIFYING THE MERCHANDISE COUNTRY OF ORIGIN.
+ FULL SET OF CLEAN ON BOARD OCEAN BILLS OF LADING MADE OUT TO ORDER OF SHIPPER AND MARKED FREIGHT PREPAID AND NOTIFY APPLICANT
+ PACKING LIST IN THREE COPIES MENTIONING NET WEIGHT AND GROSS WEIGHT AND MEAS. OF EACH CARTON.
+ GSP FORM A BY CIQ

ADDITIONAL COND. *47A:

+ THE FOLLOWING MUST APPEAR ON THE INVOICE AND B/L.

Ⅰ IMPORT REGISTRATION NO. QDF-6926

Ⅱ H. S. CODE 6210 3000 00

+ INVOICE AND PACKING LIST MUST BE CERTIFIED WITH SIGNED BY CCPIT WITH DATE.
+ L/C NO. MUST BE GIVEN ON ALL OTHER DOCUMENTS

48: PERIOD FOR PRESENTATION

15 DAYS AFTER SHIPMENT DATE BUT IN ANY CASE WITHIN THIS L/C VALIDITY

49: CONFIRMATION INSTRUCTIONS: WITHOUT

71B: CHARGE

ALL BANKING CHARGE AND COMM. OUTSIDE OF USA ARE FOR THE BENEFICIARY'S ACCOUNT

资料2:

1. INVOICE NO. BM709
2. B/L NO. VTRA1357264 B/L DATE: AUG. 19, 2013
   VESSEL NAME: VICTORIA V. 019
   CONTAINER NO.: EISU2628205 SEAL NO. 354671
3. MEASUREMENT: 0. 120CBM N. W. 50KGS G. W. 55KGS PER CARTON
4. MAKE A STANDARD SHIPPING MARK BY YOURSELF
5. FORM A NO. G133701100430718

资料 3:

COMMERCIAL INVOICE

Original

To:

Invoice No. :

Date:

L/C No. :

Contract No. :

From: ____________________ **To** ____________________

Shipping Marks	Quantities & Descpription	Unit Price	Amount

资料 4:

PACKING LIST

Original

To:

No.

Date:

L/C No. :

Contract:

From: ____________________ **To** ____________________

Shipping Marks	NO. & Kind of Pkgs: Description of the Goods	Net Weight	Gross Weight	Measurement

资料5：

No. ________	Qingdao, ________
EXCHANGE FOR	
At	sight of this First of EXCHANGE（SECOND OF THE SAME TENOR
AND DATE UNPAID)	pay to the order of ________
the sum of	
Drawn under	________
To ________	

资料6：

1. Goods Consigned from (Exporter's business name, address, country)			Reference No. CENERALIZES SYSTEM OF PREFERENCES CERTIFICATE OF ORIGIN (Combined declaration and certificate) FORM A issued in --------------- See Notes Overleaf		
2. Goods Consigned to (Consignee's name, address, country)					
3. Means of Transport and Route (as far as known)			4. For Official Use		
5. Item Number	6. Marks and Numbers of Packages	7. Number and Kind of Packages; Description of Goods	8. Origin Criterion (see Notes Overleaf)	9. Gross Weight or Other Quantity	10. Number and Date of Invoices
12. Certification It is hereby certified that the declaration by the exporter is correct.			11. Declaration by the Exporter The undersigned hereby declares that the above details and statements are correct; that all the goods were produced in and that they comply with origin requirements specified for those goods in the Generalized System of Preferences for goods exported to ------------------------------		
Place and date, signature and stamp of certifying authority			Place and date, signature and authorized signatory		

实训要求：

根据所给资料，分别填制商业发票、装箱单、汇票、普惠制原产地证。

参考答案

1. 商业发票

COMMERCIAL　　INVOICE

Original

To: FLORIC TRADING CO.
NO. 209 WALL STREET, NEW YORK AMERICA

No. BM709
Date: JUL. 28, 2013
L/C No: 66917 - QX18
Contract No: 7863JK

From: QINGDAO, CHINA　**To** NEW YORK, USA

Shipping Marks	Quantities & Descpription			Unit Price	Amount
F. T. C.	WOMEN'S DRESSES			CIFNEW YORK	
7863JK	SIZE	QUANTITY	PACKAGE		
NEW YORK	S	1560PCS	156CTNS	USD21. 00 /PC	USD32760. 00
NO. 1 - 480	M	2160PCS	216CTNS	USD21. 50 /PC	USD46440. 00
	L	1080PCS	108CTNS	USD22. 50 /PC	USD24300. 00
	TOTAL:	4800PCS	480CTNS		USD103500. 00

PACKED IN 480 CTNS.

PACKED IN CARTON EACH OF 10PCS

AS PER CONTRACT NO. 7863 DATE 20130701

WE HEREBY CERTIFY THAT THE GOODS ARE OF CHINA ORIGIN.

IMPORT REGISTRATION NO. QDF - 6926

H. S. CODE 6210 3000 00

L/C NO. 66917 - QX18

CCPIT
JUL. 30, 2013

QINGDAO SUNSHINE TRADING CO.
TOM

2. 装箱单

PACKING LIST

ORIGINAL

To: FLORIC TRADING CO.
NO. 209 WALL STREET, NEW YORK AMERICA

No. BM709
Date: JUL. 28, 2013
L/C No.: 66917－QX18
Contract NO: 7863JK

From: QINGDAO, CHINA **To** NEW YORK, USA

Shipping Marks	NO. & Kind of Pkgs: Description of the Goods			Net Weight	Gross Weight	Measurement
F. T. C.	WOMEN's DRESSES					
7863JK	SIZE	QUANTITY	PACKAGE	@50. 00KGS/CTN	@55. 00KGS/CTN	@0. 120CBM/CTN
NEW YORK	S	1560PCS	156CTNS	24000. 00KGS	8580. 00KGS	2. 496CBM
NO. 1－480	M	2160PCS	216CTNS	10800. 00KGS	11880. 00KGS	3. 456CBM
	L	1080PCS	108CTNS	5400. 00KGS	5940. 00KGS	1. 728CBM
	TOTAL:	4800PCS	480CTNS	24000. 00KGS	26400. 00KGS	7. 680CBM

PACKED IN 480CTNS OF 10PCS EACH

QINGDAO SUNSHINE TRADING CO.
TOM

3. 汇票

No. BM709 **QINGDAO,** AUG. 21, 2013

EXCHANGE FOR USD103500. 00

At 30 DAYS **sight of this First of EXCHANGE (SECOND OF THE SAME TENOR AND DATE UNPAID) pay to the order of** BANK OF CHINA, QINGDAO BRANCH

the sum of SAY U. S. DOLLARS ONE HUNDRED THREE THOUSAND AND FIVE HUNDRED ONLY.

Drawn under NATIONAL CITY BANK OF NEW YORK
L/C NO. 66917－QX18
DATED: JUL. 21, 2013

To NATIONAL CITY BANK OF NEW YORK

QINGDAO SUNSHINE TRADING CO.
TOM

4. 普惠制原产地证

<table>
<tr><td colspan="3">1. Goods Consigned from (Exporter's business name, address, country)
QINGDAO SUNSHINE TRADING CO.
NO. 62 HAIER ROAD QINGDAO CHINA</td><td colspan="3" rowspan="2">Reference No.
G133701100430718
GENERALIZES SYSTEM OF PREFERENCES
CERTIFICATE OF ORIGIN
(Combined declaration and certificate)
FORM A
issued in
CHINA
See Notes Overleaf</td></tr>
<tr><td colspan="3">2. Goods Consigned to (Consignee's name, address, country)
FLORIC TRADING CO.
NO. 209 WALL STREET, NEW YORK AMERICA</td></tr>
<tr><td colspan="3">3. Means of Transport and Route (as far as known)
FROM QINGDAO, CHINA TO NEW YORK, USA BY SEA</td><td colspan="3">4. For Official Use</td></tr>
<tr><td>5. Item Number</td><td>6. Marks and Numbers of Packages</td><td>7. Number and Kind of Packages: Description of Goods</td><td>8. Origin Criterion (see Notes Overleaf)</td><td>9. Gross Weight or Other Quantity</td><td>10. Number and Date of Invoices</td></tr>
<tr><td>1</td><td>F. T. C.
7863JK
NEW YORK
NO. 1 - 480</td><td>FOUR HUNDRED AND EIGHTY (480) CARTONS OF
WOMEN'S DRESSES
* * * * * * * *</td><td>"P"</td><td>26400.00KGS</td><td>BM709
DATE:
JUL. 28, 2013</td></tr>
<tr><td colspan="3">12. Certification
It is hereby certified that the declaration by the exporter is correct.

SHANDONG CIQ

JUL. 30, 2013 QINGDAO CHINA

Place and date, signature and stamp of certifying authority</td><td colspan="3">11. Declaration by the Exporter
The undersigned hereby declares that the above details and statements are correct; that all the goods were produced in
CHINA
and that they comply with origin requirements specified for those goods in the Generalized System of Preferences for goods exported to USA

QINGDAO SUNSHINE TRADING CO.
QINGDAO CHINA JUL. 28, 2013
TOM

Place and date, signature and authorized signatory</td></tr>
</table>

项目三

运输单据和保险单据

项目介绍

出口商在收到国外的信用证确认无误后，将立刻安排组织备货。在CFR术语下，出口商需要负责办理出口托运，订立运输合同和安排租船订舱；在CIF术语下，出口商需要负责办理出口托运，订立运输合同和安排租船订舱，并且购买保险等。本项目介绍办理运输和保险事项的单据缮制。

学习目标

知识目标

- □ 熟悉托运单的定义和作用。
- □ 熟悉海运提单的定义、作用、种类。
- □ 熟悉保险单的种类。
- □ 掌握托运单、提单、保险单的缮制规范。

能力目标

能够根据信用证条款和合同条款及商业单证，准确填写海运托运单、海运提单和保险单的相关项目。

德育目标

培养学生认真仔细、严谨负责的学习和工作态度。

项目情境

青岛海富贸易有限公司生产部门已经备好货，接下来业务员李华根据出货信息、商业发票、装箱单和其他信息制作托运单，办理订舱手续，张丽依据信用证审核并修改船公司提供的海运提单。在完成手续后，李华又根据信用证条款向保险公司办理保险，张丽根据信用证和合同条款，审核并修改从保险公司取得的保险单。

英文储备

Shipping Order	托运单
Shipper	托运人
Consignee	收货人
Notify Party	通知人
Container	集装箱
Freight Prepaid	运费预付
Freight Collect	运费到付
Vessel Name	船　名
Bill of Loading	提　单
Insurance	保　险
Insured	被保险人
Premium	费　率
Claim	索　赔
Blank Endorsed	空白背书
Issued by	出具（人）

任务分解

为了完成运输单据和保险单据项目的学习，具体可分解为以下三个任务：

（1）缮制托运单。

（2）缮制海运提单。

（3）缮制保险单。

任务一 缮制托运单

【工作认知】

一、认知托运单

（一）托运单的含义

托运单（Shipping Order）是出口商（发货人/托运人）在报关前向船方或其代理人（承运人）申请租船订舱的单据。

（二）托运单的作用

托运单是缮制提单的主要背景资料，是船公司制作提单的依据，如果托运单缮制有差错、延误等，就会影响到其他单证的流转。因此，正确、快速地制单，是保证安全收汇的前提。

（三）海运托运单样章

海运托运单样章如下页所示。

二、缮制海运托运单

（一）海运托运单格式

海运托运单的格式是统一的，一般为五联。第一联是托运人留存，其他联分别交与货物运输的相关部门。

（二）海运托运单填制规范

海运托运单的主要内容如下：

1. 托运人（Shipper）

一般情况下，填写出口公司的名称和地址。在信用证结算方式下，该栏目填写受益人的名称和地址。

2. 收货人或凭指示方（Consignee or Order）

根据信用证和合同规定，填写收货人的名称和地址。

在信用证支付的条件下，对收货人的规定常有两种表示方法：

（1）记名收货人：是直接将收货人（即买方）的名称、地址完整地表示出来。记名收货人的单据不能直接转让，不便于买卖流通，因此不常使用。

（2）指示收货人：常用空白指示和记名指示两种。

指示收货人的单据可以转让。在空白指示（不记名指示，空白指示）情况下，单据的持有人可自由转让单据。在记名指示情况下，记名人有权控制和转让单据。

Shipper（发货人）（1）		D/R No.（编号）（4）
Consignee（收货人）（2）		
Notify Party（通知人）（3）		
Pre－Carriage by（前程运输）（5）	Place of Receipt（收货地点）（6）	
Ocean Vessel（船名）（7）　Voy. No.（航次）（8）	Port of Loading（装货港）（9）	
Port of Discharge（卸货港）（10）	Port of Delivery（交货地点）（11）	Final Destination for the Merchant's Reference（12）（目的地）

Container No.（集装箱号）（13）	Seal No.（封志号）（14）Marks & No.（标记与号码）（15）	No. of Container or Pkgs（箱数或件数）（16）	Kind of Pkg., Description of Goods（包装种类与货名）（17）	Gross Weight（毛重，公斤）（18）	Measurment（尺码，立方米）（19）
TOTAL NO. OF CONTAINER OR PACKAGEES (IN WORDS)（20）集装箱数或件数合计（大写）					
CONTAINER NO.					
		Received（实收）		By Terminal Clerk（签字）	

FREIGHT & CHARGE	Prepaid at（预付地点）（21）	Payable at（到付地点）（22）	Place of Issue（签发地点）（23）
	Total Prepaid（预付总额）	No. of Original B/L（正本提单份数）（24）	BOOKING（订舱确认）APPROVED BY

Service Type on Receiving	Service Type on Delivery	Reefer Temperature Required（冷藏温度）
□－CY，□－CFS，□－DOOR	□－CY，□－CFS，□－DOOR	F　C

TYPE OF GOODS（种类）	□ Ordinary（普通）	□ Reefer（冷藏）	□ Dangerous（危险品）	□ Auto（裸装车辆）	危险品	Clase Property IMDG code page UN No.
	□ Liquid（液体）	□ Live Animal（活动物）	□ Bulk（散货）			

REMARKS（备注） 可否装船 可否分批 有效期 签章

3. 被通知人（Notify Party）

本栏填写信用证中规定的被通知人名称和地址。被通知人的职责是及时接受船方发出的到货通知并将该通知转告给最终的收货人。

4. 托运单编号（D/R Number）

一般是出让舱位的单位填写。

5. 前程运输（Pre－Carriag）

是指货物联运时，从内陆到港口的运输。

6. 收货地点（Place or Receipt）

是指装集装箱的地点。一般是工厂或仓库的地点。

7. 船名（Ocean Vessel）

海洋运输货物的船名。

8. 航次（Voy No.）

海洋运输船的本轮航次。

9. 装货港（Port of Loading）

海洋运输的启运港。

10. 卸货港（Port of Discharge）

海洋运输的卸货港。需要特别指出，港口后面，一定要加注国家，防备同名海港的混淆。

11. 交货地（Place of Delivery）

本栏按信用证的目的港填写。一般卸货港与交货地是同一地点，这一栏目空着。如果目的地是一内陆城市，根据价格术语来填写。在船方或其代理人计算运费时，是根据托运单的本项内容计算航程的。

12. 目的地（Final destination of the merchant's reference）

根据收货人或商人的要求，填写目的地。

13. 集装箱号（Container No.）

海洋运输货物的箱号。

14. 封志号（Seal No.）

海洋运输货物箱号的铅封号码。大部分托运单在出单据时，是没有集装箱号与封志号的，可以留空。

15. 标记与号码（Marks and No.）

本栏填写信用证或合同都规定的唛头，买卖合同或信用证中没有规定唛头，可填写N/M。也可自行选择一个合适的唛头。在选择唛头时，要充分考虑到买方提货的方便、买方利益和买方所在国要求，包括商业习惯、港口规定、文化传统以及政府的有关政策。

16. 箱数或件数（No. of Container or Pkgs）

托运单中的数量是指最大包装的件数。

17. 包装种类与货物说明（Kinds of Packages，Description of Goods）

本栏只写大类名称或统称。如果同时出口不同的商品，应分别填写，而不允许只填写其中的一种金额较大的商品。

18. 毛重（Gross Weight / Net Weight）

本栏运输公司习惯写毛重。如果一次装运的货物中有几种不同的包装材料或完全不同的货物，那么在填写这一栏目时，应先分别计算并填写每一种包装材料或每项货物的毛重，然后合计全部的毛重。在计算重量时，要求使用统一的计量单位。常用的计量单位是公吨或千克。

19. 尺码（Measurement）

本栏填写一批货的尺码总数，一般单位为立方米。总尺码不仅包括各件货物尺码之和，还应包括件与件之间堆放时的合理空隙所占的体积。

20. 集装箱数或件数合计大写（TOTAL No. OF CONTAINERS OR PACKAGES）

本栏用大写表示件数，以便数量的清楚准确。

21. 运费预付地点（Prepaid at）

根据价格术语或合同填写，一般填写装货港。

22. 到付地点（Payable at）

可以填写卸货港，一般不填写。

23. 签发地点（Palce of issue）

是指正本提单的签发地点，一般是装运港口。

【例 3-1-1】

PORT OF LAODING：QINGDAO，CHINA

则PLACE OF ISSUE：QINGDAO，CHINA

PORT OF LAODING：SHANCHAI，CHINA

则 PALCE OF ISSUE：SHANGHAI，CHINA

24. 提单正本份数（No. of Original B/Ls）

提单正本份数一般一式三份，三份正本提单同时有效。

【例 3-1-2】

THREE ORIGINAL BILL OF LADING，ORIGINAL BILL OF LADING IN THREE，FULL SET OF BILL OF LADING，意指全套提单，即三份正本提单

25. 其他

（1）装运日（Time of Shipment）：装运期的表示可以全部使用阿拉伯数字，也可使用英文与阿拉伯数字一起表示，如 6/5/2012，MAY 06，2012。

（2）到期日（Expiry Date）：本栏一般按信用证的规定填写。但如果装运期空白不填的话，这一栏目可以不填。

（3）存货地：内容用中文填写。

（4）转船（Trans Shipment）：填写要求与分批一致，在“允许”或“不允许”两者取一。

（5）分批（Partial Shipment）：按照合同或信用证条款填写。只能限在“允许”或“不允许”两者中取一。如果信用证或合同规定分若干批，或对分批有进一步的说明，不要将

这些说明填入本栏目，而应填写在“特别条款类”栏目中。

（6）运费（Freight）：一般不显示具体运费，只填写“运费待付”或“运费预付/已付”。

（7）托运单日期：托运单日期的填写是根据配舱的日期填写的。

（8）提单副本的份数：提单副本一般是指出口企业留底份数加寄单所需份数加信用证对正本提单要求的份数之和。

（9）特别条款：根据信用证要求或合同要求中有关运输方面的特殊条款，如危险品、冷冻品、活体物品等，需要标注的商品。

（10）签字：经办人签字，出口企业盖章。其他项目如船名、提单号码等由船方或其代理人填写。

资料卡

托运单的流转程序

（1）托运人填写托运单；

（2）托运人留下托运单中的货主留存联；

（3）外轮代理公司加注编号和所配船名；

（4）海关审核认可后，加盖海关放行章；

（5）货运代理安排将集装箱号/封箱号/件数填入托运单，集装箱进入指定的港区、场站；

（6）场站的业务员在集装箱进场后，加批实际收箱数；

（7）场站业务员在装船前及时送外轮理货员，理货员于装船时交大副；

（8）然后第一联收据由场站业务员交还托运人，作为向外轮代理公司换取收货待运提单的凭证，或装船后换取装船提单。

【工作指导】

青岛海富贸易有限公司在货物备妥后，张丽的师傅李华根据合同和信用证的要求及已经制好的商业发票、装箱单和其他相关资料，制作了一份海运托运单。

资料1：信用证

MT：700	ISSUE OF A DOCUMENTARY CREDIT	
SEQUENCE OF TOTAL	*27：	1/1
FORM OF DOC. CREDIT	*40A：	IRREVOCABLE
DOC. CREDIT NUMBER	*20：	IC01925U
DATE OF ISSUE	31C：	20130525
EXPRIRY	*31D：	DATE 20130725

IN QINGDAO		
ISSUING BANK	51A：	WACHOVIA BANK, NO. 3K STREET，RM 504 FUNGLEE COMM. BLDG. ROTTERDAM NETHERLANDS
APPLICANT	*50：	FUTURO INDUSTRIAL CO. LTD. , ROTTERDAM NETHERLANDS TEL：031 431 7295
BENEFICIARY	*59：	QINGDAO HAIFU TRADING CO. LTD. , NO. 1HONGKONG ROAD, QINGDAO CHINA
AMOUNT	*32B：	CURRENCY USD AMOUNT USD40000. 00
AVAILABLE WITH /BY	*41D：	ANY BANK BY DEF PAYMENT
DRAFT AT…	42C：	AT 60 DAYS AFTER B/L SHIPMENT DATE
DRAWEE	42A：	ISSUING BANK
PARTIAL SHIPMENT	43P：	ALLOWED
TRANSHIPMENT：	43T：	ALLOWED
LOADING IN CHARGE	44A：	QINGDAO，CHINA
FOR TRANSPORT TO	44B：	ROTTERDAM PORT，NETHERLANDS
LATEST SHIPMENT DATE	44C：	20130710
DESCRIPTION OF GOODS	45A：	

2450CARTONS（ONE CONTAINER）OF QINCDAO SPRINC ROLLS AT USD15. 50PER CTN CIF ROTTERDAM

PACKING：20G PER PC，50PCS IN A BOX，9 BOXES IN A CARTON

PACKED IN PLANT OF QINGDAO BANMU FOODS PRODUCTS CO. LTD. , QINGDAO INDUSTRIAL ZONE QINGDAO.

AS PER CONTRACT NO. MSR719 DATE：20130412

DOCUMENTS REQUIRED 46A：

+ SIGNED COMMERCIAL INVOICE IN THREE COPIES CERTIFYING COUNTRY OF ORIGIN.

+FULL SET OF ORIGINAL CLEAN ON BAORD OCEAN BILLS OF LADING CONSIGNED TO ORDER OF SHIPPER MARKED FREIGHT PREPAID NOTIFY APPLICANT AND ISSUING BANK.

资料 2：

1. TOTAL SHIPMENT 2450CARTONS

2. PACKING：2KGS X5 IN ONE CARTON，EACH CARTON 10KGS IN N. W. , 11KGS IN G. W. 0. 0205CBM/CTN

3. 运输为 40 尺冷藏，温度为 -18 摄氏度

资料3：海运托运单

Shipper（发货人）		D/R No. （编号）
Consignee（收货人）		
Notify Party（通知人）		
Pre－Carriage by（前程运输）	Place of Receipt（收货地点）	
Ocean Vessel （船名） Voy. No. （航次）	Port of Loading（装货港）	
Port of Discharge（卸货港）	Port of Delivery（交货地点）	Final Destination for the Merchant's Reference （目的地）

Container No. （集装箱号）	Seal No. （封志号） Marks & No. （标记与号码）	No. of Container or Pkgs （箱数或件数）	Kind of Pkg., Description of Goods （包装种类与货名）	Gross Weight （毛重，公斤）	Measurment （尺码，立方米）
TOTAL NO. OF CONTAINER OR PACKAGEES（IN WORDS） 集装箱数或件数合计（大写）					
CONTAINER NO.					

		Received（实收）	By Terminal Clerk（签字）
FREIGHT & CHARGE	Prepaid at（预付地点）	Payable at（到付地点）	Place of Issue（签发地点）
	Total Prepaid（预付总额）	No. of Original B/L（正本提单份数）	BOOKING（订舱确认） APPROVED BY

Service Type on Receiving □－CY，□－CFS，□－DOOR	Service Type on Delivery □－CY，□－CFS，□－DOOR	Reefer Temperature Required（冷藏温度） F C

TYPE OF GOODS （种类）	□ Ordinary （普通）	□ Reefer （冷藏）	□ Dangerous （危险品）	□ Auto （裸装车辆）	危险品	Clase Property IMDG code page UN No.
	□ Liquid （液体）	□ Live Animal （活动物）	□ Bulk （散货）			

REMARKS（备注） 可否装船 可否分批 有效期

师傅李华制作的海运托运单如下所示：

Shipper（发货人） QINGDAO HAIFU TRADING CO. LTD., NO. 1 HONGKONG ROAD, QINGDAO CHINA		D/R No. （编号）
Consignee（收货人） TO ORDER OF SHIPPER		
Notify Party（通知人） FUTURO INDUSTRIAL CO. LTD., ROTTERDAM NETHERLANDS TEL: 031 431 7295 AND WACHOVIA BANK, NO. 3 K STREET, RM 504 FUNGLEE COMM. BLDG. ROTTERDAM NETHERLANDS		

Pre－Carriage by（前程运输）		Place of Receipt（收货地点）	
Ocean Vessel （船名）	Voy. No. （航次）	Port of Loading（装货港） QINGDAO CHINA	
Port of Discharge（卸货港） ROTTERDAM PORT, NETHERLANDS		Port of Delivery（交货地点）	Final Destination for the Merchant's Reference（目的地）

Container No. （集装箱号）	Seal No. （封志号） Marks & No. （标记与号码）	No. of Container or Pkgs （箱数或件数）	Kind of Pkg., Description of Goods （包装种类与货名）	Gross Weight （毛重，公斤）	Measurment （尺码，立方米）
	N/M	2450CTNS	QINGDAO SPRING ROLLS SHIPMENT IN 1 X 40'R FREIGHT PREPAID	26950.00	50.225

TOTAL NO. OF CONTAINER OR PACKAGEES (IN WORDS) 集装箱数或件数合计（大写）	SAY: TWO TIIOUSAND FOUR HUNDRED AND FIFTY CTNS ONLY
CONTAINER NO.	

		Received（实收）	By Terminal Clerk（签字）
FREIGHT & CHARGE	Prepaid at（预付地点） QINGDAO	Payable at（到付地点）	Place of Issue（签发地点）
	Total Prepaid（预付总额）	No. of Original B/L（正本提单份数） THREE	BOOKING（订舱确认） APPROVED BY

Service Type on Receiving □－CY, □－CFS, □－DOOR	Service Type on Delivery □－CY, □－CFS, □－DOOR	Reefer Temperature Required（冷藏温度） F　　－18℃

TYPE OF GOODS （种类）	□ Ordinary （普通）	■ Reefer （冷藏）	□ Dangerous （危险品）	□ Auto （裸装车辆）	危险品	Clase Property IMDG code page UN No.
	□ Liquid （液体）	□ Live Animal （活动物）	□ Bulk （散货）			

REMARKS（备注） 可否装船　V 可否分批　V 有效期　20130710

【工作演练】

张丽在师傅李华的指导下，已经基本掌握了制作海运托运单的技能。下面请你和张丽一起根据青岛海富贸易有限公司收到的来自韩国 MERRY 公司的信用证及相关资料制作一份海运托运单。

资料1：信用证

ISSUING BANK: KOREA EXCHANGE BANK SEOUL KOREA
DOC. CREDIT NO. M06C7604RU00032
DATE OF ISSUE: 20130406
EXPIRY: DATE 20130605 PLACE CHINA
APPLICANT: MERRY CO. LTD.,
213 MAPO－KU SEOUL, KOREA
BENEFICIARY: QINGDAO HAIFU TRADING CO. LTD.,
NO. 1 HONGKONG ROAD,
QINGDAO CHINA
AMOUNT: USD70000.00
AVAILABLE WITH: ANY BANK
DRAFT AT: 60 DAYS AFTER SIGHT
DRAWEE: KOREA EXCHANGE BANK BRANCH SEOUL KOREA
PARTIAL SHIPMENTS: ALLOW
TRANSSHIPMENT: ALLOW
LOADING IN CHARGE: QINGDAO, CHINA
FOR TRANSPORT TO : BUSAN KOREA
LATEST DATE OF SHIPMENT: 20130525
DESCRIPT. OF GOODS:
ORIGIN: CHINA
P. O NO. 60489
5600CASES CANNED FOOD AT USD 15.50 PER CTN
PRICE TERM CIF BUSAN CHINA
DOCUMENTS REQUIRED:
+ SIGNED COMMERCIAL INVOICE IN 3 COPIES
+ FULL SET ORIGINAL CLEAN ON BOARD COMBINED BILL OF LADING MADE OUT TO ORDER OF KOREA EXCHANGE BANK, SEOUL NOTIFY APPLICANT B/L MUST SHOW CONTAINER SHIPMENT ONLY AND SHIPPING MARKS AS LOT 60489 HANJIN
+ MARINE INSURANCE POLICY OR CERTIFICATE IN DUPLICATE ENDORSED IN

BLANK, WITH CLAIM PAYABLE IN KOREA IN THE CURRENCY OF THE DRAFT, COVERING 110 PERCENT OF INVOICE VALUE, INCLUDING INSTITUTE WAR CLAUSE INSTITUTE CARGO CALUSES (all risks) INSTITUTE STRIKES RIOTS AND CIVIL COMMOTIONS CLAUSES.

资料2：实际发货信息

数量：5600CASES
PACKING：N. W. 5. 5KGS，G. W. 6. 00KGS，0. 006CBM/CASE
用2个20尺集装箱运输

资料3：海运托运单

<table>
<tr><td colspan="4">Shipper（发货人）</td><td colspan="2" rowspan="5">D/R No.
（编号）</td></tr>
<tr><td colspan="4">Consignee（收货人）</td></tr>
<tr><td colspan="4">Notify Party（通知人）</td></tr>
<tr><td colspan="2">Pre－carriage by（前程运输）</td><td colspan="2">Place of Receipt（收货地点）</td></tr>
<tr><td>Ocean Vessel
（船名）</td><td>Voy. No.
（航次）</td><td colspan="2">Port of Loading（装货港）</td></tr>
<tr><td colspan="2">Port of Discharge（卸货港）</td><td colspan="2">Port of Delivery（交货地点）</td><td colspan="2">Final Destination for the Merchant's Reference
（目的地）</td></tr>
<tr><td>Container No.
（集装箱号）</td><td>Seal No.
（封志号）
Marks & No.
（标记与号码）</td><td>No. of Container or Pkgs
（箱数或件数）</td><td>Kind of Pkg.，Description of Goods
（包装种类与货名）</td><td>Gross Weight
（毛重，公斤）</td><td>Measurment
（尺码，立方米）</td></tr>
<tr><td colspan="2">TOTAL NO. OF CONTAINER OR PACKAGES (IN WORDS)
集装箱数或件数合计（大写）</td><td></td><td colspan="3"></td></tr>
<tr><td colspan="6">CONTAINER NO.</td></tr>
<tr><td colspan="3"></td><td colspan="2">Received（实收）</td><td>By Terminal Clerk（签字）</td></tr>
<tr><td rowspan="2">FREIGHT
&
CHARGE</td><td colspan="2">Prepaid at（预付地点）</td><td colspan="2">Payable at（到付地点）</td><td>Place of Issue（签发地点）</td></tr>
<tr><td colspan="2">Total Prepaid（预付总额）</td><td colspan="2">No. of Original B/L（正本提单份数）</td><td>BOOKING（订舱确认）
APPROVED BY</td></tr>
</table>

<table>
<tr><td colspan="2">Service Type on Receiving
□－CY，□－CFS，□－DOOR</td><td colspan="3">Service Type on Delivery
□－CY，□－CFS，□－DOOR</td><td colspan="2">Reefer Temperature Required（冷藏温度）
F　　C</td></tr>
<tr><td rowspan="2">TYPE OF GOODS（种类）</td><td>□ Ordinary（普通）</td><td>□ Reefer（冷藏）</td><td>□ Dangerous（危险品）</td><td>□ Auto（裸装车辆）</td><td rowspan="2">危险品</td><td rowspan="2">Clase
Property
IMDG code page
UN No.</td></tr>
<tr><td>□ Liquid（液体）</td><td>□ Live Animal（活动物）</td><td colspan="2">□ Bulk（散货）</td></tr>
</table>

REMARKS（备注）
可否装船
可否分批
有效期

提示：

（1）托运单填制的品名、件数、数量、重量一定要与实物一致。

（2）填写时要注意信用证要求或合同要求中是否有有关运输方面的特殊条款，如危险品、冷冻品、活体物品等，需要标注的商品等要在托运单中标注。

【工作评价】

1. 评价标准

<table>
<tr><td colspan="4">Shipper（发货人）
QINGDAO HAIFU CO. LTD.,
NO. 1 HONGKONG ROAD，QINGDAO，CHINA</td><td colspan="3" rowspan="5">D/R No.（编号）</td></tr>
<tr><td colspan="4">Consignee（收货人）
TO ORDER OF KOREA EXCHANGE BANK，SEOOL</td></tr>
<tr><td colspan="4">Notify Party（通知人）
MERRY CO. LTD.,
213 MAPO－KU SEOUL，KOREA</td></tr>
<tr><td colspan="2">Pre－carriage by（前程运输）</td><td colspan="2">Place of Receipt（收货地点）</td></tr>
<tr><td>Ocean Vessel（船名）</td><td>Voy. No.（航次）</td><td colspan="2">Port of Loading（装货港）
QINGDAO CHINA</td></tr>
<tr><td colspan="2">Port of Discharge（卸货港）
BUSAN KOREA</td><td colspan="2">Port of Delivery（交货地点）</td><td colspan="3">Final Destination for the Merchant's Reference（目的地）</td></tr>
<tr><td>Container No.（集装箱号）</td><td>Seal No.（封志号）
Marks & No.（标记与号码）

LOT 60489
HANJIN</td><td>No. of Container or Pkgs（箱数或件数）

5600CASES</td><td colspan="2">Kind of Pkg., Description of Goods（包装种类与货名）

CANNED FOOD

SHIPMENT IN 2×20'CONTAINER</td><td>Gross Weight（毛重，公斤）

33600.00</td><td>Measurment（尺码，立方米）

33.600</td></tr>
</table>

<table>
<tr><td colspan="2">TOTAL NO. OF CONTAINER OR PACKAGEES (IN WORDS)
集装箱数或件数合计（大写）</td><td colspan="4">SAY FIVE THOUSAND AND SIX HUNDRED CASES ONLY</td></tr>
<tr><td colspan="6">CONTAINER NO.</td></tr>
<tr><td colspan="3"></td><td>Received（实收）</td><td colspan="2">By Terminal Clerk（签字）</td></tr>
<tr><td rowspan="2">FREIGHT
&
CHARGE</td><td colspan="2">Prepaid at（预付地点）
QINGDAO</td><td>Payable at（到付地点）</td><td colspan="2">Place of Issue（签发地点）</td></tr>
<tr><td colspan="2">Total Prepaid（预付总额）</td><td>No. of Original B/L（正本提单份数）
THREE</td><td colspan="2">BOOKING（订舱确认）
APPROVED BY</td></tr>
</table>

<table>
<tr><td rowspan="2">Service Type on Receiving
□ - CY, □ - CFS, □ - DOOR</td><td rowspan="2">Service Type on Delivery
□ - CY, □ - CFS, □ - DOOR</td><td colspan="2">Reefer Temperature Required（冷藏温度）</td></tr>
<tr><td></td><td>F　　C</td></tr>
</table>

<table>
<tr><td rowspan="2">TYPE
OF
GOODS
（种类）</td><td>□ Ordinary
（普通）</td><td>□ Reefer
（冷藏）</td><td>□ Dangerous
（危险品）</td><td>□ Auto
（裸装车辆）</td><td rowspan="2">危险品</td><td rowspan="2">Clase
Property
IMDG code page
UN No.</td></tr>
<tr><td>□ Liquid
（液体）</td><td>□ Live Animal
（活动物）</td><td>□ Bulk
（散货）</td><td></td></tr>
</table>

<table>
<tr><td>REMARKS（备注）
可否装船 V
可否分批 V
有效期 20130525</td></tr>
</table>

2. 评价表（见表 3－1－1）

表 3－1－1

评价指标＼评价人	自　评	互　评	师　评
独立完成情况（20 分）			
格式规范性（20 分）			
内容完整性、正确性（50 分）			
内容简明性、整洁性（10 分）			
合计总分			

任务二　缮制海运提单

【工作认知】

一、认知海运提单

（一）海运提单的含义

海运提单（Ocean Bill of Loading，B/L），是承运人收到货物后出具的货物收据，也是承运人所签署的运输契约的证明。

（二）海运提单的作用

（1）货物收据。提单作为承运人或其代理人出具的货物收据，证明承运人已收到或接管提单上所列货物。

（2）物权凭证。提单在法律上具有物权凭证的作用，承运人在货物抵达目的港后向提单的合法持有人交付货物。提单可以背书转让，也可以向银行办理抵押货款。

（3）运输契约的证明。提单是持有人和托运人之间的运输契约证明，提单背面条款规定了承运人和托运人双方的权利、义务、责任和豁免。

（三）海运提单的种类

常见海运提单的种类见表 3－2－1。

表 3－2－1　　常见海运提单的分类

根据货物是否已装船	已装船提单（Shipped on Board B/L）和备用提单（Received for Shipment B/L）。
根据货物外表状况有无不良批注	清洁提单（Clean B/L）和不清洁提单（Unclean Or Foul B/L）。
根据不同运输方式	直达提单（Direct B/L）、转船提单（Transshipment B/L）、联运提单（Through B/L）和联合运输提单（Combined Transport B/L）等。
根据提单抬头不同	记名提单（Straight B/L）、不记名提单（Bearer B/L）和指示提单（Order B/L）。

此外，还有全式提单和简式提单；运费预付提单和运费到付提单；正本提单和副本提单；租船合同下的提单；舱面提单、倒签提单、预借提单等。

（四）海运提单样章

海运提单样章如下所示：

<table>
<tr><td colspan="2">Shipper
1. 托运人</td><td rowspan="6">B/L No.
4. 提单号</td></tr>
<tr><td colspan="2">Consignee or Order
2. 收货人或指示</td></tr>
<tr><td colspan="2">Notify Party
3. 被通知方</td></tr>
<tr><td>Pre－carriage by
5. 前程运输</td><td>Port of Loading
8. 装货港</td></tr>
<tr><td>Vessel and Voy No.
6. 船名航次</td><td>Port of Discharge
9. 卸货港</td></tr>
<tr><td>Sailing on or about
7. 开船日期</td><td>Final Destination
10. 最终目的地</td></tr>
</table>

<table>
<tr><td>Marks & Nos.</td><td>Number and kind of Packages</td><td>Gross Weight</td><td>Measurement（cbm）</td></tr>
<tr><td>Container No. & Seal No.
11. 唛头
12. 集装箱号
13. 铅封号</td><td>Description of Goods
14. 件数和包装种类
货物描述</td><td>15. 毛重</td><td>16. 尺码</td></tr>
<tr><td colspan="4">22. 提单要求的批注</td></tr>
<tr><td colspan="4">TOTAL NUMBER OF CONTAINERS
17. 包装总数（大写）</td></tr>
</table>

<table>
<tr><td>Freight and Charges
18. 运费和费用</td><td>No. of Original B(s)/L
19. 正本数</td><td>Place and Date of Issue
20. 签单日期和地点</td></tr>
<tr><td colspan="2"></td><td>Signed for the Carrier
21. 承运人签字</td></tr>
</table>

二、缮制海运提单

（一）海运提单的格式

海运提单的格式由各海运公司自行确定，形式各有特色，但主要包括了以下内容。

1. 提单正面的内容

根据1993年7月1日公布实施的《中华人民共和国海商法》第七十三条的规定，提单正面应记载以下各项：（1）货物的品名、标志、包数或者件数、重量或者体积以及运输危险货物时对危险性质的说明；（2）承运人的名称和主要营业场所；（3）船舶名称；（4）托运人的名称；（5）收货人的名称；（6）装货港和在装货港接受货物的日期；（7）卸货港；（8）多式联运提单增列接收货物地点；（9）提单的签发日期、地点和份数；（10）运费的支付；（11）承运人或者其代表。

《中华人民共和国海商法》第七十三条还同时规定："提单缺少本款规定的一项或者几项的，不影响提单的性质。"提单正面记载的事项，在法律上具有初步证据。

2. 提单背面的内容

提单背面印定的条款规定了承运人与货方之间的权利、义务和责任豁免，是双方当事人处理争议时的主要法律依据。在正本提单的背面，列有许多条款，各国船公司签发的提单背面条款略有差异，但基本上可以归纳为以下内容：定义条款、管辖权条款、责任期限条款、损失赔偿条款、运费条款、共同海损和碰撞条款、变更航线条款等。

（二）海运提单的缮制规范

海运提单的主要填写内容如下：

1. 托运人（Shipper）

托运人是指委托运输的人，一般为信用证中的受益人，即合同的卖方。如果开证人为了贸易上的需要，要求做第三者提单（Third Party B/L），也可照办。

2. 收货人（Consignee）

提单收货人，又称“抬头人”，与托运单收货人栏目的填写完全一致。提单的抬头决定了海运提单的性质和货权的归属。在进出口贸易中多使用指示抬头以便提单可以流通转让。

托运方式下的提单，本栏一般填“TO ORDER”或“TO ORDER OF SHIPPER”均可，然后由托运人背书。本栏不能做成凭收货人提示或凭代收行提示。

信用证支付方式下，应严格按照信用证规定填制，本栏常见填法主要有三种：

（1）指示式。这种方式最普遍，多数信用证使用这种方式，分为空白指示式和记名指示式。空白指示式本栏填“TO ORDER”，然后在整本提单背面由托运人签字盖章背书（ENDORSEMENT）。记名指示式又分为发货人指示式、银行指示式、收货人指示式三种。其中，发货人指示式本栏填“TO ORDER OF SHIPPER”，托运人必须在正本提单背面背书，可以是空白背书，也可以是记名背书，根据信用证或合同规定填制。银行指示式本栏填“TO ORDER OF XXX BANK”。收货人指示式本栏填“TO ORDER OF XXX CO.，LTD.”银行指示式和收货人指示式，托运人均不需要背书。

【例 3-2-1】

如信用证规定“FULL SET ORIGINAL CLEAN ON BOARD BILLS OF LADING MADE OUT TO ORDER OF SHIPPER AND ENDORSED IN BLANK AND MARKED FREIGHT PREPAID NOTIFY APPLICANT AND ISSUING BANK”，则此处应填 TO ORDER OF SHIPPER.

资料卡

背书（Endorsement）又分为空白背书和记名背书，空白背书由背书人在正本提单背面签字盖章而不记载被背书人的名称；记名背书除了背书人在正本提单背面签字盖章外，还要记载被背书人的名称。

（2）记名式。本栏直接填某某公司的名称，如填“XXX CO. LTD.”，托运人不需要背书。记名式除收货人外，提单不能转让，目前这种做法比较少见，主要用于 T/T 支付方式下。

（3）不记名式。本栏留空不填，或填“TO BEARER”（来人抬头），谁持有该提单，其物权就归谁。不记名提单可以转让，不需背书或任何转让手续，风险较大，国际上很少使用。

3. 被通知人（Notify Party）

这是船公司在货物到达目的港时发送到货通知的收件人，有时即为进口人。在信用证项下的提单，如信用证上对提单被通知人有权具体规定时，则必须严格按信用证要求填写。如果是记名提单或收货人指示提单，且收货人又有详细地址的，则此栏可以不填。如果是空白指示提单或托运人指示提单，则此栏必须填写被通知人名称及详细地址，否则船方就无法与收货人联系，收货人也不能及时提货，甚至会因超过海关规定申报时间被没收。

【例 3-2-2】

如信用证规定“FULL SET ORIGINAL CLEAN ON BOARD BILLS OF LADING MADE OUT TO ORDER OF SHIPPER AND ENDORSED IN BLANK AND MARKED FREIGHT PREPAID NOTIFY APPLICANT AND ISSUING BANK”，则通知人应填写开证申请人和开证行名称及详细地址。

4. 提单号（B/L No.）

一般列在提单右上角，以便工作联系和查核。发货人向收货人发送装船通知（SHIPMENT ADVICE）时，也要列明船名和提单号码。

5. 前程运输（Pre-Carriage by）

指联合运输过程中在装货港装船前的运输。海运提单一般此处不填。

6. 船名航次（Vessel and Voy No.）

应填写货物所装的船名及航次。

7. 开船日期（Sailing on or About）

货物装船的日期，按照实际装船日期填写，时间不应超过信用证规定的“最迟装运期”（LATEST DATE OF SHIPMENT）。

【例 3-2-3】 如信用证规定：“LATEST DATE OF SHIPMENT：130120”，则开船日期必须在 2013 年 1 月 20 日之前。

8. 装货港（Port of Loading）

应填列实际装船港口的具体名称。

（1）如信用证只笼统规定“CHINESE PORT”，制单时应填写具体的港口名称；如货物实际在青岛发运，应填写“QINGDAO，CHINA”。

（2）如来证同时列明几个装货港，如“DALIAN/QINGDAO/TANGSHAN”则提单只能填写其中一个实际装运的港口名称。

9. 卸货港（Port of Discharge）

填写货物实际卸下的港口名称。

（1）货物如需转运，装货港后面没有注明中转港，则可在目的港之后加注“WITH TRANSSHIPMENT AT HONGKONG”，简写为“W/T HONGKONG”，如“SINGAPORE W/T HONGKONG”（目的港新加坡，在香港转船）。

（2）如货运目的港再运至内地某处，或利用邻国港口过境，需在目的港后加注“IN TRANSIT（TO）某地”，如“KUWAIT IN TRANSIT TO SAUDI ARABIA”（目的港科威特转运沙特阿拉伯)。

10. 最终目的地(Final Destination)

指联合运输的终点站。应是当次运输的运费截止地。如果是港至港的海运提单,则本栏不填或仍填卸货港名称。

11. 唛头 (Marks)

按照托运人填制的订舱委托书填写,格式与商业发票中唛头的缮制要求一致。若无唛头,则填写“N/M”。

12. 集装箱号 (Container No.)

填写装货集装箱号码。

13. 铅封号 (Seal No.)

填写铅封号。

14. 件数和包装种类 (NUMBER AND KIND OF PACKAGES);货名 (DESCRIPTION OF GOODS)

在信用证项下货名按照信用证规定填写,并与发票等单据一致。

件数是指本海运提单项下的商品总包装件数。

(1) 对于包装货物,本栏应注明包装数量和包装单位,如“2000 BALES”,“230 DRUMS”。

(2) 如是散装货,如煤炭、石油等,此栏填写“IN BULK”。

(3) 如果是裸装货,应加件数,如一台汽车,此栏填写“1 UNIT”。

(4) 如是集装箱运输,由托运人装箱的整箱货可只注明集装箱数量,如“2 CONTAINER”等。只要海关已对集装箱封箱,承运人对箱内的内容和数量不负责任,提单内应加注“SHIPPER'S LOAD & COUNT”(托运人装货并计数)。如须注明集装箱箱内小件数量时,数量前应加“SAID TO CONTAIN…”。

(5) 如是托盘装运,此栏应填写托盘数量,同时应用括号加注货物的包装件数,如“6 PALLETS (50 CARTONS)”,提单内还应加注“SHIPPER'S LOAD & COUNT”。

(6) 如是多种包装,如“200 BAGS”、“300 CARTONS”、“100BALES”,件数栏内要逐项列明,同时下面应合计数量,如上述包装数量可合计为600PACKAGES。

15. 毛重 (Gross Weight)

除信用证另有规定者外,一般以公斤为单位列出货物的毛重。如果没有毛重只有净重,应先加注“N. W.”,再列明具体净重。

16. 尺码 (Measurement)

除信用证另有规定者外,一般以立方米列出货物体积。立方米以下保留小数点后三位。

17. 包装总数 (Total Number of Containers or Packages in words)

与14栏“包装总数”对应,此处应为包装数的英文大写加包装单位。

【例3-2-4】 例如,数量为100 CARTONS,此处应填写“SAY ONE HUNDRED CARTONS ONLY”。

18. 运费和费用 (Freight and Charges)

一般为预付(FREIGHT PREPAID)或到付(FREIGHT COLLECT)。

如果是 CIF 或 CFR 出口，一般均填上运费预付字样。千万不可漏填，否则收货人会因运费问题提不到货，虽可查清情况，但拖延提货时间，也将造成损失。如果是 FOB 出口，则运费可制作“运费到付”字样，除非收货人委托发货人垫付运费。

（1）运费预付——FREIGHT PREPAID。

（2）运费到付——FREIGHT PAYABLE AT DESTINATION / FREIGHT COLLECT。

19. 正本提单的签发份数（No. of Original B/L）

船公司一般按照托运人的要求出具相应的份数，如果信用证规定要求出口方提供“全套海运提单”（FULL SET OR COMPLETE SET B/L），实际业务中应提供三份海运提单正本，因此此处一般填写“THREE（3）”。

20. 签单地点和日期（Place and Date of Issue）

海运提单签发地点一般为装货港，提单签发日期与提单第 7 栏一致，即提单上所签的日期必须与信用证或合同上所要求的最后装船期一致或先于装船期。

21. 承运人签章（Signed for the Carrier）

提单必须由承运人或船长或他们的代理签发，并应明确表明签发人身份。一般表示方法有“CARRIER”、“CAPTAIN”，或“AS AGENT FOR THE CARRIER：XXX”等。

22. 提单要求的批注

信用证要求提交“清洁已转船”提单时，如果提单上没有事先印就的“已装船”或“清洁”字样，制单时应加注“SHIPPED ON BOARD & CLEAN”。另外，正本要注明“ORIGINAL”，有时还要按照信用证要求注明货物的交接方式（如“CY－CY”）或声明船龄船籍等条款（“THE VESSEL IS NOT OLDER THAN 15 YEARS”）。

【工作指导】

青岛海富贸易有限公司收到的来自荷兰 FUTURO 公司申请开出的信用证，张丽的师傅李华根据信用证、海运托运单及相关资料制作了一份海运提单。

资料 1：信用证

MT：700		**ISSUE OF A DOCUMENTARY CREDIT**
SEQUENCE OF TOTAL	*27：	1/1
FORM OF DOC. CREDIT	*40A：	IRREVOCABLE
DOC. CREDIT NUMBER	*20：	IC01925U
DATE OF ISSUE	31C：	20130525
EXPRIRY	*31D：	DATE 20130725 IN QINGDAO
ISSUING BANK	51A：	WACHOVIA BANK, NO. 3K STREET, RM 504 FUNGLEE COMM. BLDG. ROTTERDAM NETHERLANDS
APPLICANT	*50：	FUTURO INDUSTRIAL CO. LTD. , ROTTERDAM NETHERLANDS TEL：031 431 7295

BENEFICIARY *59: QINGDAO HAIFU TRADING CO. LTD.,
NO. 1HONGKONG ROAD,
QINGDAO CHINA
AMOUNT *32B: CURRENCY USD AMOUNT USD40000. 00
AVAILABLE WITH /BY *41D: ANY BANK BY DEF PAYMENT
DRAFT AT… 42C: AT 60 DAYS AFTER B/L SHIPMENT DATE
DRAWEE 42A: ISSUING BANK
PARTIAL SHIPMENT 43P: ALLOWED
TRANSHIPMENT: 43T: ALLOWED
LOADING IN CHARGE 44A: QINGDAO, CHINA
FOR TRANSPORT TO 44B: ROTTERDAM PORT, NETHERLANDS
LATEST SHIPMENT DATE 44C: 20130710
DESCRIPTION OF GOODS 45A:
2450CARTONS (ONE CONTAINER) OFQINGDAO SPRING ROLLS AT USD15. 50PER CTN CIFROTTERDAM
PACKING: 20G PER PC, 50PCS IN A BOX, 9 BOXES IN A CARTON
PACKED IN PLANT OF QINGDAO BANMU FOODS PRODUCTS CO. LTD., QINGDAO INDUSTRIAL ZONE QINGDAO.
AS PER CONTRACT NO. MSR719 DATE: 20130412
DOCUMENTS REQUIRED 46A:
+ SIGNED COMMERCIAL INVOICE IN THREE COPIES CERTIFYING COUNTRY OF ORIGIN.
+ FULL SET OF ORIGINAL CLEAN ON BAORD OCEAN BILLS OF LADING CONSIGNED TO ORDER OF SHIPPER MARKED FREIGHT PREPAID NOTIFY APPLICANT AND ISSUING BANK.
+ PACKING LIST IN THREE COPIES.
+ MARINE INSURANCE POLICY OR CERTIFICATE IN DUPLICATE ENDORSED IN BLANK, WITH CLAIM PAYABLE IN NETHLANDS IN THE CURRENCY OF THE DRAFT, COVERING 110 PERCENT OF INVOICE VALUE, INCLUDING ICC (A) AND ICC WAR CLAUSE AS PER INSTITUTE CARGO CLAUSE DATED 1/1/1982.
+ SHIPPING ADVICE HAS BEEN SENT TO APPLICANT WITHIN 3 DAYS FROM DATE OF SHIPMENT INDICATING L/C NO., INVOICE NO., AMOUNT, DETAILS OF GOODS, NAME OF VESSEL, VOYAGE NO., DATE OF SHIPMENT, PORT OF LOADING, B/L NO., CONTAINER NO., SEAL NO., ESTIMATED TIME OF ARRIVAL.
+ CERTIFICATE OF ORIGINAND GSP FORM A SIGNED BY C. I. Q.
+ COPY OF BENEFICIARY CERTIFICATE CERTIFY THAT ONE COMPLETE SET OF N/N DOCUMENTS HAS BEEN SENT TO APPLICANT BY COURIER WITHIN FIVE DAYS OF THE B/L DATE.
ADDITIONAL COND. 47A:
+SHIPMENT DOCUMENTS EVIDENCE THIS L/C NO.
+THE INVOICE SEPARATELY MENTION FOB VALUE, FREIGHT CHARGE.
+B/L MUST MARK THAT THE GOODS SHIPPED IN 40 HR CONTAINER AND SET AT -18 DEGREES CENTIGRADE OR LOWER.
DETAILS OF CHARGES: 71B:
ALL BANK CHARGES OUTSIDEROTTERDAM ARE FOR ACCOUNT OF BENEFICIARY.
CONFIRMATION INSTRUCTIONS *49: WITHOUT
"ADVISE THROUGH" BANK 57A: BANK OF CHINA LTD., SHANDONG BRANCH

资料2：海运托运单

<table>
<tr><td colspan="4">Shipper（发货人）
QINGDAO HAIFU TRADING CO. LTD.,
NO. 1 HONGKONG ROAD, QINGDAO CHINA</td><td colspan="3">D/R No.
（编号）</td></tr>
<tr><td colspan="4">Consignee（收货人）
TO ORDER OF SHIPPER</td><td colspan="3"></td></tr>
<tr><td colspan="4">Notify Party（通知人）
FUTURO INDUSTRIAL CO. LTD., ROTTERDAM NETHERLANDS
TEL: 031 431 7295 AND
WACHOVIA BANK, NO. 3 K STREET, RM 504 FUNGLEE COMM. BLDG. ROTTERDAM NETHERLANDS</td><td colspan="3"></td></tr>
<tr><td colspan="2">Pre - carriage by（前程运输）</td><td colspan="2">Place of Receipt（收货地点）</td><td colspan="3"></td></tr>
<tr><td>Ocean Vessel
（船名）</td><td>Voy. No.
（航次）</td><td colspan="2">Port of Loading（装货港）
QINGDAO CHINA</td><td colspan="3"></td></tr>
<tr><td colspan="2">Port of Discharge（卸货港）
ROTTERDAM PORT,
NETHERLANDS</td><td colspan="2">Port of Delivery（交货地点）</td><td colspan="3">Final Destination for the Merchant's Reference（目的地）</td></tr>
<tr><td>Container No.
（集装箱号）</td><td>Seal No.
（封志号）
Marks & No.
（标记与号码）
F. I. C.
MSR719
ROTTERDAM
N O. 1 - 2450</td><td>No. of Container or Pkgs
（箱数或件数）
2450CTNS</td><td colspan="2">Kind of Pkg., Description of Goods
（包装种类与货名）
QINGDAO SPRING ROLLS
SHIPMENT IN 1 × 40'R
FREIGHT PREPAID</td><td>Gross Weight
（毛重，公斤）
26950.00</td><td>Measurment
（尺码，立方米）
47.775</td></tr>
<tr><td colspan="2">TOTAL NO. OF CONTAINER OR PACKAGEES (IN WORDS)
集装箱数或件数合计（大写）</td><td colspan="5">1 - 2450
SAY: TWO THOUSAND FOUR HUNDRED AND FIFTY CTNS ONLY</td></tr>
<tr><td colspan="7">CONTAINER NO.</td></tr>
<tr><td colspan="3"></td><td colspan="2">Received（实收）</td><td colspan="2">By Terminal Clerk（签字）</td></tr>
<tr><td rowspan="2">FREIGHT
&
CHARGE</td><td colspan="2">Prepaid at（预付地点）
QINGDAO</td><td colspan="2">Payable at（到付地点）</td><td colspan="2">Place of Issue（签发地点）</td></tr>
<tr><td colspan="2">Total Prepaid（预付总额）</td><td colspan="2">No. of Original B/L（正本提单份数）
THREE</td><td colspan="2">BOOKING（订舱确认）
APPROVED BY</td></tr>
</table>

<table>
<tr><td colspan="2">Service Type on Receiving
☐ - CY, ☐ - CFS, ☐ - DOOR</td><td colspan="2">Service Type on Delivery
☐ - CY, ☐ - CFS, ☐ - DOOR</td><td colspan="2">Reefer Temperature Required（冷藏温度）
F -18℃</td></tr>
<tr><td rowspan="2">TYPE
OF
GOODS
（种类）</td><td colspan="3">☐ Ordinary（普通） ■ Reefer（冷藏） ☐ Dangerous（危险品） ☐ Auto（裸装车辆）</td><td rowspan="2">危险品</td><td rowspan="2">Clase
Property
IMDG code page
UN No.</td></tr>
<tr><td colspan="3">☐ Liquid（液体） ☐ Live Animal（活动物） ☐ Bulk（散货）</td></tr>
</table>

<table>
<tr><td>REMARKS（备注）
可否装船 V
可否分批 V
有效期 20130710</td></tr>
</table>

资料3：

INVOICE NO.：QD528
C/O. NO. G370213070203
H. S. CODE：19022200
VESSEL NAME：SITCQINGDAO V. 23 B/L NO. SITC229173
CONTAINER NO. SITC1292748 SEAL NO. 006265
FREIGHT CHARGE：USD3150. 00
PACKINGPER CTN：N. W. 9. 00KGS / G. W. 10. 00KGS / MEASUREMENT 0. 0195CBM
THE CARRIER AS NYK LING SHIPPING CO.,
MARK：MAKE A STANDARD MARK BY SELF

师傅李华制作的海运提单如下所示：

<table>
<tr><td colspan="3">Shipper
QINGDAO HAIFU TRADING CO. LTD.,
NO. 1 HONGKONG ROAD,, QINGDAO CHINA</td><td colspan="2" rowspan="7">B/L No. SITC229173</td></tr>
<tr><td colspan="3">Consignee or Order
TO ORDER OF SHIPPER</td></tr>
<tr><td colspan="3">Notify Party
FUTURO INDUSTRIAL CO. LTD., ROTTERDAM NETHERLANDS
TEL：031 431 7295 AND WACHOVIA BANK, NO. 3 K STREET,
RM 504 FUNGLEE COMM. BLDG. ROTTERDAM NETHERLANDS</td></tr>
<tr><td colspan="2">Pre-carriage by</td><td>Port of Loading
QINGDAO, CHINA</td></tr>
<tr><td colspan="2">Vessel and Voy No.
SITC QINGDAO V. 23</td><td>Port of Discharge
ROTTERDAM PORT, NETHERLANDS</td></tr>
<tr><td colspan="2">Sailing on or about
JULY 9, 2013</td><td>Final Destination</td></tr>
<tr><td colspan="3"></td></tr>
<tr><td>Marks & Nos.
Container No. & Seal No.</td><td colspan="2">Number and Kind of Packages
Description of Goods</td><td>Gross Weight</td><td>Measurement (cbm)</td></tr>
<tr><td>F. I. C.
MSR719
ROTTERDAM
NO. 1-2450

CONTAINER NO.：SITC1292748
SEAL NO.：006265</td><td colspan="2">2450CARTONS (ONE CONTAINER) OF
QINGDAO SPRING ROLLS

THE GOODS SHIPPED IN 40HR CONTAINER AND SET AT -18 DEGREES
CENTIGRADE OR LOWER
L/C NO. ICO1925U

ON BOARD</td><td>26950. 00KGS</td><td>47. 775CBM</td></tr>
<tr><td>TOTAL NUMBER OF CONTAINERS OR PACKAGES (IN WORDS)</td><td colspan="4">SAY TWO THOUSAND FOUR HUNDRED AND FIFTY CARTONS ONLY</td></tr>
<tr><td>Freight and Charges
FREIGHT PREPAID</td><td>No. of Original B(s)/L
THREE</td><td colspan="3">Place and Date of Issue
QINGDAO, CHINA
JULY 9, 2013</td></tr>
<tr><td colspan="2"></td><td colspan="3">Signed for the Carrier
NYK LING SHIPPING CO.
* * *</td></tr>
</table>

【工作演练】

张丽在师傅李华的指导下，已经基本掌握了制作海运提单的技能。下面请你和张丽一起根据青岛海富贸易有限公司收到的来自日本的 SHITAYA KINZOKU 公司的信用证及相关资料独立制作一份海运提单。

资料 1：信用证

ISSUING BANK：THE SUMITOMO BANK LTD.，TOKYO JAPAN
TO：BANK OF CHINA，SHANDONG BRANCH
L/C NO. SCN1200N9
DATE：SEP. 25，2009
EXPIRY DATE AND PALCE：DEC. 10，2009—CHINA
APPLICANT：SHITAYA KINZOKU CO.
4 – 1 – 7 CHOME – KU TOKYO JAPAN
BENEFICIARY：QINGDAO HAIFU CO. LTD.，
NO. 1HONGKONG ROAD，QINGDAO CHINA
AMOUNT：USD13430.00（U. S. DOLLARS THIRTEENTHOUSAND FOUR HUNDRED AND THIRTY）
DRAFTS：AT 30DAYS AFTER B/L DATE FOR FULL INVOICE VALUE OF GOODS DRAWN ON OURSELVES
PARTIAL SHIPMENTS：ALLOWED
TRANSHIPMENT：PROHIBITED
SHIPMENT FROM ANY PORT INCHINA TO TOKYO JAPAN AT LATEST NOV. 20，2009
DESCRIPTION OF GOODS：
MEN's LEATHER SHOES
400PAIRS BLACK COLOR SIZE 39 – 41 @ USD12.00PER PAIR
300PAIRS WHITE COLOR SIZE 38 – 42 @ USD13.00PER PAIR
350PAIRS BROWN COLOR SIZE 40 – 44 @ USD13.50PER PAIR
CFRTOKYO PACKED 10 PAIRS IN ONE CARTON EACH
AS PER BUYER's ORDER NO. SK682 DD. 20090921
DOCUMENTS：
+ SIGNED COMMERCIAL INVOICE IN TRIPLICANT CERTIFYING MERCHANDISE COUNTRY OF ORIGIN AND SHOWING FOB VALUE
+ FULL SET ORIGINAL CLEAN ON BOARD BILLS OF LADING MADE OUT TO ORDER OF SHIPPER AND ENDORSED IN BLANK AND MARKED FREIGHT PREPAID NOTIFY APPLICANT AND ISSUING BANK

SPECIAL CONDITIONS：
+ THE GOODS HAVE SHIPPED IN 40H CONTAINER APPEAR IN B/L
+ INSURANCE IS TO BE EFFECTED BY BUYER
+ THE IMPORT REGISTRATION NO. LS－325 APPEAR ON INVOICE
+ ALL DOCUMENTS MUST EVIDENCE THIS CREDIT NO.

资料 2：

1. INVOICE NO. SHC0932
2. B/L NO. OSCN72183　　B/L DATE：NOV. 18，2009　VESSEL NAME：OOCL SANO V. 035E　CONTAINER NO.：KKLU3240801　SEAL NO. 516727
3. EACH OF PACKING：MEASUREMENTS0. 35CBM　G. W. 21KGS
4. FREIGHT CHARGE：USD350. 00
5. 自制标准唛头

资料 3：海运提单

<table>
<tr><td colspan="4"></td><td colspan="2" rowspan="7">B/L No.</td></tr>
<tr><td colspan="4">Shipper</td></tr>
<tr><td colspan="4">Consignee or Order</td></tr>
<tr><td colspan="4">Notify Party</td></tr>
<tr><td colspan="2">Pre－carriage by</td><td colspan="2">Port of Loading</td></tr>
<tr><td colspan="2">Vessel and Voy No.</td><td colspan="2">Port of Discharge</td></tr>
<tr><td colspan="2">Sailing on or about</td><td colspan="2">Final Destination</td></tr>
<tr><td>Marks & Nos.
Container No. & Seal No.</td><td colspan="3">Number and Kind of Packages
Description of Goods</td><td>Gross Weight</td><td>Measurement（cbm）</td></tr>
<tr><td></td><td colspan="3"></td><td></td><td></td></tr>
<tr><td colspan="6">TOTAL NUMBER OF CONTAINERS</td></tr>
<tr><td>Freight and Charges</td><td colspan="2">No. of Original B(s)/L</td><td colspan="3">Place and Date of Issue</td></tr>
<tr><td colspan="3"></td><td colspan="3">Signed for the Carrier</td></tr>
</table>

提示：

（1）提单的通知方一栏必须严格按照信用证要求填写，地址和电话要填写准确，以免货到联系不到收货人。

（2）提单中货物描述一栏只需填写货物的名称和总包装数，不必将货物的种类、花色等内容列入此栏。

【工作评价】

1. 评价标准

<table>
<tr><td colspan="2"></td><td colspan="2" rowspan="7">B/L No.
OSCN72183</td></tr>
<tr><td colspan="2">Shipper
QINGDAO HAIFU CO. LTD.,
NO. 1 HONGKONG ROAD, QINGDAO CHINA</td></tr>
<tr><td colspan="2">Consignee or Order
TO ORDER OF SHIPPER</td></tr>
<tr><td colspan="2">Notify Party
SHITAYA KINZOKU CO.
4-1-7 CHOME-KU TOKYO JAPAN
AND THE SUMITOMO BANK LTD., TOKYO JAPAN</td></tr>
<tr><td>Pre-carriage by</td><td>Port of Loading
QINGDAO, CHINA</td></tr>
<tr><td>Vessel and Voy No.
OOCL SANO V. 035E</td><td>Port of Discharge
TOKYO, JAPAN</td></tr>
<tr><td>Sailing on or about
NOV. 18, 2009</td><td>Final Destination</td></tr>
<tr><td>Marks & Nos.
Container No. & Seal No.</td><td>Number and Kind of Packages
Description of Goods</td><td>Gross Weight</td><td>Measurement (cbm)</td></tr>
<tr><td>S. K. C.
SK682
TOKYO
NO. 1-105

CONTAINER NO.: KKLU3240801

SEAL NO. 516727</td><td>MEN'S LEATHER SHOES
105CARTONS

THE GOODS HAVE SHIPPED IN 40H CONTAINER
L/C NO. SCN1200N9</td><td>2205.00KGS</td><td>36.750CBM

ON BOARD</td></tr>
<tr><td>TOTAL NUMBER OF CONTAINERS</td><td colspan="3">SAY ONE HUNDRED AND FIVE CARTONS ONLY.</td></tr>
<tr><td>Freight and Charges
FREIGHT PREPAID</td><td>No. of Original B(s)/L
THREE</td><td colspan="2">Place and Date of Issue
QINGDAO, CHINA
NOV. 18, 2009</td></tr>
<tr><td colspan="2"></td><td colspan="2">Signed for the Carrier
×××</td></tr>
</table>

2. 评价表（见表 3－2－1）

表 3－2－1

评价人 评价指标	自 评	互 评	师 评
独立完成情况（20 分）			
格式规范性（20 分）			
内容完整性、正确性（50 分）			
内容简明性、整洁性（10 分）			
合计总分			

任务三　缮制保险单

【工作认知】

一、认知保险单

（一）保险单的含义

保险单（Insurance Policy）是保险公司向投保人出具的承保证明，并规定了双方的权利和义务关系，又是被保险人凭以向保险公司索赔和保险公司进行理赔的依据。在国际贸易中，保险单经背书后可以随货物所有权的转移而转让。

（二）保险单的种类

1. 保险单（Insurance Policy）

保险单，俗称“大保单”，是保险人与被保险人订立保险合同的正式书面证明，是目前我国进出口贸易中使用最广泛的一种正规的保险单据，一般由保险公司签发。除正面项目外，背面载有保险双方当事人的权利、义务条款。

2. 保险凭证（Insurance Certificate）

保险凭证，俗称“小保单”，是一种简化的保险单据，其正面内容与保险单基本一致，但背面不列有保险人与被保险人双方权利义务条款。保险凭证与保险单具有相同的法律效力。但保险条款仍以保险单的保险条款为准。

3. 联合保险凭证（Combined Insurance Certificate）

联合保险凭证一般无固定格式，是一种比保险凭证更为简化的保险单据。保险公司不另出保险单，而是在商业发票的空白处加打保险条款，并加盖印戳，其他项目均以发票所列为准。这种联合保险凭证不是专用单据，不能转让，仅适用于我国港澳地区中资银行来证，现已很少使用。

4. 预约保险单（Open Policy，Open Cover）

预约保险单是一种长期性的货物运输保险合同。合同中规定了承保范围、险别、费率、责任、赔款处理等项目。凡属合同约定的运输货物在合同有效期内自动承保。其往往与保险通知书和保险声明书一起使用。当交易以 FOB 及 CFR 价格出口时，由进口方办理手续。一般进口商和保险公司订有较长期的预约保险单。每当货物装船后，由出口方把货物的详细情况，包括品名、数量、重量、金额、运输工具、运输日期以及信用证中的预约保险单号码直接通知保险公司和进口商，并以其作为正式保单生效的依据。

5. 批单（Endorsement）

批单是指保险公司应投保人或被保险人的要求出具的修改或更改保险合同内容的书面文件，其实质是对保险合同内容的变更，一经签发，就成为保险合同的重要组成部分。如果批改内容涉及保险金额的增加和保险责任范围的扩大等重大修改，那么保险公司必须在证实货物未发生出险事故的情况下，方可同意办理。保险单经过批改后，保险公司即按批改后的内容来承担责任。批单原则上需粘贴在保险单上，并加盖骑缝章，作为保险单不可分割的一部分。

（三）保险单样章

保险单样章如下所示：

中国人民保险公司

The People's Insurance Company of China

货物运输保险单

Cargo Transportation Insurance Policy

发票号（INVOICE　NO.）　　　　保单号次

合同号（CONTRACT　NO.）　　　POLICY　NO.

信用证号（L/C　NO.）

被保险人：

Insured：

MARKS & NOS	QUANTITY	DESCRIPTION OF GOODS	AMOUNT INSURED

总保险金额：

TOTAL AMOUNT INSURED：

保费：　　　　开航日期：

PREMIUM：　　　DATE OF COMMENCEMENT：

装载运输工具：
PER CONVEYANCES：
自　　　　　　　经　　　　　　　至
FROM ________ VIA ________ TO ________
承保险别：
CONDITIONS：
所保货物，如发生保险单项下可能引起索赔的损失或损坏，应立即通知本公司下述代理人查勘。如有索赔，应向本公司提交保单正本（本保单共有______份正本）及有关文件。
IN THE EVENT OF LOSS OR DAMAGE WHICH MAY RESULT IN A CLAIM UNDER THIS POLICY, IMMEDIATE NOTICE MUST BE GIVEN TO THE COMPANY's AGENT AS MENTIONDE HEREUNDER CLAIMS, IF ANY, ONE OF THE ORIGINAL POLICY WHICH HAS BEEN ISSUED IN ______ ORIGINAL（S）TOGETHER WITH THE RELEVANT DOCUMENTS SHALL BE SURRENDERED TO THE COMPANY.
保险代理人（Name Survey Agent）
赔款偿付地点和币别：
CLAIM PAYABLE AT：　　　IN

中国人民保险公司
The People's Insurance Company of China
出单日期：
DATE：

二、缮制保险单

（一）保险单的格式

保险单根据保险公司的不同具有不同的格式，但基本内容一致。

（二）保险单的缮制规范

保险单的主要内容如下：

1. 被保险人（Insured）

被保险人，又称“抬头”。由于保险单可以转让，被保险人只要在保险单背面签章，保险单的权益就转让给了任何保险单持有人。常见的填写方法有以下几种：

第一，一般情况下，信用证如果无明确规定，被保险人填写出口人名称，并由出口人在保险单背面做空白背书。

第二，如果信用证规定被保险人为受益人以外的某公司或某银行，保险单应直接写该公司或银行的名称。如果信用证在被保险人名称前注有“to the order of…”，保险单也照样加上，受益人不做背书。

第三，如果信用证要求保险单做成“to order”，应在被保险人一栏内直接填写“to order”，并由受益人作背书。

第四，如果信用证规定被保险人做成“to order of bearer”，保险单可照打，或在“to order of”之后注明受益人名称，这两种方式均应由受益人做背书。

2. 唛头或标记（Marks & Nos.）

按信用证规定，保险单上标记应与发票、提单上的唛头相同。

若来证无特殊规定或无唛头，打“N/M”。此栏也可做成“As per Invoice No. …”，因为保险索赔时需要提供发票。

3. 包装及数量（Quantity）

本栏填制大包装件数，并应与提单上同一栏目内容相同。一般情况下，除了散装货物和信用证另有规定外，保险单上不需要填写重量，但需要显示包装数量。

【例3-3-1】

“袋”（Bag）、“箱”（Case）、“集装箱”（Container）。裸装货物要注明本身件数；煤炭、石油等散装货注明“IN BULK”，再填净重。

4. 保险货物名称（Description of Goods）

货物名称应与信用证或商业发票上的名称一致。

一般允许使用统称，但不同类别的多种货物应注明不同类别的各自总称。

5. 保险金额（Amount Insured）

第一，保险金额应与信用证一致，并且填小写金额。

第二，保险金额的加成百分比应严格按照信用证规定掌握，如没有规定，应按CIF或CIP价格的110%投保。

第三，小数点后的尾数一律上升为整数。

【例3-3-2】（USD102×110%）=USD112.20，则进位后为USD113.00，应填SAY UNITED STATES DOLLARS（U.S. DOLLARS）ONE HUNDRED AND THIRTEEN ONLY。

如果发票金额扣除佣金时，保险金额应按扣佣前的毛额（发票金额）加成投保。

资料卡

保险金额=CIF（CIP）价×（1+投保加成率）

保险金额，又称“投保金额”，是指货物发生保险范围内的损失时，保险公司向被保险人赔付的最高金额。按保险市场的习惯做法，保险金额一般是按照CIF或CIP价值的110%计算，即在CIF或CIP金额上再加10%。

6. 总保险金额（Total Amount Insured）

本栏填写保险金额的合计大写，币种与信用证的规定一致，而且使用币种的全称（如美元不能用“USD”，而应写“U.S. DOLLARS”）。同时注意，大小写金额必须相符，并且由于保险金额精确到个位，所以大写金额后应加上“ONLY”字样，以防涂改。

7. 保费（Premium）和费率（Rate）

一般由保险公司在出保险单时填入“as arranged”字样，出口公司在填保险单时无需填写。但信用证如注明“保费已付”（Premium Paid），可以将原先印制的“as arranged”删掉，然后改为“Paid”或“Prepaid”。

8. 开航日期（Slg On or Abt）

本栏填写提单中的签发日期或签发日期前5天内的任何一天的日期，也可以填写“As Per B/L”；空运可以填写“As Per AWB”。

9. 装载运输工具（Per Conveyance）

海运方式下填写船名和航次，如果采取直达轮船运输货物，则在此栏填写船名；如果中途需要转船，填写第一程轮船名或已知的第二程轮船名，中间用“/”隔开。

【例3-3-3】 提单中一程船名为“DONGXING”，二程船为“HUAIHAI”，则填“DONGXING/HUAIHAI”。

10. 起至地点（From…To…）

在“From”之后填写装运港，在“To”之后填写目的港。如需转船，应在目的港后加注“W/T at …（转运港名称）”。

【例3-2-4】 FROM QINGDAO，CHINA TO NEW YORK，USA VIA HONGKONG（OR W/T HONGKONG）。

当信用证中未明确列明具体的起运港口和目的地的港口时（如“ANY CHINESE PORT”或“ANY JAPANESE PORT”），填制时应根据货物实际装运选定一个具体的港口（如SHANGHAI或OSAKA等）。

11. 承保险别（Conditions）

本栏是保险单的核心内容，填写时应注意保险险别及文句与信用证严格一致，应根据信用证或合同中的保险条款要求填制，即使信用证中有重复语句，为了避免混乱和误解，最好按信用证规定的顺序填写。投保的险别除注明险别名称外，还应注明险别适用的文本及日期。

在实际操作中一般是由出口公司在制单时，先在副本上填写这一栏的内容，当全部保险单填好交给保险公司审核确认后，才由保险公司把承保险别的详细内容加注在正本保单上。

【例3-3-5】 来证要求“INSURANCE POLICY COVERING THE FOLLOWING RISKS: ALL RISKS AND WAR RISK AS PER CHINA INSURANCE CLAUSE（C. I. C）”，则制单时应打上“ALL RISKS AND WAR RISK AS PER CHINA INSURANCE CLAUSE（C. I. C）”。

12. 保险单份数

一般情况保险单为两份正本。

13. 保险代理人（Name Survey Agent）

保险人选择的查勘代理人应位于货运目的地，此栏除了填写查勘代理人的名称外，还须有详尽的地址以及联系方式，以便被保险人在货物出险后与其联系。

14. 赔付地点和币别（Claim Payable at）

第一，如果信用证规定了赔付地点，按信用证规定填写；如果信用证未规定赔付地点，则填写目的港。

第二，赔付的货币通常为信用证所使用的货币；如果信用证未规定赔付货币，可写美元。

15. 出单人（Issued by）

保险单必须在表面上由保险公司或保险人或两者的代理人开立和签署。

16. 出单地点和日期（Place and Date of Issue）

出单地点按出单公司的实际所在地填写。出单日期是保险人开始对承保货物承担保险责任的日期。应注意的是，保险单日期必须早于提单日期。

【工作指导】

青岛海富贸易有限公司收到来自荷兰 FUTURO 公司申请开出的信用证，张丽的师傅李华根据信用证所给内容及相关资料制作了一份保险单。

资料 1：信用证

MT：700	ISSUE OF A DOCUMENTARY CREDIT	
SEQUENCE OF TOTAL	*27：	1/1
FORM OF DOC. CREDIT	*40A：	IRREVOCABLE
DOC. CREDIT NUMBER	*20：	IC01925U
DATE OF ISSUE	31C：	20130525
EXPRIRY	*31D：	DATE 20130725 PLACE IN QINGDAO
ISSUING BANK	51A：	WACHOVIA BANK, NO. 3K STREET，RM 504 FUNGLEE COMM. BLDG. ROTTERDAM NETHERLANDS
APPLICANT	*50：	FUTURO INDUSTRIAL CO. LTD. , ROTTERDAM NETHERLANDS TEL：031 431 7295
BENEFICIARY	*59：	QINGDAO HAIFU TRADING CO. LTD. , NO. 1HONGKONG ROAD, QINGDAO CHINA
AMOUNT	*32B：	CURRENCY USD AMOUNT USD40000. 00
AVAILABLE WITH /BY	*41D：	ANY BANK BY DEF PAYMENT
DRAFT AT…	42C：	AT 60 DAYS AFTER B/L SHIPMENT DATE
DRAWEE	42A：	ISSUING BANK
PARTIAL SHIPMENT	43P：	ALLOWED
TRANSHIPMENT：	43T：	ALLOWED
LOADING IN CHARGE	44A：	QINGDAO，CHINA
FOR TRANSPORT TO	44B：	ROTTERDAM PORT，NETHERLANDS
LATEST SHIPMENT DATE	44C：	20130710

DESCRIPTION OF GOODS 45A:

2450CARTONS (ONE CONTAINER) OFQINGDAO SPRING ROLLS AT USD15. 50PER CTN CIFROTTERDAM

PACKING: 20G PER PC, 50PCS IN A BOX, 9 BOXES IN A CARTON

PACKED IN PLANT OF QINGDAO BANMU FOODS PRODUCTS CO. LTD., QINGDAO INDUSTRIAL ZONE QINGDAO.

AS PER CONTRACT NO. MSR719 DATE: 20130412

DOCUMENTS REQUIRED 46A:

+ SIGNED COMMERCIAL INVOICE IN THREE COPIES CERTIFYING COUNTRY OF ORIGIN.

+ FULL SET OF ORIGINAL CLEAN ON BAORD OCEAN BILLS OF LADING CONSIGNED TO ORDER OF SHIPPER MARKED FREIGHT PREPAID NOTIFY APPLICANT AND ISSUING BANK.

+ PACKING LIST IN THREE COPIES.

+ MARINE INSURANCE POLICY OR CERTIFICATE IN DUPLICATE ENDORSED IN BLANK, WITH CLAIM PAYABLE IN NETHLANDS IN THE CURRENCY OF THE DRAFT, COVERING 110 PERCENT OF INVOICE VALUE, INCLUDING ICC (A) AND ICC WAR CLAUSE AS PER INSTITUTE CARGO CLAUSE DATED 1/1/1982.

+ SHIPPING ADVICE HAS BEEN SENT TO APPLICANT WITHIN 3 DAYS FROM DATE OF SHIPMENT INDICATING L/C NO., INVOICE NO., AMOUNT, DETAILS OF GOODS, NAME OF VESSEL, VOYAGE NO., DATE OF SHIPMENT, PORT OF LOADING, B/L NO., CONTAINER NO., SEAL NO., ESTIMATED TIME OF ARRIVAL.

+ CERTIFICATE OF ORIGINAND GSP FORM A SIGNED BY C. I. Q.

+ COPY OF BENEFICIARY CERTIFICATE CERTIFY THAT ONE COMPLETE SET OF N/N DOCUMENTS HAS BEEN SENT TO APPLICANT BY COURIER WITHIN FIVE DAYS OF THE B/L DATE.

ADDITIONAL COND. 47A:

+ SHIPMENT DOCUMENTS EVIDENCE THIS L/C NO.

+ THE INVOICE SEPARATELY MENTION FOB VALUE, FREIGHT CHARGE.

+ B/L MUST MARK THAT THE GOODS SHIPPED IN 40 HR CONTAINER AND SET AT -18 DEGREES CENTIGRADE OR LOWER

DETAILS OF CHARGES: 71B:

ALL BANK CHARGES OUTSIDEROTTERDAM ARE FOR ACCOUNT OF BENEFICIARY.

CONFIRMATION INSTRUCTIONS *49: WITHOUT

"ADVISE THROUGH" BANK 57A: BANK OF CHINA LTD., SHANDONG BRANCH

资料 2：

INVOICE NO. QD528　AMOUNT：USD37975. 00
保险单号码：PIC2013007096
VESSEL NAME：SITC QINGDAO　V. 23　B/L DATE：JULY 9，2013
数量：2450CTNS。运输为 40 尺冷藏。

师傅李华制作的保险单如下所示：

中国人民保险公司
The People's Insurance Company of China
货物运输保险单
Cargo Transportation Insurance Policy

发票号（INVOICE　NO.）QD528　保单号次
合同号（CONTRACT　NO.）MSR719　POLICY　NO. PIC2013007096
信用证号（L/C　NO.）IC01925U
被保险人：QINGDAO HAIFU TRADING CO. LTD.，
Insured：

MARKS & NOS	QUANTITY	DESCRIPTION OF GOODS	AMOUNT INSURED
F. I. C. MSR719 ROTTERDAM NO. 1 -2450	2450CARTONS	QINGDAO SPRING ROLLS	USD41773. 00

总保险金额：
TOTAL AMOUNT INSURED：U. S. DOLLARS FOURTY ONE THOUSAND SEVEN HUNDRED AND SEVENTY -THREE ONLY.
保费：　AS ARRANGE　开航日期：JULY 9，2013
PREMIUM：as arranged　DATE OF COMMENCEMENT：as per B/L
装载运输工具：SITC QINGDAO V. 023
PER CONVEYANCES：
自　经　至
FROM QINGDAO，CHINA VIA ________ TO ROTTERDAM，NETHERLANDS
承保险别：INCLUDING INSTITUTE WAR CLAUSE INSTITUTE CARGO CALUSES（all risks）INSTITUTE STRIKES RIOTS AND CIVIL COMMOTIONS CLAUSES.
CONDITIONS：
所保货物，如发生保险单项下可能引起索赔的损失或损坏，应立即通知本公司下述代理人查勘。如有索赔，应向本公司提交保单正本（本保单共有 2 份正本）及有关文件。
IN THE EVENT OF LOSS OR DAMAGE WHICH MAY RESULT IN A CLAIM UNDER THIS

POLICY, IMMEDIATE NOTICE MUST BE GIVEN TO THE COMPANY's AGENT AS MENTIONDE HEREUNDER CLAIMS, IF ANY, ONE OF THE ORIGINAL POLICY WHICH HAS BEEN ISSUED IN TWO ORIGINAL (S) TOGETHER WITH THE RELEVANT DOCUMENTS SHALL BE SURRENDERED TO THE COMPANY.

保险代理人（Name Survey Agent）THE INSURANCE OF ROTTERDAM

赔款偿付地点和币别：ROTTERDAM，NETHERLANDS

CLAIM PAYABLE AT： IN USD

中国人民保险公司

The People's Insurance Company of China

出单日期：

DATE：JULY 8，2013

【工作演练】

张丽在师傅李华的指导下，已经基本掌握了制作保险单的技能。下面请你和张丽一起根据青岛海富贸易有限公司收到的来自美国的 JIMMY IMPORT AND EXPORT COMPANY 公司的信用证及相关资料制作一份保险单。

资料1：信用证

L/C NO. A66789

APPLICANT：JIMMY IMPORT AND EXPORT COMPANY，NEW YORK

BENEFICIARY：QINGDAO HAIFU TRADING CO. LTD.，NO. 1 HONGKONG ROAD，QINGDAO，CHINA

GOODS：GIRLS'S KIRTS，CIF NEW YORK，TTL AMOUNT：USD59，000. 00

DOCUMENTS REQUIRED：INSURANCE POLICY IN DUPLICATE IN NEGOTIABLE FORM BLANK EDDORSED FOR 110 PERCENT OF INVOICE VALUE COVERING OCEAN TRANSPORTATION CLAUSES OF PICC，INCLUDING WAREHOUSE TO WAREHOUSE，CLAIMS PAYABLE AT NEW YORK IN THE CURRENCY OF DRAFT.

资料2：

发票号码：JS06011

保险单号码：PYIE20133702100052

发票显示：DESCRIPTIONS OF GOODS：

GIRLS'S KIRTS，CIF NEW YORK AMOUNT：USD59，000. 00 120CARTONS

提单显示：

PORT OF LOADING：NINGBO PORT OF DISCHARGE：NEW YORK

VESSEL：FREEDOM V. 23 ON BOARD DATE：JAN. 3，2013
SHIPPING MARKS：JIMMY/NEW YORK/NO. 1 –120
保险代理：PICC NEW YORK BRANCH
666 CARNEY STREET，NEW YORK，U. S. A.
001 –65432143
保险单据的投保日期与提单的装船日期相同。

资料3：

中国人民保险公司
The People's Insurance Company of China
货物运输保险单
Cargo Transportation Insurance Policy

发票号（INVOICE NO.） 保单号次
合同号（CONTRACT NO.） POLICY NO.
信用证号（L/C NO.）
被保险人：
Insured：

MARKS & NOS	QUANTITY	DESCRIPTION OF GOODS	AMOUNT INSURED

总保险金额：
TOTAL AMOUNT INSURED：
保费： 开航日期：
PREMIUM： DATE OF COMMENCEMENT：
装载运输工具：
PER CONVEYANCES：
自 经 至
FROM ________ VIA ________ TO ________
承保险别：
CONDITIONS：
所保货物，如发生保险单项下可能引起索赔的损失或损坏，应立即通知本公司下述代理人查勘。如有索赔，应向本公司提交保单正本（本保单共有______份正本）及有关文件。
IN THE EVENT OF LOSS OR DAMAGE WHICH MAY RESULT IN A CLAIM UNDER THIS POLICY, IMMEDIATE NOTICE MUST BE GIVEN TO THE COMPANY'S AGENT AS MENTIONDE HEREUNDER CLAIMS, IF ANY, ONE OF THE ORIGINAL POLICY WHICH HAS

BEEN ISSUED IN TWO ORIGINAL (S) TOGETHER WITH THE RELEVANT DOCUMENTS SHALL BE SURRENDERED TO THE COMPANY.

保险代理人 (Name Survey Agent)

赔款偿付地点和币别:
CLAIM PAYABLE AT: IN

中国人民保险公司
The People's Insurance Company of China

出单日期:
DATE:

提示:

(1) 保单金额必须是整数,如有小数,小数一律往整数位进1。例如,USD12.10 应填为 USD13.00。

(2) 保费栏一般填写为 AS ARRANGED。

(3) 承保险别必须与信用证一致。

【工作评价】

1. 评价标准

中国人民保险公司
The People's Insurance Company of China
货物运输保险单
Cargo Transportation Insurance Policy

发票号 (INVOICE NO.) JS06011 保单号次:
合同号 (CONTRACT NO.) POLICY NO. PYIE20133702100052
信用证号 (L/C NO.) A66789
被保险人: QINGDAO HAIFU TRADING CO. LTD., NO.1 HONGKONG ROAD, QINGDAO, CHINA
Insured:

MARKS & NOS	QUANTITY	DESCRIPTION OF GOODS	AMOUNT INSURED
JIMMY/NEW YORK/NO. 1 – 120	120CARTONS	GIRLS'S KIRTS	USD64900.00

总保险金额:
TOTAL AMOUNT INSURED: SAY U.S. DOLLARS SIXTY FOUR THOUSAND NINE HUNDRED ONLY.

保费：　　　　　　　　　开航日期：
PREMIUM：AS ARRANGED　DATE OF COMMENCEMENT：AS PER B/L DATE {JAN. 3，2013}
装载运输工具：
PER CONVEYANCES：FREEDOM V. 23
自　　　　　　　　　　　　　　经　　　　　至
FROM NINBO PORT，CHINA VIA ______ TO NEW YORK，USA
承保险别：
CONDITIONS：
OCEAN TRANSPORTATION CLAUSES OF PICC，INCLUDING WAREHOUSE TO WAREHOUSE，

所保货物，如发生保险单项下可能引起索赔的损失或损坏，应立即通知本公司下述代理人查勘。如有索赔，应向本公司提交保单正本（本保单共有 2 份正本）及有关文件。
IN THE EVENT OF LOSS OR DAMAGE WHICH MAY RESULT IN A CLAIM UNDER THIS POLICY，IMMEDIATE NOTICE MUST BE GIVEN TO THE COMPANY's AGENT AS MENTIONDE HEREUNDER CLAIMS，IF ANY，ONE OF THE ORIGINAL POLICY WHICH HAS BEEN ISSUED IN TWO ORIGINAL（S）TOGETHER WITH THE RELEVANT DOCUMENTS SHALL BE SURRENDERED TO THE COMPANY.
保险代理人（Name Survey Agent）PICC NEW YORK BRANCH
666 CARNEY STREET，NEW YORK，U. S. A.
001 -65432143

赔款偿付地点和币别：
CLAIM PAYABLE AT：　NEW YORK IN THE CURRENCY OF DRAFT

中国人民保险公司
The People's Insurance Company of China
出单日期：2013 年 1 月 3 日
DATE：JAN. 3，2013

2. 评价表（见表 3 -3 -1）

表 3 -3 -1

评价指标 \ 评价人	自　评	互　评	师　评
独立完成情况（20 分）			
格式规范性（20 分）			
内容完整性、正确性（50 分）			
内容简明性、整洁性（10 分）			
合计总分			

项目实训

资料1：

APPLICATION HEADER	* 0 700: CHO HUNG BANK, SEOUL KOREA
MSG USER REF.	* 108: 02 - 0045 - 09
RECEVING BANK	* AGRICULTURAL BANK OF CHINA SHANDONG BRANCH
FORM OF DOC. CREDIT	* 40A: IRREVOCABLE
DOC. CREDIT NUMBER	* 20: MUNK0903N005
DATE OF ISSUE	* 31C: MAR. 5, 2014
APPLICABLE RULES	* 40E: UCP LATEST VERSION
EXPIRY	* 31D: DATE MAR. 29, 2014 PLACE IN CHINA
APPLICANT BANK	* 51A: KOREA CO., LTD., NO. 12 QUEEN ROAD SEOUL KOREA
APPLICANT	* 50 CHO HUNG BANK, SEOUL KOREA
BENEFICIARY	* 59: QINGDAO HAISHAN IMPORT AND EXPORT CORP. NO. 1132 CHONGQIN ROAD QINGDAO CHINA
AMOUNT	* 32B: CURRENCY USD AMOUNT 13000. 00
AVAILABLE WITH/BY	* 41D: ANY BANK IN CHINA BY DRAFT
DRAFTS AT	* 42C: 30 DAYS AFTER B/L DATE FOR 95 PERCENT OF CIF VALUE
DRAWEE	* 42A: THE ISSUE BANK
PARTIAL SHIPMENTS	* 43P: ALLOWED
TRANSHIPMENT	* 43T: ALLOWED
PORT OF LOADING	* 44E: ANY PORT OF CHINA
PORT OF DISCHARGE	* 44F: BUSAN KOREA
LATEST DATE OF SHIP.	* 44C: MAR. 15, 2014
DESCRIPT. OF GOODS	*45A:

AGRICULTURAL IMPLEMENT

300DOZEN S301B SHOVEL AT USD 19. 00 PER DOZEN

200DOZEN S302B SHOVEL AT USD 20. 00 PER DOZEN

100DOZEN S303B SHOVEL AT USD 21. 00 PER DOZEN

PACKING EXPORT STANDARD PACKINGCHINA ORIGIN CIFC2 BUSAN

DOCUMENTS REQUIRED *46A:

+ SIGNED COMMERCIAL INVOICE IN THREE COPIES

+ FULL SET OF CLEAN ON BOARD OCEAN BILLS OF LADING MADE OUT TO ORDER OF SHIPPER AND MARKED FREIGHT PREPAID NOTIFY ACCOUNTEE.
+ PACKING LIST IN TWO CIPIES INDICATION QUANTITY N. W. G. W. OF EACH PACKAGE ADDITIONAL COND. ＊47A：
+ THE DOCUMENT PRIOR APPROVAL OF L/C DATE NOT ACCEPTANCE.
+ THE CARRIER AS SINO TRANSPORTATION SHANGDONG CO.
+ SHIPMENT MUST BE EFFECTED IN 20′ CONTAINER FCL/FCL BASIS. THE B/L MUST BE SHOW IT.
+ INVOICE AND PACKING LIST MUST BE CERTIFICATE WITH SIGNED BY CCPIT WITH DATE
+ ALL DOCUMENTS TO BE IN ENGLISH LANGUAGE AND MUST BEAR L/C NO. AND DATE
+ THE WORDS "IMPORT UNDER CFER LCAF NO. 194181 IRC NO. BA－78607 AND H. S. CODE NO. 4411 12 00 MUST APPEAR ON THE INVOICE AND PACKING LIST

资料2：

INVOICE NO. MN9078
PACKING：2 DOZENS IN ONE CARTON， N. W. 44KGS/G. W. 48KGS 0. 07CBMEACH CTN
VESSEL NAME：MAYFLOWER V. 023　B/L NO. TMBL529317
CONTAINER NO.：APZU3028274
SEAL NO. 401710
MADE A STANDARD MARK ON DOCUMENTS

资料3：

<table>
<tr><td colspan="4"></td><td colspan="2" rowspan="7">B/L No.</td></tr>
<tr><td colspan="4">Shipper</td></tr>
<tr><td colspan="4">Consignee or Order</td></tr>
<tr><td colspan="4">Notify Party</td></tr>
<tr><td colspan="2">Pre－carriage by</td><td colspan="2">Port of Loading</td></tr>
<tr><td colspan="2">Vessel and Voy No.</td><td colspan="2">Port of Discharge</td></tr>
<tr><td colspan="2">Sailing on or about</td><td colspan="2">Final Destination</td></tr>
<tr><td>Marks & Nos.
Container No. & Seal No.</td><td colspan="3">Number and Kind of Packages
Description of Goods</td><td>Gross Weight</td><td>Measurement （cbm）</td></tr>
<tr><td></td><td colspan="3"></td><td></td><td></td></tr>
<tr><td colspan="6">TOTAL NUMBER OF CONTAINERS</td></tr>
<tr><td>Freight and Charges</td><td colspan="2">No. of Original B(s)/L</td><td colspan="3">Place and Date of Issue</td></tr>
<tr><td colspan="3"></td><td colspan="3">Signed for the Carrier</td></tr>
</table>

实训要求：

根据所给资料，填制一份海运提单。

参考答案

1. 海运提单

<table>
<tr><td colspan="4"></td><td rowspan="7">B/L
No. TMBL529317</td></tr>
<tr><td colspan="4">Shipper
QINGDAO HAISHAN IMPORT AND EXPORT CORP.
NO. 1132 CHONGQIN ROAD QINGDAO CHINA</td></tr>
<tr><td colspan="4">Consignee or Order
TO ORDER OF SHIPPER</td></tr>
<tr><td colspan="4">Notify Party
KOREA CO., LTD.,
NO. 12 QUEEN ROAD SEOUL KOREA</td></tr>
<tr><td colspan="2">Pre – carriage by</td><td colspan="2">Port of Loading
QINGDAO, CHINA</td></tr>
<tr><td colspan="2">Vessel and Voy No.
MAYFLOWER V. 023</td><td colspan="2">Port of Discharge
BUSAN, KOREA</td></tr>
<tr><td colspan="2">Sailing on or about
MAR. 14, 2014</td><td colspan="2">Final Destination</td></tr>
<tr><td>Marks & Nos.
Container No. & Seal No.</td><td colspan="2">Number and Kind of Packages
Description of Goods</td><td>Gross Weight</td><td>Measurement (cbm)</td></tr>
<tr><td>K. C.
BUSAN
NO. 1 – 300

CONTAINER NO.:
APZU3028274

SEAL NO. 401710</td><td colspan="2">AGRICULTURAL IMPLEMENT
300CTNS

SHIPMENT HAS BEEN EFFECTED IN 20'CONTAINER FCL/FCL BASIS

L/C NO.: MUNK0903N005 DATED MAR. 5, 2014</td><td>14400.00KGS</td><td>21.000CBM

ON BOARD</td></tr>
<tr><td colspan="2">TOTAL NUMBER OF CONTAINERS OR PACKAGES (IN WORDS)</td><td colspan="3">SAY THREE HUNDRED CARTONS ONLY</td></tr>
<tr><td>Freight and Charges
FREIGHT PREPAID</td><td>No. of Original B(s)/L
THREE</td><td colspan="3">Place and Date of Issue
QINGDAO, CHINA
MAR. 14, 2014</td></tr>
<tr><td colspan="2"></td><td colspan="3">Signed for the Carrier
SINO TRANSPORTATION SHANGDONG CO.
* * *</td></tr>
</table>

项目四

通 关 单 据

项目介绍

出口商在货物装运前，应向有关海关办理出口货物报关手续，根据国家相关法规对出口货物还需进行检验检疫的，在报关前还需办理出口货物的报检手续。该项目介绍报检、报关中的单据缮制。

学习目标

知识目标

- □ 熟悉出入境报检单的定义和分类。
- □ 熟悉进出口货物报关单的定义和分类。
- □ 掌握报检单、报关单的缮制规范。

能力目标

能够根据信用证条款或合同条款及商业单证，准确填写报检单和报关单的相关项目。

德育目标

培养学生认真仔细、严谨负责的学习和工作态度。

项目情境

张丽进入青岛海富贸易有限公司业务部实习后，在师傅李华的指导下，很快掌握了进出口贸易实际业务中相关单证的缮制，得到了好评。李华又安排张丽到报关报检部实习，一个月后，要求张丽根据出口合同、信用证及全套商业单据缮制一份出口货物报检单和一份出口货物报关单。

英文储备

Ducuments against Payment	D/P	付款交单
Ducuments against Acceptance	D/A	承兑交单
Certificate on Damaged Cargo		货物残损验证证书
Certificate on Performance		包装性能检验证书
Certificate on Tank/Hold		船舱检验证书
Inspection Certificate of Aflatoxin		黄曲霉毒素检验证书
Inspection Certificate of Fumigation		熏蒸检验书
Inspection Certificate of Packing		包装检验证书
Fumigation/Disinfection Certificate		熏蒸、消毒证书
Certificate of Plant Quarantine		植物检疫证书

任务分解

为了完成通关单据项目的学习，具体可分解为以下两个任务：

（1）缮制报检单。

（2）缮制报关单。

任务一　缮制报检单

【工作认知】

一、认知出入境货物报检单

（一）报检及报检单的含义

进出口商品报检是指进出口商品的收发货人或其代理人，根据《中华人民共和国进出口商检法》等有关法律、法规，对法定检验的进出口商品，在检验检疫机构规定的时限和地点，向检验检疫机构申请办理检验、配合检验、付费、取得商检单证等手续的全过程。

报检单是国家检验检疫部门根据检验检疫、鉴定工作的需要，为保证检验检疫工作规范化和程序化而设制的。它是报检人根据有关法律、行政法规或合同约定申请检验检疫机构对其某种货物实施检验检疫、鉴定意愿的书面凭证，它表明了申请人正式向检验检疫机构申请检验检疫、鉴定，以取得该批货物进出口的合法凭证。

（二）常用报检单的分类

报检时必须使用国家质检总局统一印制的报检单，经常使用的报检单类型有：“出境货物报检单”、“入境货物报检单”、“出入境货物包装检验申请单”。

（三）出入境货物报检单样章

1. 出境货物报检单样章

出境货物报检单样章如下所示：

中华人民共和国出入境检验检疫

出境货物报检单

报检单位（加盖公章）： *编　号 ____________

报检单位登记号： 联系人： 电话： 报检日期： 年 月 日

发货人	（中文）				
	（外文）				
收货人	（中文）				
	（外文）				
货物名称（中/外文）	H. S. 编码	产地	数/重量	货物总值	包装种类及数量

运输工具名称号码		贸易方式		货物存放地点	
合同号		信用证号		用途	
发货日期	输往国家（地区）		许可证/审批号		
启运地	到达口岸		生产单位注册号		
集装箱规格、数量及号码					

合同、信用证订立的检验检疫条款或特殊要求	标 记 及 号 码	随附单据（划“✓”或补填）	
		□合同 □信用证 □发票 □换证凭单 □装箱单 □厂检单	□包装性能结果单 □许可/审批文件 □ □ □ □

需要证单名称（划“✓”或补填）				*检验检疫费	
□品质证书 □重量证书 □数量证书 □兽医卫生证书 □健康证书 □卫生证书 □动物卫生证书	_正_副 _正_副 _正_副 _正_副 _正_副 _正_副 _正_副	□植物检疫证书 □熏蒸/消毒证书 □出境货物换证凭单 □出境货物通关单 □ □ □	_正_副 _正_副	总金额（人民币元） 计费人 收费人	

报检人郑重声明：	领 取 证 单	
1. 本人被授权报检。 2. 上列填写内容正确属实，货物无伪造或冒用他人的厂名、标志、认证标志，并承担货物质量责任。 签名：____________	日期	
	签名	

注：有“*”号栏由出入境检验检疫机关填写。 ◆国家出入境检验检疫局制

[1-2（2001.1.1）*1]

2. 入境货物报检单样章

入境货物报检单样章如下所示：

中华人民共和国出入境检验检疫

入境货物报检单

报检单位（加盖公章）： ＊编　号

报检单位登记号： 联系人： 电话： 报检日期： 年 月 日

收货人	（中文）		企业性质（划“✓”）	□合资 □合作 □外资
	（外文）			
发货人	（中文）			
	（外文）			

货物名称（中/外文）	H. S. 编码	原产国（地区）	数/重量	货物总值	包装种类及数量

运输工具名称号码				合同号	
贸易方式		贸易国别（地区）		提单/运单号	
到货日期		启运国家（地区）		许可证/审批号	
卸毕日期		启运口岸		入境口岸	
索赔有效期至		经停口岸		目的地	
集装箱规格、数量及号码					
合同订立特殊条款以及其他要求				货物存放地点	
				用途	

随附单据（划“✓”或补填）		标 记 及 号 码	＊外商投资财产（划“✓”）	□是□否
□合同	□到货通知		＊检验检疫费	
□发票	□装箱单			
□提/运单	□质保书		总金额（人民币元）	
□兽医卫生证书	□理货清单			
□植物检疫证书	□磅码单			
□动物检疫证书	□验收报告		计费人	
□卫生证书	□			
□原产地证	□		收费人	
□许可/审批文件	□			

报检人郑重声明： 1. 本人被授权报检。 2. 上列填写内容正确属实。 签名：________	领 取 证 单	
	日期	
	签名	

注：有“＊”号栏由出入境检验检疫机关填写。

◆国家出入境检验检疫局制

［1－1（2000. 1. 1）］

二、缮制出入境货物报检单

（一）“出境货物报检单”的缮制规范

1. 编号

“编号”是指检验检疫机构受理本批货物报检后生成的正式编号。

本栏由检验检疫机构受理报检人员填写，前6位为检验检疫机构代码，第7位为报检类别，第8、9位为年代码，第10至15位为流水号。实行电子报检后，该编号可在受理电子报检的回执中自动生成。

2. 报检单位

报检单位是指由检验检疫机构核准，在检验检疫机构备案或注册登记，有权从事报检业务的法人。

本栏填写报检单位的中文名称，并加盖与名称一致的公章。

资料卡

报检单位

- 自理报检单位：根据法律法规规定自行办理检验检疫报检/申报手续的进出境收发货人。自理报检单位在首次报检时须办理备案登记手续，取得自理报检单位备案登记号。
- 代理报检单位：获得检验检疫机构注册登记后，接受进出境收发货人委托，为委托人办理报检的从事代理报检业务的境内企业。

3. 报检单位登记号

报检单位登记号是指报检单位在检验检疫机构备案或注册登记后取得的登记证号码。

本栏填写10位数登记证号码。

4. 联系人

联系人是指本批货物的报检员。本栏填写报检员姓名及其联系电话。

5. 报检日期

报检日期是指检验检疫机构实际受理报检的日期。本栏由检验检疫机构受理报检人员填写。

6. 发货人

发货人是指外贸合同中的卖方。

本栏填写外贸合同中的卖方或信用证中的受益人，中英文名称均须填写。

7. 收货人

收货人是指外贸合同中的买方。

本栏填写外贸合同中的买方或信用证中的开证申请人。由于出境货物的收货人一般为国外公司，可能没有相对应的中文名称，因此，收货人中文一栏可以填写“ *** ”。

8. 货物名称

货物名称是指申请报检的出境货物的名称、规格、型号、成分及英文对照。

本栏填写应与外贸合同、信用证、发票等所列一致。另外应注意：废旧货物必须注明。

9. H. S 编码

本栏填写商品10位编号，以当年海关公布的商品税则编码分类为准。

10. 产地

产地是指本批货物的生产（加工）地，本栏填写生产地的省、市、县的中文名称。

注意事项：

（1）难以判定具体行政区名称的货物，如海洋资源，可填制为“中国”。

（2）进口货物复出口的，可填制为“境外”。

11. 数/重量

本栏填写实际申请检验检疫的货物的数/重量，并注明单位。应与合同、发票上所列一致。重量一般填写净重。

填写数/重量时，对于H. S. 编码对应的第一计量单位必须输入，且不得对计量单位进行修改。

【例4-1-1】 出口报检一批服装，H. S. 编码为6201121000，数量为1 000件，重量为500KGS，该编码的第一计量单位为件。则数/重量一栏应填写：1 000件/500千克。

12. 货物总值

本栏填写本批货物实际成交的总价及币种，应与外贸合同、发票上所列的货物总值一致。

13. 包装种类及数量

本栏填写本批货物实际运输的外包装的种类及数量，一般情况下以装箱单为依据，并且应当注明包装的材质。例如，包装为木箱，则必须填制为“木箱”，不得填制为“箱”。

14. 运输工具名称号码

本栏填写装运本批货物出境的运输工具的名称和号码，如船名航次等。

15. 贸易方式

贸易方式是指该批进出口货物的交易方式。

本栏填写本批货物进出口的贸易方式。

16. 货物存放地点

本栏填写本批货物存放的具体地点、厂库。

17. 合同号

本栏填写对外贸易合同（包括协议和订单）的编号或形式发票的号码。特殊情况无合同号的，应注明原因。

18. 信用证号

本栏填写本批货物对应的信用证编号。对于不以信用证方式结汇的，应注明结汇方式，如“T/T”。

19. 用途

用途是指出口货物的实际应用范围。本栏填写本批货物的用途。根据“用途代码表”和实际情况选填：种用或繁殖、食用、奶用、观赏或演艺、伴侣动物、实验、药用、饲用、介质土、食品包装材料、食品加工设备、食品添加剂、食品容器、食品洗涤剂、食品消毒剂、其他。对于选择“其他”的，应在报检单中手填具体的用途。

20. 发货日期

本栏填写出境货物预定装运发货的日期。日期为8位数字，顺序为年、月、日。例如，

2013 年 5 月 1 日，填写为 20130501。

21. 输往国家（地区）

输往国家（地区）是指出口货物离开我国关境直接运抵的国家或地区，或者在运输中转国（地区）未发生任何商业性交易的情况下最后运抵的国家或地区。

本栏填写出境货物最终输往的国家或地区，或合同注明的最终运抵国家和地区。

22. 许可证/审批号

对已实施许可/审批制度管理的货物，报检时填写质量许可证编号或审批单编号。例如，对于须办理注册登记或备案登记的木制品、机电产品、玩具、食品等，应填写已取得的相关注册或备案证书的号码。没有许可证或审批单的出境货物，本栏免填。

23. 启运地

本栏填写出境货物最后离境的口岸/出境货物报关地的口岸名称。

24. 到达口岸

本栏填写出境货物境外运抵口岸。货物经海运至某口岸再陆运至最终收货地点的，按货物最终卸离船舶的口岸为到达口岸。

【例 4－1－2】 出境货物先通过海运由上海出发，经新加坡运至比利时安特卫普，然后再通过陆运至瑞士。则到达口岸一栏应填写“安特卫普”。

25. 生产单位注册号

本栏填写生产、加工本批货物的单位在检验检疫机构备案登记的 10 位数代码。

26. 集装箱规格、数量及号码

本栏应填写装载出口货物（包括拼箱货物）的集装箱的规格、数量及号码。

27. 合同订立的特殊条款以及其他要求

本栏填写在外贸合同中特别订立的有关质量、卫生等条款或报检单位对本批货物检验检疫的特别要求。

28. 标记及号码

本栏填写货物的运输标志（唛头）中除了图形以外的所有文字和数字，应与合同、发票等有关外贸单据保持一致。若没有标记号码则填“N/M”。

29. 随附单据

随附单据是指报检企业实际向检验检疫机构提供的单据。本栏在对应的“□”上打“√”或补填。

30. 需要证单名称

需要证单名称是指报检企业向检验检疫机构申请出具的证单。本栏根据所需，在对应的“□”上打“√”或补填，并注明所需证单的正副本数量。

31. 报检人郑重声明

报检人郑重声明是报检员申报此批货物信息的确认。本栏必须由报检员亲笔签名，不得打印。

32. 检验检疫费

本栏由检验检疫机构计/收费人员填写。

33. 领取证单

本栏由报检人在领取证单时填写领证日期并签名。

(二)“入境货物报检单”的缮制规范

“入境货物报检单”与“出境货物报检单”有许多相同的栏目，这部分内容已经在《出境货物报检单》中做了详尽的介绍，下面我们将主要介绍与之不同的栏目。

1. 报检日期

报检日期是指检验检疫机构实际受理报检的日期。

2. 原产国（地区）

本栏填写申报货物生产/加工的国家或地区。对经过几个国家或地区加工制造的货物，以最后一个对货物进行实质性加工的国家或地区作为该货物的原产国。

注意事项：

(1) 同一批货物，原产地不同的，应当分别填报原产国（地区）。

(2)“退运货物”原产国填制为“中国”。

(3) 在保税区或加工区进行了实质性加工的货物出区输往国内时，原产国填制为“中国”。

3. 贸易国别（地区）

贸易国别（地区）一般是指外贸合同卖方所在的国家（地区）。填写合同或信用证中的卖方所在国。

4. 提单/运单号

本栏填写本批货物海运提单号或空运单号或铁路运单号。

5. 到货日期

到货日期是指运载所申报进口货物的运输工具到达进境口岸的日期。

本栏填写货物准确到达口岸的日期。

6. 启运国家（地区）

启运国家（地区）是指进口货物起始发出直接运抵我国的国家（地区），或者在运输中转国（地区）未发生任何商业性交易的情况下运抵我国的国家（地区）。

注意事项：

(1) 发生运输中转的货物，如在中转地没有任何商业性交易，启运国家不变；如发生商业性交易，则中转地作为启运国家。

(2) 从中国境内保税区、出口加工区入境的，启运国家填写“保税区”或者“出口加工区”。

7. 卸毕日期

卸毕日期是指本批货物在口岸卸毕的日期。本栏填写货物在口岸卸离运输工具的实际日期。

8. 启运口岸

启运口岸是指装运本批货物的交通工具起始发出直接运抵我国的口岸。

注意事项：

(1) 货物从内陆国家经陆运至他国海港口岸装船出运的，按第一海港口岸填制。

【例4-1-3】 进口货物从瑞士经陆运运至比利时安特卫普，从安特卫普装船经新加坡转船运至中国上海口岸。则报检单中“启运口岸”应填写“安特卫普”。

（2）从中国境内保税区、出口加工区入境的，填制“保税区”或者“出口加工区”。

9. 入境口岸

本栏填写入境货物从运输工具卸离的第一个境内口岸。

10. 索赔有效期至

索赔有效期是指贸易合同约定的进口货物不合格对外提出索赔要求的有效期限。

本栏填写按贸易合同签定的索赔有效期的天数填写，如60天、90天等。合同未约定索赔有效期的，应注明“无索赔期”。

11. 经停口岸

经停口岸是指货物随运输工具启运后，在抵达入境口岸之前所抵靠的发生货物装卸的境外口岸。如未经停任何口岸，本栏填写“ *** ”。

12. 目的地

目的地是指已知的进境货物在我国国内的消费、使用地区或最终运抵的地点。

13. 合同订立的特殊条款以及其他要求

合同对检验检疫有相关要求的或收货人对检验检疫有特殊要求的，应在此栏注明。如有其他检验检疫机构要求特别备注的情况，此栏兼作备注栏使用。

【例4-1-4】 （1）入境参展物品，备注“入境非销售展览物品、展毕退运出境”。

（2）进口旧机电产品，备注“进口旧机电产品登记备案”。

（3）进口废物原料，备注“合同卖方的注册编号： *** ”。

（4）入境的误发（如货物发错港口、发错收货人等）及其他非不符合检验检疫报检有关规定原因的货物，货主申请同进同出，直接退运出境的，备注“误发货物，申请同进同出，直接退运出境”或者“因 *** 原因，申请同进同出，直接退运出境”。

14. 外商投资财产

外商投资财产是确认进口的设备是否属于外商投资财产。本栏由检验检疫机构报检受理人员填写。

【工作指导】

青岛海富贸易有限公司在货物出境装运前7天，由张丽的师傅李华根据已制作的全套单据及其他相关资料制作一份出境货物报检单。

资料 1：商业发票

QINGDAO HAIFU TRADING CO. LTD.
NO. 1 HONGKONG ROAD，QINGDAO　CHINA
TEL：86 －0532 －85896210　FAX：86 －0532 －85896211

COMMERCIAL　INVOICE

Original
To：FUTURO INDUSTRIAL CO. LTD
FUTUROINDUSTRIAL CO. LTD.
ROTTERDAM NETHERLANDS
TEL：031 431 7295

No.　QD528
Date：　JUNE. 25，2013
L/C No.：　IC01925U
Contract：　MSR719

From：　QINGDAO，CHINA　　To　ROTTERDAM PORT，NETHERLANDS

Shipping Marks	Quantities & Descpription	Unit Price	Amount
F. I. C. MSR719 ROTTERDAM 1 －2450	2450CARTONS（ONE CONTAINER）OF QINGDAO SPRING ROLLS	CIF ROTTERDAM @ USD15. 50/ CTN	USD37975. 00

H. S. CODE：1902220000
PACKING：20GPERPC，50PCSINABOX，9BOXESINACARTON
AS PER CONTRACT NO. MSR719　DATE：APR. 12，2013
PACKED IN PLANT OF QINGDAO BANMU FOODS PRODUCTS CO. LTD.，
QINGDAO INDUSTRIAL ZONE　QINGDAO
FREIGHT CHARGE：USD3150. 00
FOB VALUE：USD34825. 00
WE HEREBY　CERTIFY THAT THE GOODS ARE OFCHINA ORIGIN

QINGDAO HAIFU TRADING CO. LTD.，
LIHUA

资料 2：装箱单

PACKING LIST

Original
To：　FUTURO INDUSTRIAL CO. LTD.，
　ROTTERDAM　NETHERLANDS
TEL：031 431 7295

No. QD528
Date：JUNE. 25，2013
L/C No.：IC01925U
Contract：MSR719

om：　QINGDAO，CHINA　　To　ROTTERDAM PORT，NETHERLANDS

Shipping Marks	NO. & Kind of Pkgs：Description of the Goods	Net Weight	Gross Weight	Measurement
F. I. C. MSR719 ROTTERDAM NO. 1 －2450	2450CARTONS（ONE CONTAINER）OF QINGDAO SPRING ROLLS	@ 9. 00KGS/CTN	@ 10. 00KGS/CTN	@ 0. 0195CBM/CTN
	TOTAL：	22050. 00KGS	24500. 00KGS	47. 775CBM

PACKING：20G PER . PC 50 PCS IN A BOX.

QINGDAO HAIFU TRADING CO. LTD.，
LIHUA

资料 3：

报检单位登记号：3700166892

报检员：李华 电话：13953209966

报检受理日期：2013－6－30

VESSEL NAME：SITCQINGDAO　V. 23

40' CONTAINER

CONTAINER NO. SITC1292748　SEAL NO. 006265

货物存放地点：青岛海关监管 3 号仓库

发货日期：2013－7－8

师傅李华制作的出境货物报检单如下所示：

中华人民共和国出入境检验检疫
出境货物报检单

报检单位（加盖公章）：青岛海富贸易有限公司　　＊编　　号＿＿＿＿＿＿＿＿

报检单位登记号：3700166892　　联系人：李华　　电话：13953209966　　报检日期：2013 年 6 月 30 日

发货人	（中文）	青岛海富贸易有限公司 3700166892
	（外文）	QINGDAO HAIFU TRADING CO. LTD. ,
收货人	（中文）	***
	（外文）	FUTURO INDUSTRIAL CO. LTD. ,

货物名称（中/外文）	H. S. 编码	产地	数/重量	货物总值	包装种类及数量
青岛春卷 QINGDAO SPRING ROLLS	1902220000	山东青岛	2 450 纸箱/ 22 050. 00 千克	37 975. 00 美元	2 450 纸箱

运输工具名称号码	SITC QINGDAO　V. 23	贸易方式	一般贸易	货物存放地点	青岛海关监管 3 号仓库
合同号	MSR719	信用证号	IC01925U	用途	食用
发货日期	2013. 07. 08	输往国家（地区）	荷兰	许可证/审批号	***
启运地	青岛	到达口岸	鹿特丹	生产单位注册号	3700166892
集装箱规格、数量及号码	1×40' SITC1292748				

合同、信用证订立的检验检疫条款或特殊要求	标记及号码	随附单据（划"✓"或补填）	
***	F. I. C. MSR719ROTTERDAM 1－2450	☑合同 ☑信用证 ☑发票 ☐换证凭单 ☑装箱单 ☑厂检单	☑包装性能结果单 ☐许可/审批文件 ☐ ☐ ☐ ☐

需要证单名称（划"✓"或补填）				＊检验检疫费	
☐品质证书	＿正＿副	☐植物检疫证书	＿正＿副	总金额（人民币元）	
☐重量证书	＿正＿副	☐熏蒸/消毒证书	＿正＿副		
☐数量证书	＿正＿副	☐出境货物换证凭单		计费人	
☐兽医卫生证书	＿正＿副	☑出境货物通关单			
☐健康证书	＿正＿副	☐		收费人	
☐卫生证书	＿正＿副	☐			
☐动物卫生证书	＿正＿副	☐			

报检人郑重声明：	领取证单	
1. 本人被授权报检。 2. 上列填写内容正确属实，货物无伪造或冒用他人的厂名、标志、认证标志，并承担货物质量责任。	日期	
签名：＿＿李华＿＿	签名	

注：有"＊"号栏由出入境检验检疫机关填写。　　◆国家出入境检验检疫局制

［1－2（2001. 1. 1）＊1］

【工作演练】

张丽在师傅李华的指导下，已经基本掌握了填写出入境货物报检单的基本技能。请你和张丽一起根据下列相关资料独立填写一份出境货物报检单。

青岛阳光贸易有限公司3700138721向韩国GEO贸易有限公司生产并出口一批货物，货物存放于青岛港场站12号位。由青岛京川物流公司（注册号：3700956549）代理报检，报检员张刚（电话：18753210900）于2014年3月1日发送电子报检数据并予当日受理。货物于2014年3月9日出境。根据下列资料填写一份出境货物报检单。

资料1：

QINGDAO HAIFU TRADING CO. LTD.

NO. 1 HONGKONG ROAD, QINGDAO CHINA

TEL: 86 -0532 -85896210 FAX: 86 -0532 -85896211

COMMERCIAL INVOICE

Original

To: GEO ENTERPRISE CO., LTD.
104 -2 E - MOY - DONGJANGAN - KU KOREA

No. SDT2105
Date: DEC. 27, 2013
L/C No.: M0912NS19
Contract: 0112T

From: QINGDAO, CHINA To BUSAN, KOREA

Shipping Marks	Quantities & Descpription		Unit Price	Amount
GEO 0112T	BABY TOYS		CFR BUSAN KOREA	
BUSAN	WWP -2A	350PCS	USD3. 20/PC	USD1 120. 00
NO. 1 -107	WWB -2A	200PCS	USD4. 15/PC	USD830. 00
	WGF -1B	520PCS	USD4. 50/PC	USD2 340. 00
	TOTAL:	1 070PCS		USD4 290. 00

PACKED IN 107CARTONS AND ONE PCS IN PLASTIC BAG TEN PCS IN ONE PACKAGE

AS PER CONTRACT NO. 0112T DATED NOV. 15, 2013

WE CERTIFY THAT THE MERCHANDISE ARE OFWEIHAI, CHINA ORIGIN

H. S CODE: 95031000

QINGDAO SUNNY BRIGHT TRADING CO.
ZHANGGANG

资料2：

PACKING LIST

Original

To:	GEO ENTERPRISE CO. , LTD.	No.	SDT2105
	104 - 2 E - MOY - DONG JANGAN - KU KOREA	Date:	DEC. 27, 2013
		L/C No. :	M0912NS19
		Contract:	0112T
From:	QINGDAO, CHINA	To	BUSAN, KOREA

Shipping Marks	NO. & Kind of Pkgs: Description of the Goods			Net Weight	Gross Weight	Measurement
GEO 0112T	BABY TOYS					
BUSAN	ART NO.	QUANTITY	PACKAGE	@5. 00KGS/PKG	@6. 00KGS/PKG	@0. 350CBM/PKG
NO. 1 - 107	WWP - 2A	350PCS	35 CARTONS	175. 00KGS	210. 00KGS	12. 250CBM
	WWB - 2A	200PCS	20 CARTONS	100. 00KGS	120. 00KGS	7. 000CBM
	WGF - 1B	520PCS	52 CARTONS	260. 00KGS	312. 00KGS	18. 200CBM
	TOTAL:	1 070PCS	107 CARTONS	535. 00KGS	642. 00KGS	37. 450CBM

PACKING: ONE PCS IN PLASTIC BAG TEN PCS IN ONECARTON.

WE HEREBY CERTIFY THAT THE OUTER CARTONS HAVE BEEN

MARKED WITH THE SHIPPING MARKS

QINGDAO SUNNY BRIGHT TRADING CO.
ZHANGGANG

资料3：

VESSEL NAME AND VOY. NO. : YANGMING HEQD V. 025E

SHIPMENT IN 20′ CONTAINER

CONTAINER NO：COLU3922101

需要证单：CERTIFICATE OF QUALITY IN ONE ORIGINAL AND ONE COPY

资料4：出境货物报检单

中华人民共和国出入境检验检疫
出境货物报检单

报检单位（加盖公章）：　　　　　　　　　　　　　　　　＊编　　号 ________

报检单位登记号：　　　　联系人：　　　　电话：　　　　报检日期：　　年　月　日

发货人	（中文）	
	（外文）	
收货人	（中文）	
	（外文）	

货物名称（中/外文）	H. S. 编码	产地	数/重量	货物总值	包装种类及数量

运输工具名称号码		贸易方式		货物存放地点	
合同号		信用证号		用途	
发货日期		输往国家（地区）		许可证/审批号	
启运地		到达口岸		生产单位注册号	
集装箱规格、数量及号码					

合同、信用证订立的检验检疫条款或特殊要求	标 记 及 号 码	随附单据（划“✓”或补填）	
		□合同	□包装性能结果单
		□信用证	□许可/审批文件
		□发票	□
		□换证凭单	□
		□装箱单	□
		□厂检单	□

需要证单名称（划“✓”或补填）				＊检验检疫费	
□品质证书	__正__副	□植物检疫证书	__正__副	总金额（人民币元）	
□重量证书	__正__副	□熏蒸/消毒证书	__正__副		
□数量证书	__正__副	□出境货物换证凭单			
□兽医卫生证书	__正__副	□出境货物通关单		计费人	
□健康证书	__正__副	□			
□卫生证书	__正__副	□		收费人	
□动物卫生证书	__正__副	□			

报检人郑重声明：	领 取 证 单	
1. 本人被授权报检。	日期	
2. 上列填写内容正确属实，货物无伪造或冒用他人的厂名、标志、认证标志，并承担货物质量责任。		
签名：________	签名	

注：有“＊”号栏由出入境检验检疫机关填写。　　　　◆国家出入境检验检疫局制

［1－2（2001.1.1）＊1］

提示：

（1）填制报检单过程中，必须注意与其他单据不同，应用中文填写，且中英文对照应一致。

（2）熟悉不同货物的报检要求，并且认真审核信用证，准确标明报检单中的随附单据和所需要的证单。

【工作评价】

1. 评价标准

中华人民共和国出入境检验检疫
出境货物报检单

报检单位（加盖公章）：青岛京川物流公司　　　　＊编　　号 ________

报检单位登记号：3700956549　　联系人：张刚　　电话：18753210900　　报检日期：2014 年 3 月 1 日

发货人	（中文）	青岛阳光贸易有限公司 3700138721
	（外文）	QINGDAO SUNNY BRIGHT TRADING CO.
收货人	（中文）	***
	（外文）	GEO ENTERPRISE CO. , LTD.

货物名称（中/外文）	H. S. 编码	产地	数/重量	货物总值	包装种类及数量
婴儿玩具 BABY TOYS WGF－1B WWB－2A WWP－2A	95031000	山东青岛	1 070 个/ 535. 00 千克	4 290. 00 美元	107 纸箱

运输工具名称号码	YANGMING HEQD V. 025E	贸易方式	一般贸易	货物存放地点	青岛港场站 12 号位
合同号	0112T	信用证号	M0912NS19	用途	其他
发货日期	2014. 03. 09	输往国家（地区）	韩国	许可证/审批号	***
启运地	青岛	到达口岸	釜山	生产单位注册号	3700138721
集装箱规格、数量及号码	1×20′　COLU3922101				

合同、信用证订立的检验检疫条款或特殊要求	标 记 及 号 码	随附单据（划“✓”或补填）	
***	GEO BUSAN NO. 1－107	☑合同 ☑信用证 ☑发票 ☐换证凭单 ☑装箱单 ☑厂检单	☑包装性能结果单 ☐许可/审批文件 ☐ ☐ ☐ ☐

需要证单名称（划“✓”或补填）				＊检验检疫费	
☐品质证书	__正__副	☐植物检疫证书	__正__副	总金额（人民币元）	
☐重量证书	__正__副	☐熏蒸/消毒证书	__正__副		
☐数量证书	__正__副	☐出境货物换证凭单		计费人	
☐兽医卫生证书	__正__副	☑出境货物通关单			
☐健康证书	__正__副	☐			
☐卫生证书	__正__副	☐		收费人	
☐动物卫生证书	__正__副	☐			

报检人郑重声明	领 取 证 单	
报检人郑重声明： 1. 本人被授权报检。 2. 上列填写内容正确属实，货物无伪造或冒用他人的厂名、标志、认证标志，并承担货物质量责任。 签名：　张刚	日期	
	签名	

注：有“＊”号栏由出入境检验检疫机关填写。　　　　◆国家出入境检验检疫局制

［1－2（2001. 1. 1）＊1］

2. 评价表（见表4－1－1）

表4－1－1

评价指标＼评价人	自　评	互　评	师　评
独立完成情况（20分）			
格式规范性（20分）			
内容完整性、正确性（50分）			
内容简明性、整洁性（10分）			
合计总分			

任务二　缮制报关单

【工作认知】

一、认知进出口货物报关单

（一）报关单的含义

进出口货物报关单是指进出口货物的收发货人或其代理人，按照海关规定的格式对进出口货物的实际情况做出书面申明，以此要求海关对其货物按适用的海关制度办理通关手续的法律文书。

（二）报关单的类型

（1）按进出口状态分：进口货物报关单、出口货物报关单。

（2）按表现形式分：纸质报关单、电子数据报关单。

（3）按海关监管方式分：进料加工进出口货物报关单（粉红色）、来料加工及补偿贸易进出口货物报关单（浅绿色）、一般贸易及其他贸易进出口货物报关单（白色）。

（4）按用途分：报关单录入凭单、预录入报关单、电子数据报关单、报关单证明联。

（三）进出口货物报关单各联的名称

（1）纸质进口货物报关单一式四联，分别是：海关作业联、企业留存联、海关核销联、进口付汇证明联。

（2）纸质出口货物报关单一式五联，分别是：海关作业联、企业留存联、海关核销联、出口收汇证明联、出口退税证明联。

（四）进出口货物报关单样章

1. 出口货物报关单样章

出口货物报关样章如下所示：

中华人民共和国海关出口货物报关单

1. 预录入编号：　　　　2. 海关编号：

3. 出口口岸	4. 备案号	5. 出口日期	6. 申报日期
7. 经营单位	8. 运输方式　9. 运输工具名称		10. 提运单号
11. 发货单位	12. 贸易方式	13. 征免性质	14. 结汇方式
15. 许可证号　16. 运抵国（地区）		17. 指运港	18. 境内货源地
19. 批准文号	20. 成交方式	21. 运费　22. 保费　23. 杂费	
24. 合同协议号	25. 件数　26. 包装种类	27. 毛重（公斤）	28. 净重（公斤）
29. 集装箱号	30. 随附单据		31. 生产厂家
32. 标记唛码及备注			
33. 项号 34. 商品编号 35. 商品名称、规格型号 36. 数量及单位 37. 最终目的国（地区）38. 单价 39. 总价 40. 币制 41. 征免			
42. 税费征收情况			
43. 录入员　44. 录入单位	兹声明以上申报无讹并承担法律责任	47. 海关审单批注及放行日期（签章）	
报关员		审单　审价	
单位地址	45. 申报单位（签章）	征税　统计	
邮编　电话	46. 填制日期	查验　放行	

2. 进口货物报关单样章

进口货物报关样章如下所示：

中华人民共和国海关进口货物报关单

1. 预录入编号：　　　　　　　　　　2. 海关编号：

3. 进口口岸	4. 备案号	5. 进口日期		6. 申报日期
7. 经营单位	8. 运输方式	9. 运输工具名称		10. 提运单号
11. 收货单位	12. 贸易方式	13. 征免性质		14. 征税比例
15. 许可证号	16. 起运国（地区）	17. 装货港		18. 境内目的地
19. 批准文号	20. 成交方式	21. 运费	22. 保费	23. 杂费
24. 合同协议号	25. 件数	26. 包装种类	27. 毛重（公斤）	28. 净重（公斤）
29. 集装箱号	30. 随附单据			31. 用途
32. 标记唛码及备注				
33. 项号 34. 商品编号 35. 商品名称、规格型号 36. 数量及单位 37. 原产国（地区）38. 单价 39. 总价 40. 币制 41. 征免				
42. 税费征收情况				
43. 录入员　44. 录入单位	兹声明以上申报无讹并承担法律责任		47. 海关审单批注及放行日期（签章）	
报关员			审单	审价
单位地址	45. 申报单位（签章）		征税	统计
邮编　电话	46. 填制日期		查验	放行

二、缮制进出口货物报关单

进出口货物报关单的主要内容如下：

1. 预录入编号

填写预录入报关单的编号。预录入编号规则由接受申报的海关决定，计算机自动打印。

2. 海关编号

填写海关接受申报时给予报关单的编号。一份报关单对应一个海关编号。此栏由海关填写。

3. 进口口岸/出口口岸

进（出）口口岸是特指货物实际进（出）我国关境的口岸海关。

本栏目应填写海关规定的“关区代码表”中相应的口岸海关的名称及代码。

【例4-2-1】 在上海浦江海关办理货物出口报关手续，出口口岸栏目应填写浦江海关2201。

4. 备案号

备案号是指进出口货物收发货人办理海关手续时，应递交的海关备案审批文件的编号，如加工贸易手册编号、征免税证明编号。备案号长度为12位，其中第一位是备案的标记代码。常用备案号的字头标记代码与备案或审批文件的对应关系见表4-2-1。

表4-2-1 常用备案号的字头标记代码与备案或审批文件的对应关系

首位代码	备案审批文件
B	来料加工加工贸易手册
C	进料加工加工贸易手册
E	加工贸易电子账册
Z	征免税证明
Y	原产地证书

一份报关单只允许填写一个备案号。无备案审批文件的报关单，本栏目免于填写。

【例4-2-2】 某企业出口皮鞋，其来料加工加工贸易手册的编号52084400153，备案号栏目应填写B52084400153。

5. 进口日期/出口日期

进口日期是指运载所申报进口货物的运输工具申报进境的日期。出口日期是指运载所申报出口货物的运输工具办结出境手续的日期。

本栏目日期均为8位数字，顺序为年（4位）、月（2位）、日（2位）。出口日期在申报时免于填写。

【例4-2-3】 运输工具申报进境日期为2012年9月15日，进口日期栏目应填写为20120915。

6. 申报日期

申报日期指海关接受进出口货物的收发货人或其代理人向海关申报进出口货物的日期。本栏目在申报时免于填写。

7. 经营单位

经营单位特指对外签订并执行进出口贸易合同的中国境内法人、其他组织或个人。经营单位编码是指海关为注册的经营单位设置的注册登记编码，一般为10位数字。

本栏目在申报时应填写经营单位的中文名称及编码。特殊情况的填写：

（1）如果对外签订合同和执行合同的不是同一单位，则填写执行合同的单位。

（2）国内的企业委托有进出口经营权的企业进出口，经营单位应填写代理方的中文名称及编码。

【例4-2-4】 舟山海洋渔业公司（经营单位编码3309913303）出口一批鱼罐头，经营单位栏目应填写舟山海洋渔业公司3309913303。

【例4-2-5】 上海城建局委托上海土产进出口公司（3101915031）进口黄桐木材，应填报为上海土产进出口公司3101915031。

8. 运输方式

运输方式是指载运货物进出关境所使用的运输工具的分类，即海关规定的运输方式。本栏目应根据实际运输方式按海关规定的《运输方式代码表》选择填写相应的运输方式名称或代码。常用的运输方式代码表见表4-2-2。

表4-2-2 常用的运输方式代码表

代码	名称	代码	名称
2	水路运输	4	公路运输
3	铁路运输	5	航空运输

9. 运输工具名称

运输工具名称是指载运货物进出境所使用的运输工具的名称或运输工具编号。

航次号是指载运货物进出境的运输工具的航次编号。

本栏目填写运输工具名称或编号以及航次编号。一份报关单只允许填写一个运输工具名称。

10. 提运单号

提运单号是指进出口货物提单或运单的编号。本栏目填写进出口货物提单或运单的编号。

一份报关单只允许填写一个提运单号，一票货物对应多个提运单时，应分单填写。

11. 收货单位/发货单位

收货单位指已知的进口货物在境内的最终消费、使用单位。

发货单位指出口货物在境内的生产或销售单位。

本栏目应填写收发货单位中文名称及企业编码。没有编码的，填写其中文名称。

12. 贸易方式

贸易方式（监管方式）指以国际贸易中进出口货物的交易方式为基础，结合海关对进出口货物监督管理综合设定的进出口货物的管理方式，即海关监管方式。根据实际情况，按海关规定的《贸易方式代码表》（见表4－2－3）选择填写相应的贸易方式简称或代码。

一份报关单只允许填写一种贸易方式。

表4－2－3　　常用贸易方式代码表

代　码	简　称	全　称
0110	一般贸易	一般贸易
0214	来料加工	来料加工装配贸易进口料件及加工出口货物
0615	进料对口	进料加工
2025	合资合作设备	合资合作企业作为投资进口的设备物品
2225	外资设备物品	外资企业作为投资进口的设备物品

13. 征免性质

征免性质是指海关根据《中华人民共和国海关法》、《中华人民共和国关税条例》及国家有关政策对进出口货物实施的征、减、免税管理的性质类别。本栏目应按海关规定的《征免性质代码表》（见表4－2－4）选择填写相应的征免性质简称或代码。

一份报关单只允许填写一种征免性质。

表4－2－4　　常见征免性质代码表

代　码	简　称	全　称
101	一般征税	一般征税进出口货物
502	来料加工	来料加工装配和补偿贸易进口料件及出口成品
503	进料加工	进料加工贸易进口料件及出口成品
601	中外合资	中外合资经营企业自产出口的货物
602	中外合作	中外合作经营企业自产出口的货物
603	外资企业	外商独资企业自产出口的货物
789	鼓励项目	国家鼓励发展的内外资项目进口设备

14. 征税比例/结汇方式

进口报关单征税比例栏免于填写。

结汇方式指出口货物的发货人或其代理人收结外汇的方式。

出口报关单应按海关规定的《结汇方式代码表》（见表4－2－5）选择填写相应的结汇方式名称或代码。

表4－2－5 常用结汇方式代码表

代码	结汇方式	英文缩写	英文名称
1	信汇	M/T	Mail Transfer
2	电汇	T/T	Telegraphic Transfer
3	票汇	D/D	Remittance by Banker's Demand Draft
4	付款交单	D/P	Documents against Payment
5	承兑交单	D/A	Documents against Acceptance
6	信用证	L/C	Letter of Credit

15. 许可证号

许可证号是指由商务主管部门签发的进出口许可证的编号。

本栏目填写进出口货物许可证的编号。一份报关单只允许填报一个许可证号。对于非许可证管理的商品本栏目为空。

16. 起运国（地区）/运抵国（地区）

起运国（地区）指进口货物起始发出的国家（地区）。

运抵国（地区）指出口货物直接运抵的国家（地区）。

本栏目应按海关规定的《国别（地区）代码表》（见表4－2－6）选择填写相应的国别（地区）的中文名称或代码。

表4－2－6 常用主要国别（地区）代码表

国别代码	中文名称	国别代码	中文名称
110	中国香港	116	日本
133	韩国	142	中国
143	中国台澎金马关税区	303	英国
304	德国	502	美国
305	法国	344	俄罗斯联邦

17. 装货港/指运港

装货港是指进口货物在运抵我国关境前的最后一个境外装运港。

指运港是指出口货物运往境外的最终目的港。

本栏目应根据实际情况按海关规定的《港口航线代码表》选择填写相应的港口中文名称或代码。

资料卡

中转货物起运国/运抵国、装货港/指运港的填报：

（1）对于发生运输中转而未发生任何买卖关系的货物，其起运国（地区）或运抵国（地区）不变。

（2）对于发生运输中转并发生了买卖关系的货物，其中转地为起运国（地区）或运抵国（地区）；最后一个中转港就是装货港，指运港不受中转影响。

【例 4－2－6】 青岛某进出口公司与香港某公司签约进口 100 台日本产丰田轿车，从日本东京启运经香港中转运抵境内，则进口货物报关单启运国栏目应填写中国香港，装货港栏目应填写香港。

18. 境内目的地/境内货源地

境内目的地是指已知的进口货物在我国关境内的消费、使用地区或最终运抵的地点。

境内货源地是指出口货物在我国关境内的产地或原始发货地。

本栏目按海关规定的《国内地区代码表》选择填写相应的国内地区名称或代码。

19. 批准文号

进出口货物报关单批准文号栏免于填报。

20. 成交方式

在我国进出口贸易活动中常见的成交方式有 CIF、CFR、FOB 等。

值得注意的是，报关单填制中的“CIF、CFR、FOB”等成交方式与《2000 年通则》、《2010 年通则》中的贸易术语内涵并非完全一致。

本栏目应根据实际成交价格条款，按海关规定的《成交方式代码表》（见表 4－2－7）选择填写相应的成交方式代码。

表 4－2－7 成交方式代码表

成交方式代码	成交方式名称	成交方式代码	成交方式名称
1	CIF	4	C&I
2	CFR（C&F/CNF）	5	市场价
3	FOB	6	垫 仓

21. 运费

运费是指进出口货物从始发地到目的地的国际运输所需要的各种费用。

本栏目应填写该份报关单所含全部货物的国际间运输费用，即进口成交方式为 FOB 或出口成交方式为 CIF、CFR 的，应在运费栏目填写运费。运保费合并计算的，运保费填写在“运费”栏中。

22. 保费

保费专指进出口货物在国际运输中，由被保险人付给保险人的保险费用。

本栏目应填写该份报关单所含全部货物的国际间保险费用，进口成交方式为 FOB、CFR 或出口成交方式为 CIF 的，应在保费栏目填写保费。运保费合并计算的，运保费填写在“运费”栏中，“保费”栏免于填写。

23. 杂费

杂费是指成交价格以外的，应计入完税价格或应从完税价格中扣除的费用，如手续费、佣金、折扣等。

本栏目应填写应根据具体情况选择杂费总价或杂费率两种方式之一填写，同时注明杂费标记并按海关规定的《货币代码表》选择填报相应的币种代码。应计入完税价格的杂费填报为正值或正率；应从完税价格中扣除的杂费填报为负值或负率。无杂费时，本栏免于填写。

24. 合同协议号

合同协议号是指进出口货物合同（协议）的编号。

本栏目应填写进出口货物合同的全部字头和号码。

25. 件数

件数是指有外包装的单件进出口货物的实际件数。

本栏目应填写有外包装进出口货物的实际件数。件数应大于1或等于1，不得填写为“0”。散装、裸装货物应填写为1。

26. 包装种类

包装种类是指进出口货物在运输过程中外表所呈现的状态，一般情况下，应以装箱单或提运单据所反映的货物处于运输状态时的最外层包装向海关申报，并相应计算件数。

本栏目按进出口货物实际外包装种类，选择填写相应的包装种类，如木箱、纸箱、铁桶、散装、裸装、托盘等。散装或裸装货物应填写为散装或裸装。

27. 毛重

毛重是指货物及其包装材料的重量之和。

毛重栏填写进出口货物的实际毛重，不得为空，计量单位为千克。毛重应大于或等于1，不足1千克的填写为“1”。

28. 净重

净重是指减去外包装材料后剩下的商品本身重量。

净重栏填写进出口货物的实际净重，不得为空，计量单位为千克。净重应大于或等于1，不足1千克的都填写为“1”。

29. 集装箱号

集装箱号是在每个集装箱箱体两侧标示的全球唯一的编号。其组成规则是：箱主代号（3位字母）+设备识别号（U）+顺序号（6位数字）+校验码（1位数字），如“EASU9808849”。

本栏目应填写集装箱号+“/”+规格+“/”+自重。涉及多个集装箱的，第一个集装箱号填报在“集装箱号”栏中，其余的依次填报在“标记唛码与备注”栏中。非集装箱货物，填报为“0”。

【例4-2-7】 一个20英尺集装箱，箱号为TGHU8491952，自重2275公斤，集装箱号栏目应填写为TGHU8491952/20/2275。

30. 随附单据

随附单据是指随进出口货物报关单一并向海关递交的，除商业、货运单证及许可证号栏填写的进出口许可证以外的监管证件。

本栏目填报监管证件的代码及编号，格式为：监管证件的代码+“：”+监管证件编号。所申报货物涉及多个监管证件的，第一个监管证件代码和编号填写在随附单据栏，其余监管证件代码和编号填写在标记唛码及备注栏中。

31. 用途/生产厂家

用途是指进口货物在境内实际应用的范围。

生产厂家是指出口货物的中国境内生产企业的名称。

进口货物填写用途，应根据进口货物的实际用途，按海关规定的“用途代码表”选择填写相应的用途名称或代码。出口货物填写生产厂家，应填写中国境内生产企业的名称。

32. 标记唛码及备注

进出口货物报关单上标记唛码专指货物的运输标志。一般与发票相同。

备注是指填制报关单时需要备注的事项。

标记唛码栏填写除图形以外的所有文字和数字。

33. 项号

项号是指申报货物在报关单中的商品排列序号及该项商品在加工贸易手册等备案单证中的顺序编号。

本栏目分两行填报：第一行填报货物在报关单中的商品排列序号。第二行专用于加工贸易等已备案的货物，填报该项货物在加工贸易手册中的备案项号。

34. 商品编号

商品编号是指按《进出口税则》确定的进出口货物的海关监管商品代码。商品编号由10位数组成，本栏目应填报10位海关商品编号。

35. 商品名称、规格型号

商品名称是指缔约双方同意买卖的商品的名称。一般是指进出口货物规范的中文名称。

商品的规格型号是指能反映商品性能、品质和规格的一系列指标，如成分、等级、大小、长短等。

本栏目分两行填报：第一行填写进出口货物规范的中文名称。如果发票中的商品名称为非中文名称，则需翻译成规范的中文名称填报，仅在必要时加注原文。第二行填写规格型号。

36. 数量及单位

报关单上的数量及单位是指进出口商品的成交数量和计量单位，以及海关法定计量单位和按照海关法定计量单位计算的数量。

本栏目分三行填报：第一行应填写第一计量单位及数量。第二行应填写第二计量单位及数量。第三行应填写成交计量单位及数量。

37. 原产国/最终目的国

原产国是指进口货物的生产、开采或加工制造的国家（地区）。

最终目的国是指已知的出口货物的最终实际消费、使用或进一步加工制造的国家（地区）。

本栏目应按海关规定的《国别（地区）代码表》选择填报相应的国家（地区）的中文名称或代码。

38. 单价

单价是指进出口货物实际成交的商品单位价格的金额部分。

单价栏目应填写同一项号下进出口货物实际成交的商品单位价格的数字部分。

39. 总价

总价是指进出口货物实际成交的商品总价的金额部分。

总价栏目填写同一项号下进出口货物实际成交的商品总价的数字部分。

40. 币制

币制是指进出口货物实际成交价格的计价货币的名称。

币制栏目根据实际成交情况按海关规定的《货币代码表》（见表4－2－8）选择填写相应的货币名称或代码。常用货币代码表见表4－2－8。

表4－2－8 货币代码表

币制代码	币制符号	币制名称	币制代码	币制符号	币制名称
110	HKD	港 币	116	JPY	日 元
142	CNY	人民币	300	EUR	欧 元
303	GBP	英 镑	502	USD	美 元

41. 征免

征免指海关对进出口货物进行征税、减税、免税或特案处理的实际操作方式。

本栏目应填写海关规定的“征减免税方式代码表”中相应的征减免税方式的名称。

42. 税费征收情况

本栏目供海关批注进出口货物税费征收及减免情况。

43. 录入员

本栏目用于记录预录入操作人员的姓名。

44. 录入单位

本栏目用于记录预录入单位名称。

45. 申报单位

自理报关的，本栏目填写进出口企业的名称及海关注册编码；委托代理报关的，本栏目填写经海关批准的报关企业名称及海关注册编码。

本栏目还包括报关单左下方用于填报申报单位有关情况的相关栏目，包括报关员、报关单位地址、邮政编码和电话号码等栏目。

46. 填制日期

本栏目填写申报单位填制报关单的日期。本栏目为8位数字，顺序为年（4位）、月（2位）、日（2位）。

47. 海关审单批注及放行日期（签章）

本栏目供海关作业时签注。

【工作指导】

青岛海富贸易有限公司在办理货物报检后，由张丽的师傅李华根据已经制作好的商业发票和装箱单及其他相关资料制作一份出口货物报关单。

资料1：

青岛海富贸易有限公司（市南区）生产发货，海关注册编号为370291xxxx，法定计量单位为千克，货物于2013年7月6日向大港海关（关区代码4427）办理出口申报手续。出境货物通关单编号：370100213111021000。结汇方式为L/C。提单号：SITC229173。CONTAINER 1×40’ SITC1292748，TARE WGT3250KG。保险费率是0.28%。

资料2：商业发票

QINGDAO HAIFU TRADING CO. LTD.

NO. 1 HONGKONG ROAD, QINGDAO CHINA

TEL: 86－0532－85896210 FAX: 86－0532－85896211

COMMERCIAL INVOICE

Original

To: FUTURO INDUSTRIAL CO. LTD.,
ROTTERDAM NETHERLANDS
TEL: 031 431 7295

No. QD528
Date: JUNE. 25, 2013
L/C No.: 1C01925U
Contract: MSR719

From: QINGDAO, CHINA　　To ROTTERDAM PORT, NETHERLANDS

Shipping Marks	Quantities & Description	Unit Price	Amount
F. I. C. MSR719	2450CARTONS (ONE CONTAINER) OF	CIF ROTTERDAM	
ROTTERDAM 1－2450	QINGDAO SPRING ROLLS	@USD15.50/CTN	USD37975.00

H. S. CODE: 19022000

PACKING: 20G PER PC, 50PCS IN A BOX, 9 BOXES IN A CARTON

AS PER CONTRACT NO. MSR719 DATE: APR. 12, 2013

PACKED IN PLANT OF QINGDAO BANMU FOODS PRODUCTS CO. LTD.,

QINGDAO INDUSTRIAL ZONE QINGDAO

FREIGHT CHARGE: USD3150.00

FOB VALUE: USD34825.00

WE HEREBY CERTIFY THAT THE GOODS ARE OF CHINA ORIGIN

QINGDAO HAIFU TRADING CO. LTD.,
LIHUA

资料3：装箱单

PACKING LIST

Original

To: FUTURO INDUSTRIAL CO. LTD.,
ROTTERDAM NETHERLANDS
TEL: 031 413 7295

No. QD528
Date: JUNE. 25, 2013
L/C No.: IC01925U
Contract: MSR719

From: QINGDAO, CHINA To ROTTERDAM PORT, NETHERLANDS

Shipping Marks	NO. & Kind of Pakgs: Description of the Goods	Net Weight	Gross Weight	Measurement
F. I. C. MSR719	2450CARTONS (ONE CONTAINER) OF			
ROTTERDAM	QINGDAO SPRING ROLLS	@9.00KGS/CTN	@10.00KGS/CTN	@0.0195CBM/CTN
1-2450	TOTAL:	22050.00KGS	24500.00KGS	47.775CBM

PACKING: 20G PER PC, 50PCS IN A BOX, 9 BOXES IN A CARTON

Vessel and Voy No.: SITC QINGDAO V.23

QINGDAO HAIFU TRADING CO. LTD.,
LIHUA

师傅李华制作的出口货物报关单如下所示：

中华人民共和国海关出口货物报关单

预录入编号：　　　　　　　　海关编号：

出口口岸	备案号	出口日期	申报日期
大港海关 4427			

经营单位	运输方式	运输工具名称	提运单号
青岛海富贸易有限公司 370291xxxx	2	SITC QINGDAO/23	SITC229173

发货单位	贸易方式	征免性质	结汇方式
青岛海富贸易有限公司 370291xxxx	一般贸易	一般征税	信用证

许可证号	运抵国（地区）	指运港	境内货源地
	荷兰	鹿特丹	青岛市南区

批准文号	成交方式	运费	保费	杂费
	1	502/3150/3	0.28/1	

合同协议号	件数	包装种类	毛重（公斤）	净重（公斤）
MSR719	2450	纸箱	24500	22050

集装箱号	随附单据	生产厂家
SITC1292748/40/3250	B：370100213111021000	青岛海富贸易有限公司

标记唛码及备注
F. I. C.
MSR719
ROTTERDAM
1－2450

项号	商品编号	商品名称、规格型号	数量及单位	最终目的国（地区）	单价	总价	币制	征免
01	19022000	春卷	22050 千克 2450 纸箱	荷兰	15.50	37975.00	美元	照章征税

42. 税费征收情况

43. 录入员　　44. 录入单位	兹声明以上申报无讹并承担法律责任	47. 海关审单批注及放行日期（签章）
报关员		审单　　审价
单位地址	45. 申报单位（签章）	征税　　统计
邮编　　电话	46. 填制日期	查验　　放行

【工作演练】

张丽在师傅李华的指导下，已经基本掌握了填写进出口货物报关单的基本技能。请你和张丽一起根据下列相关资料独立填写一份进口货物报关单。

资料1：

青岛海富贸易有限公司（市南区），海关注册编号为370291xxxx，所申报商品位列B52084400256号登记手册备案料件第2项，法定计量单位为千克。货物于2012年7月16日运抵口岸，当日向大港海关（关区代码4427）办理进口申报手续。保险费率为0.25%。入境货物通关单编号：370100112265797000。

资料2：

COMMERCIAL INVOICE

CONSIGNEE:
QINGDAO HAIFU CO. LTD.,
NO. 1 HONGKONG ROAD
QINGDAO, CHINA

SHIPPER:
ABC (HONG KONG) LTD.
ROOM 101 SHATIN GALLERIA
MEI STREET, FOTAN, SHATIN, N.T.,
HONG KONG

INVOICE NO. BL04060643　　DATE: 07/07/12

CONTRACT NO: ABC—1001　　REFERENCE No: HB184004

SHIPMENT FROM KUNSAN, KOREA TO QINGDAO CHINA VIA HONG KONG

SHIPPING MARKS	DESCRIPTION	QUANTITY	UNIT PRICE	AMOUNT
N/M	"HI—Q" BRAND ART PAPER 039—44	16350kg 16ROLLS	0.8040	CFR HUANGPU US $ 13, 145. 40

TOTAL: US $ 13, 145. 40　　16ROLLS　　16350kg

SINFNED BY ABC (HONG KONG) LTD.

资料3：

PACKING LIST

DATE：07/07/12

TO：QINGDAO HAIFU CO. LTD.，

NO. 1 HONGKONG ROAD，QINGDAO CHINA

SHIPMENT FROM KUNSAN，KOREA TO QINGDAO， CHINA VIA HONGKONG

Vessel and Voage No.：穗顺航 30/4Y0708

B/L NO：SG40746

DESCRIPTION	QTY	WEIGHT（GROSS）	NETWEIGHT	MEASUREMENT
"HI—Q" BRAND	16350KGS	16400	16350	
ART PAPER	16 ROLLS			
039—44				
H. S：48101300				
		16400	16350	

1X20' CONTAINER

TEXU2263978 TARE WGT2280kg

资料4：进口货物报关单

中华人民共和国海关进口货物报关单

预录入编号：　　　　　　　　海关编号：

进口口岸	备案号		进口日期	申报日期
经营单位	运输方式		运输工具名称	提运单号
收货单位	贸易方式		征免性质	征税比例
许可证号	起运国（地区）		装货港	境内目的地
批准文号	成交方式		运费	保费　杂费
合同协议号	件数	包装种类	毛重（公斤）	净重（公斤）
集装箱号	随付单据			用途
标记唛码及备注				

项号	商品编号	商品名称、规格型号	数量及单位	原产国（地区）	单价	总价	币制	征免

税费征收情况

录入员　录入单位	兹声明以上申报无讹并承担法律责任	海关审单批注及放行日期（签章）
报关员		审单　审价
单位地址	申报单位（签章）	征税　统计
邮编　电话	填制日期	查验　放行

提示：

（1）出口日期在申报时免于填写。

（2）批准文号进出口报关单均免于填写。

（3）结汇方式栏目应填结汇方式名称或代码，而不能填写英文缩写。

（4）进口成交方式为CFR的，运费栏免于填写、保费栏目应填写；出口成交方式为CFR的，运费栏应填写、保费栏免于填写。

（5）海关法定计量单位为千克的，净重就是数量。

【工作评价】

1. 评价标准

中华人民共和国海关进口货物报关单

预录入编号：　　　　　　海关编号：

<table>
<tr><td>进口口岸
大港海关 4427</td><td colspan="2">备案号
B52084400256</td><td>进口日期
20120716</td><td colspan="2">申报日期</td></tr>
<tr><td>经营单位
青岛海富贸易有限公司 370291xxxx</td><td colspan="2">运输方式
水路运输</td><td>运输工具名称
穗顺航 30/4Y0708</td><td colspan="2">提运单号
SG40746</td></tr>
<tr><td>收货单位
青岛海富贸易有限公司 370291xxxx</td><td colspan="2">贸易方式
来料加工</td><td>征免性质
来料加工</td><td colspan="2">征税比例</td></tr>
<tr><td>许可证号</td><td colspan="2">起运国（地区）
中国香港</td><td>装货港
香港</td><td colspan="2">境内目的地
青岛市市南区</td></tr>
<tr><td>批准文号</td><td colspan="2">成交方式
2</td><td>运费</td><td>保费
0.25/1</td><td>杂费</td></tr>
<tr><td>合同协议号
ABC－1001</td><td>件数
16</td><td>包装种类
卷</td><td>毛重（公斤）
16400</td><td colspan="2">净重（公斤）
16350</td></tr>
<tr><td>集装箱号
TEXU2263978/20/2280</td><td colspan="3">随付单据
A：370100112265797000</td><td colspan="2">用途
加工返销</td></tr>
<tr><td colspan="6">标记唛码及备注
N/M</td></tr>
</table>

项号	商品编号	商品名称、规格型号	数量及单位	原产国（地区）	单价	总价	币制	征免
01	48101300	韩松铜版纸	16350 千克	韩国	0.8040	13145.40	美元	全免
02		039－44						

<table>
<tr><td colspan="3">税费征收情况</td></tr>
<tr><td>录入员　　　录入单位</td><td rowspan="2">兹声明以上申报无讹并承担法律责任</td><td>海关审单批注及放行日期（签章）</td></tr>
<tr><td>报关员</td><td>审单　　　审价</td></tr>
<tr><td colspan="2">单位地址　　　　　　　申报单位（签章）</td><td>征税　　　统计</td></tr>
<tr><td colspan="2">邮编　　　电话　　　填制日期</td><td>查验　　　放行</td></tr>
</table>

2. 评价表（见表4－2－9）

表4－2－9

评价人 评价指标	自　评	互　评	师　评
独立完成情况 （20分）			
格式规范性 （20分）			
内容完整性、正确性 （50分）			
内容简明性、整洁性 （10分）			
合计总分			

项目实训

资料1：

青岛阳光贸易有限公司（市南区）生产发货，海关注册编号为370291xxxx，报检单位登记号：3700138721，货物存放在青岛海关监管1号仓库，并于2013年11月1日向青岛出入境检验检疫局报检。报检员为王丽，联系电话：18661859356。

该批货物为蜂王浆，HS：0410004100，法定计量单位为千克。货物于2013年11月6日向大港海关（关区代码4427）办理出口申报手续，于2013年11月10日出境。出境货物通关单编号：370100213111011000。结汇方式为L/C。提单号：SITC273291，船名航次：SITC DALIAN V. 21。CONTAINER 1×40’ SITC1248927，TARE WGT3250KG。运费：2500美元，保险费率为0. 25%。

资料 2：商业发票

COMMERCIAL　INVOICE

ORIGINAL

To: GREENWOOD TRADING CO. LTD. ,
NO. 42GOLDEN GARDEN STREET,
AMSTERDAM NETHERLANDS0

No. SK528
Date: OCT. 29, 2013
L/C No. : IC01925U
Contract: TP5623

From: QINGDAO, CHINA　**To** AMSTERDAM, NETHERLANDS

Shipping Marks	Quantities & Descpription	Unit Price	Amount
G. T. C.			
TP5623	CHINESE ROYAL JELLY	CIF AMTERDAM	
AMSTERDAM	DECENOIC ACID: 2.1 MIN		
NO. 1－400	MOISTURE: 67.00% MAX		
	QUANTITY: 40000PLASTIC BOTTLES	@ USD12.00/CTN	USD48000.00

PACKED IN 400CTNS AND 1KG IN A PLASTIC BOTTLE

10KGS NETWEIGHT PER CARTON　11KGS GROSS WEIGHT

PACKING IN REFRIGERATURE CONTAINER

PRODUCT DATE: MAY 15, 2013

ALL PRODUCT ARE OFCHINA ORIGIN

APPLICANT ' S REF NO. FU5102

THIS SHIPMENT CONTAINS NO SOLID WOOD PACKING MATERIAL

QINGDAO SUNSHINE TRADING CO. LTD. ,

WANGLI

资料 3：装箱单

PACKING LIST

ORIGINAL

To: GREENWOOD TRADING CO. LTD.,
NO. 42 GOLDEN GARDEN STREET,
AMSTERDAM NETHERLANDS

No. SK528
Date: OCT. 29, 2013
L/C No.: IC01925U
Contract: TP5623

From: QINGDAO, CHINA **To** AMSTERDAM, NETHERLANDS

Shipping Marks	NO. & Kind of Pakgs: Description of the Goods		Net Weight	Gross Weight	Measurement
G. T. C.					
TP5623	CHINESE ROYAL JELLY				
AMTERDAM	QUANTITY	PACKING	@10.00KGS/CTN	@11.00KGS/CTN	@0.0095CBM/CTN
NO. 1-400	40000 BOTTLES	400CTNS	40000KGS	44000KGS	38.000CBM

PACKED IN 400CTNS AND 1KG IN A PLASTIC BOTTLE

10KGS NETWEIGHT PER CARTON 11KGS GROSS WEIGHT

PACKING IN REFRIGERATURE CONTAINER

APPLICANT'S REF
NO. FU5102

PRODUCT DATE: MAY 15, 2013

QINGDAO SUNSHINE TRADING CO. LTD.,

WANGLI

资料4：出口货物报检单

中华人民共和国出入境检验检疫
出境货物报检单

报检单位（加盖公章）：　　　　　　　　　　　　　　　　　　*编　　号＿＿＿＿＿＿

报检单位登记号：　　　　　联系人：　　　　　电话：　　　　　报检日期：　　年　　月　　日

发货人	（中文）	
	（外文）	
收货人	（中文）	
	（外文）	

货物名称（中/外文）	H. S. 编码	产地	数/重量	货物总值	包装种类及数量

运输工具名称号码		贸易方式		货物存放地点	
合同号		信用证号		用途	
发货日期		输往国家（地区）		许可证/审批号	
启运地		到达口岸		生产单位注册号	
集装箱规格、数量及号码					

合同、信用证订立的检验检疫条款或特殊要求	标 记 及 号 码	随附单据（划“✓”或补填）	
		□合同	□包装性能结果单
		□信用证	□许可/审批文件
		□发票	□
		□换证凭单	□
		□装箱单	□
		□厂检单	□

需要证单名称（划“✓”或补填）				*检验检疫费	
□品质证书	＿正＿副	□植物检疫证书	＿正＿副	总金额（人民币元）	
□重量证书	＿正＿副	□熏蒸/消毒证书	＿正＿副		
□数量证书	＿正＿副	□出境货物换证凭单		计费人	
□兽医卫生证书	＿正＿副	□出境货物通关单			
□健康证书	＿正＿副	□		收费人	
□卫生证书	＿正＿副	□			

报检人郑重声明：	领 取 证 单	
1. 本人被授权报检。 2. 上列填写内容正确属实，货物无伪造或冒用他人的厂名、标志、认证标志，并承担货物质量责任。	日期	
签名：＿＿＿＿＿＿	签名	

注：有“*”号栏由出入境检验检疫机关填写。　　　　◆国家出入境检验检疫局制

［1-2（2001.1.1）*1］

资料 5：出口货物报关单

中华人民共和国海关出口货物报关单

预录入编号：　　　　海关编号：

出口口岸	备案号	出口日期	申报日期	
经营单位	运输方式	运输工具名称	提运单号	
发货单位	贸易方式	征免性质	结汇方式	
许可证号	运抵国（地区）	指运港	境内货源地	
批准文号	成交方式	运费	保费	杂费
合同协议号	件数	包装种类	毛重（公斤）	净重（公斤）
集装箱号	随附单据	生产厂家		
标记唛码及备注				

项号	商品编号	商品名称、规格型号	数量及单位	最终目的国（地区）	单价	总价	币制	征免

42. 税费征收情况				
43. 录入员	44. 录入单位	兹声明以上申报无讹并承担法律责任	47. 海关审单批注及放行日期（签章）	
报关员			审单	审价
单位地址		45. 申报单位（签章）	征税	统计
邮编	电话	46. 填制日期	查验	放行

实训要求：

（1）根据所给资料，填制一份出境货物报检单和一份出口货物报关单。

参考答案

1. 出境货物报检单

中华人民共和国出入境检验检疫

出境货物报检单

报检单位（加盖公章）：青岛阳光贸易有限公司　　　　*编　号______

报检单位登记号：3700138721　联系人：王丽　电话：18661859356　报检日期：2013 年 11 月 1 日

发货人	（中文）	青岛阳光贸易有限公司 3700138721
	（外文）	QINGDAO SUNSHINE TRADING CO. LTD. ,
收货人	（中文）	* * *
	（外文）	GREENWOOD TRADING CO. LTD. ,

货物名称（中/外文）	H. S. 编码	产地	数/重量	货物总值	包装种类及数量
中国蜂王浆 CHINESE ROYAL JELLY MOISTURE：67. 00% MAX DECENOIC ACID：2. 1 MIN	0410004100	山东青岛	40000 瓶/44000. 00 千克	48000. 00. 美元	400 纸箱

运输工具名称号码	SITCDALIAN V. 21	贸易方式	一般贸易	货物存放地点	青岛海关监管 1 号仓库		
合同号	TP5623	信用证号	IC01925U	用途	食用		
发货日期	2013. 11. 10	输往国家（地区）	荷兰	许可证/审批号	* * *		
启运地	青岛	到达口岸	阿姆斯特丹	生产单位注册号	3700138721		
集装箱规格、数量及号码	1 ×40’ SITC1248927						

合同、信用证订立的检验检疫条款或特殊要求	标 记 及 号 码	随附单据（划“✓”或补填）	
* * *	G. T. C. AMSTERDAM NO. 1 – 400	☑合同 ☑信用证 ☑发票 ☐换证凭单 ☑装箱单 ☑厂检单	☑包装性能结果单 ☐许可/审批文件 ☐ ☐ ☐ ☐

需要证单名称（划“✓”或补填）				* 检验检疫费	
☐品质证书	__正__副	☐植物检疫证书	__正__副	总金额（人民币元）	
☐重量证书	__正__副	☐熏蒸/消毒证书	__正__副		
☐数量证书	__正__副	☐出境货物换证凭单		计费人	
☐兽医卫生证书	__正__副	☑出境货物通关单			
☐健康证书	__正__副	☐		收费人	
☐卫生证书	__正__副	☐			
☐动物卫生证书	__正__副	☐			

报检人郑重声明：	领 取 证 单	
1. 本人被授权报检。 2. 上列填写内容正确属实，货物无伪造或冒用他人的厂名、标志、认证标志，并承担货物质量责任。	日期	
签名：王丽	签名	

注：有“*”号栏由出入境检验检疫机关填写。　　◆国家出入境检验检疫局制

［1 – 2（2001. 1. 1）*1］

2. 出口货物报关单

中华人民共和国海关出口货物报关单

预录入编号：　　　　　　　　　　海关编号：

出口口岸 大港海关 4427	备案号	出口日期	申报日期

经营单位 青岛阳光贸易有限公司 370291xxxx	运输方式 水路运输	运输工具名称 SITC DALIAN/21	提运单号 SITC273291
发货单位 青岛阳光贸易有限公司 370291xxxx	贸易方式 一般贸易	征免性质 一般征税	结汇方式 信用证
许可证号	运抵国（地区） 荷兰	指运港 阿姆斯特丹	境内货源地 青岛市南区

批准文号	成交方式 1	运费 502/2500/3	保费 0. 25/1	杂费
合同协议号 TP5623	件数 400	包装种类 纸箱	毛重（公斤） 44000	净重（公斤） 40000

集装箱号 SITC1248927/40/3250	随附单据 B：370100213111011000	生产厂家 青岛阳光贸易有限公司

标记唛码及备注
G. T. C.
TP5623
AMSTERDAM
NO. 1 – 400

项号	商品编号	商品名称、规格型号	数量及单位	最终目的国（地区）	单价	总价	币制	征免
01	04100041	中国蜂王浆 DECENOIC ACID：2. 1 MIN MOISTURE：67. 00% MAX	40000 千克 400 纸箱	荷兰	12. 00	48000. 00	美元	照章征税

42. 税费征收情况

43. 录入员　　44. 录入单位	兹声明以上申报无讹并承担法律责任	47. 海关审单批注及放行日期（签章）	
报关员		审单	审价
单位地址	45. 申报单位（签章）	征税	统计
邮编　　电话	46. 填制日期	查验	放行

项目五

综 合 练 习

任务一 综合制单练习

【制单练习一】

根据下列交易磋商中的资料，填制一份售货合同。

资料：

（1）合同编号：NT0961552

合同日期：2013 年 5 月 28 日

（2）出口方：山东宏达进出口有限公司

SHANDONG HONGDA IMP. & EXP. CO. , LTD

中国青岛市中山路 50 号

NO. 50 ZHONGSHAN ROAD, QINGDAO, CHINA

电话/传真：0086 - 0532 - 68474718

进口方：KNIT CREATIO CO. , LTD

84 - 6, KAMITAKAOKA MIKI - CHO, TOKYO JAPAN

出口方代表：赵凯 进口方代表：田中俊彦

（3）商品名称及规格、包装：

GIRLS WOVEN SKIRTS

数量：10000 件

唛头：K. C. / TOKYO/ NO. 1 - UP

单价：CIF 东京 每件 12. 80 美元

装运期限：不迟于 2014 年 1 月 15 日

装运港：青岛港

目的港：东京港

分批装运：不允许

转船：不允许

付款条件：即期不可撤销信用证

（4）合同其他要求：

①买方应于 2013 年 11 月 1 日前开出信用证。

②卖方按货值 110% 的投保加成率投保一切险。

（5）售货确认书：

______________________公司
____
____
____

售货确认书
SALES CONFIRMATION

Tel：______________　　　　编号：No. ______________
Fax：______________　　　　日期：Date ______________
TO Messrs：
____
____

谨启者：兹确认授予你方下列货品，其成交条款如下：

Dear Sirs：We hereby confirm having sold to you the following goods on the terms and conditions as specified below：

（1）货物名称及规格 Name of Commodity and Specification	（2）数量 Quantity	（3）单价 Unit Price	（4）总价 Amount

（5）装运期限：Time of Shipment：LATEST DATE OF SHIPMENT __________

（6）装运港：Port of Loading：__________

（7）目的港：Port of Destination：__________

（8）分批装运：Partial Shipment：__________

（9）转船：Transshipment：__________

（10）付款条件：Terms of Payment：__________

（11）运输标志：Shipping Marks：____________________

（12）保险：Insurance：The Seller should cover insurance for ______ % of the total invoice value against ______ as per Ocean Marine Cargo Clauses of PICC dated 1/1/1981.

（13）仲裁：

Arbitration：All disputes arising from the execution of, or in connection with this Sales Confirmation, shall be settled amicably through friendly negotiation. In case no settlement can be reached through negotiation, the case shall then be submitted to China International Economic and Trade Arbitration Commission, Shanghai Commission for arbitration in accordance with Rules of Arbitration of China International Economic and Trade Arbitration Commission. The award made by the Commission should be accepted as final and binding upon both parties.

(14) REMARKS：买方须于______年______月______日前开出本批交易的信用证（或通知售方进口许可证号码）。否则，售方有权不经过通知取消本确认书，或向买方提出索赔。

The Buyer shall establish the covering Letter of Credit (or notify the Import License Number) before ______, falling which the Seller reserves the right to rescind without further notice, or to accept whole or any part of this Sales Confirmation non——fulfilled by the Buyer, or, to lodge claim for direct losses sustained, if any.

凡以 CIF 条件成交的业务，保额为发票价的______，投保险别以售货确认书中所开列的为限，买方如果要求增加保额或保险范围，应于装船前经卖方同意，因此而增加的保险费由买方负责。

For transaction conclude on CIF basis, it is understood that the insurance amount will be for ______ of the invoice value against the risks specified in Sales Confirmation. If additional insurance amount or coverage is required, the buyer must have consent of the Seller before Shipment, and the additional premium is to be borne by the Buyer.

由于发生人力不可抗拒的原因，致使本合约不能履行，部分或全部商品延误交货，卖方概不负责。本合同所指的不可抗力系指不可干预、不能避免且不能克服的客观情况。

The Seller shall not be held liable for failure of delay in delivery of the entire lot or a portion of the goods under this Sales Confirmation in consequence of any Force Majeure incidents.

买方在开给卖方的信用证上请填注本确认书号码。

The Buyer is requested always to quote THE NUMBER OF THIS SALES CONFIRMATION in the Letter of Credit to be opened in favour of the Seller.

买方收到本售货确认书后请立即签回一份，如买方对本确认书有异议，应于收到后五天内提出，否则认为买方已同意接受本确认书所规定的各项条款。

The buyer is requested to sign and return one copy of the Sales Confirmation immediately after the receipt of same, Objection, if any, should be raised by the Buyer within five days after the receipt of this Sales Confirmation, in the absence of which it is understood that the Buyer has accepted the terms and condition of the Sales Confirmation.

买方　　　　　　　　　　　　　　　　卖方

【制单练习二】

根据所给资料，分别填制商业发票、提单和汇票。

资料1：信用证

FORM OF DOC. CREDIT　　　　*40A：IRREVOCABLE

DOC. CREDIT NUMBER	*20: FP7051
DATE OF ISSUE	*31C: 2014-3-23
EXPIRY	*31D: DATE 2014-5-20 PLACE IN CHINA
ISSUING BANK	*51A: UNION BANK OF SWIZERLAND, FRANCE
APPLICANT	*50: SAGIR BROTHERS CO. 27 ASADGONI MARSEILLEFRANCE
BENEFICIARY	*59: QINGDAO HAIQING TRADING CO. LTD. 52 HONGKONG ROAD QINGDAO CHINA
AMOUNT:	*32B: CURRENCY USD AMOUNT 24000.00
AVAILABLE WITH/BY	*41D: ANY BANK IN CHINA BY DRAFT
DRAFTS AT	*42C: SIGHT
DRAWEE	*42A: ISSUING BANK
PARTIAL SHIPMENTS	*43P: ALLOWED
TRANSHIPMENT	*43T: ALLOWED
PORT OF LOADING:	*44E: ANY PORT IN CHINA
PORT OF DISCHARGE	*44F: MARSEILLE FRANCE
LATEST DATE OF SHIPMENT	*44C: 2014-4-8
DESCRIPT. OF GOODS	*45A:

KING BRAND COTTON SOCKS CFR MARSEILLE

SIZE	QUANTITY	PACKAGE	UNIT PRICE
W280L	4400PAIRS	44CTNS	USD1.20 / PAIR
B260M	6000PAIRS	60CTNS	USD1.10 / PAIR
P270XL	7600PAIRS	76CTNS	USD1.50 / PAIR

PACKING: 10 PAIRS IN ONE DOZEN, 10 DOZEN IN ONE CARTON

AS PER CONTRACT NO. CS1002H DATE: FEB. 5, 2014

DOCUMENTS REQUIRED *46A:

+SIGNED COMMERCIAL INVOICE IN 3 COPIES CERTIFYING MERCHANDISE COUNTRY OF ORIGIN AND SHOWING FREIGHT CHARGE

+FULL SET OF SHIPPED ON BOARD B/L MADE OUT TO ORDER OF SHIPPER AND MARKED FREIGHT PREPAID NOTIFY APPLICANT AND ISSUING BANK.

ADDITIONAL COND. *47A:

+B/L SHOWING THAT THE CARRYING VESSEL IS NOT OLDER THAN 15 YEARS.

+ONE SET OF COPY DOCUMENTS HAS BEEN SENT TO THE APPLICANT APPEAR ON INVOICE.

+YANGMING SHIPPING CO. AS CARRIER APPEAR IN B/L.

+H. S. CODE 61159500 APPEAR ON INVOICE.

+THE GOODS SHIPPED IN 20'HR CONTAINER APPEAR IN B/L.

48: PERIOD FOR PRESENTAYION

15 DAYS AFTER SHIPMENT DATE BUT IN ANY CASE WITHIN THIS L/C VALIDITY
49：CONFIRMATION INSTRUCTIONS：WITHOUT
71B：CHARGE
ALL BANKING CHARGE AND COMM. OUTSIDE OF FRANCE ARE FOR THE BENEFICIARY'S ACCOUNT

资料2：

1. INVOICE NO. CS152
2. B/L NO. QDYM52146
   B/L DATE：APR. 6，2014
   VESSEL NAME：COSCO HN V. 029E
   CONTAINER NO. LINU4132517
   SEAL NO. 130251
3. GROSS WEIGHT：4KGS/CARTON
   NET WEIGHT：3. 5KGS/CARTON
   MEARSUREMENT：0. 0342CBM/CARTON
4. FREIGHT CHARGE：USD320. 00
5. 自制标准唛头

资料3：商业发票

COMMERCIAL INVOICE

Original

To：

Invoice No.：
Date：
L/C No.：
Contract No.：

From： ______________________ **To** ______________________

Shipping Marks	Quantities & Description	Unit Price	Amount

资料4：提单

<table>
<tr><td colspan="4"></td><td rowspan="7">B/L No.</td></tr>
<tr><td colspan="4">Shipper</td></tr>
<tr><td colspan="4">Consignee or Order</td></tr>
<tr><td colspan="4">Notify Party</td></tr>
<tr><td colspan="2">Pre - carriage by</td><td colspan="2">Port of Loading</td></tr>
<tr><td colspan="2">Vessel and Voy No.</td><td colspan="2">Port of Discharge</td></tr>
<tr><td colspan="2">Sailing on or about</td><td colspan="2">Final Destination</td></tr>
<tr><td>Marks & Nos.
Container No. & Seal No.</td><td colspan="2">Number and Kind of Packages
Description of Goods</td><td>Gross Weight</td><td>Measurement （cbm）</td></tr>
<tr><td colspan="5">TOTAL NUMBER OF CONTAINERS</td></tr>
<tr><td>Freight and Charges</td><td>No. of Original B （s） /L</td><td colspan="3">Place and Date of Issue</td></tr>
<tr><td colspan="2"></td><td colspan="3">Signed for the Carrier</td></tr>
</table>

资料5：汇票

No. ____________ Qingdao, ____________

EXCHANGE FOR

At sight of this First of EXCHANGE（SECOND OF THE SAME TENOR AND DATE UNPAID） pay to the order of ____________

the sum of

Drawn under ____________

____

To ____________

____

【制单练习三】

根据所给资料，分别填制商业发票、装箱单、提单和汇票。

资料1：信用证

FROM：HONG LEONG BANK BERHAD KUALA LUMPUR
TO： BANK OF CHINA LTD.，SHANDONG BRANCH
L/C NO.LCCG042201
DATE：AUG. 21 2013
EXPIRY DATE AND PLACE：SEP. 30，2013—CHINA
APPLICANT：
THIAM HUNG TRADING CO.
NO.41 LOTUS ROAD，SIBU SARAWAK
BENEFICIARY：
QINGDAO TRADING CO.
68 ZHONGSHAN ROAD QINGDAO CHINA
AMOUNT：USD13500.00（U. S. DOLLARSTHIRTEEN THOUSANDFIVE HUNDRED）
AVAILABLE WITH ANY BANK BY NEGOTIATION
DRAFTS： AT 90 DAYS AFTER B/L DATE FOR FULL INVOICE VALUE
DRAWEE： ISSUING BANK
PARTIAL SHIPMENTS： ALLOWED
TRANSHIPMENT： PROHIBITED
SHIPMENT FROM ANY CHINESE PORT TO SIBU SARAWAK AT LATEST SEP. 15，2013

DESCRIPTION OF GOODS:

PAPER PRODUCT

QUANTITY	DESCRIPTION	UNIT PRICE PER M/T	PACKING/CTN NET/GROSS
5 MTS	PAPER DUST	USD420.00	2X 5KGS/12KGS
0.80MTS	PAPER BOARD	USD5100	1X 10KGS /12KGS
1.20MTS	PAPER BAG	USD6000	2.5X 4KGS /12KGS

PACKING IN 10KGS NET WEIGHT 12KGS GROSS WEIGHT PER PACKAGE

CIF SIBU MALAYSIA

AS PER CONTRACT NO. SD201025 DATE JUNE 22, 2013

DOCUMENTS:

+ SIGNED COMMERCIAL INVOICE IN TRIPLICATE ORIGINALS CERTIFYING MERCHANDISE COUNTRY OF ORIGIN.
+ FULL SET ORIGINAL CLEAN ON BOARD BILLS OF LADING MADE OUT TO ORDER OF ISSUING BANK AND OOCL CONTAINER LINERS AS CARRIER MARKED FREIGHT PREPAID AND NOTIFY APPLICANT.
+ PACKING LIST IN TRIPLICATE.

SPECIAL CONDITIONS:

+ DOCUMENTS TO EVIDENCE THE SHIPPING MARKS: THT/SD200725/SIBU/1 - UP
+ THIS CREDIT NO. WHICH MUST BE GIVEN ON ALL OTHER DOCUMENTS.
+ THE B/L SHOWING ARE LINER B/L.
+ THE GOODS HAVE SHIPPED IN CONTAINER APPEAR IN B/L SHOWING CONTAINER NO. AND SEAL NO.
+ INVOICE TO SHOW A DEDUCTION OF 2% BEING COMMISSION TO OPENER.
+ BILL OF LADING MUST SHOW NAME ADDRESS AND TELEPHONE NUMBER OF LOCAL SHIPPING AGENT AT PORT OF DESTINATION.
+ USANCE DRAFT DRAWN UNDER THIS LETTER OF CREDIT SHOULD BE NEGOTIATED ON A SIGHT BASIS.
+ REIMBURSEMENT BY TELECOMMUNICATION IS PROHIBITED

资料2:

1. INVOICE NO. GHA0215
2. B/L NO. OOCL5821645

   B/L DATE: SEP. 12 2013

   VESSEL NAME: OOCL CERMANY V.015

   CONTAINER NO.: OOCL521521

   SEAL NO. 652525
3. MEASUREMENTS OF PACKING: 0.0572CBM/CTN

4. SHIPPING AGENT AT SIBU：CHEUNG OTOK BV CO. MALAYSIA TEL：94－25－0765

资料3：商业发票

COMMERCIAL INVOICE

Original

To：

Invoice No.：

Date：

L/C No.：

Contract No.：

From： ______________________ **To** ______________________

Shipping Marks	Quantities & Description	Unit Price	Amount

资料4：装箱单

PACKING LIST

Original

To：

No.

Date：

L/C No.：

CONTRACT：

FROM： ______________________ **TO** ______________________

Shipping Marks	NO. & Kind of Pkgs：Description of the Goods	Net Weight	Gross Weight	Measurement

资料5：提单

<table>
<tr><td colspan="2"></td><td rowspan="7">B/L No.</td></tr>
<tr><td colspan="2">Shipper</td></tr>
<tr><td colspan="2">Consignee or Order</td></tr>
<tr><td colspan="2">Notify Party</td></tr>
<tr><td>Pre – carriage by</td><td>Port of Loading</td></tr>
<tr><td>Vessel and Voy No.</td><td>Port of Discharge</td></tr>
<tr><td>Sailing on or about</td><td>Final Destination</td></tr>
</table>

<table>
<tr><td>Marks & Nos.</td><td>Number and Kind of Packages</td><td>Gross Weight</td><td>Measurement （cbm）</td></tr>
<tr><td>Container No. & Seal No.</td><td>Description of Goods</td><td></td><td></td></tr>
<tr><td colspan="4">TOTAL NUMBER OF CONTAINERS</td></tr>
</table>

<table>
<tr><td>Freight and Charges</td><td>No. of Original B（s）/L</td><td>Place and Date of Issue</td></tr>
<tr><td colspan="2"></td><td>Signed for the Carrier</td></tr>
</table>

资料6：汇票

No. ____________________ Qingdao, ____________________

EXCHANGE FOR

At sight of this First of EXCHANGE (SECOND OF THE SAME TENOR AND DATE UNPAID) pay to the order of ____________________

the sum of

Drawn under ____

____

To ____________________

____

【制单练习四】

根据所给资料，分别填制商业发票、装箱单、提单和汇票。

资料1：信用证

FORM OF DOC. CREDIT	*40A: IRREVOCABLE
DOC. CREDIT NUMBER	*20: S-9007NU-30
DATE OF ISSUE	*31C: 2009-3-19
APPLICABLE RULES	*40E: UCP LATEST VERSION
EXPIRY	*31D: DATE APR. 30, 2009 PLACE IN CHINA
ISSUE BANK	*51A: HANG SENG BANK, TOKYO BRANCH
APPLICANT	*50: NISSON KAISHA LTD., CHUO-KU 1-4 TOKYO JAPAN
BENEFICIARY	*59: SHANDONG TRADING IMPORT CO. QINGDAO
AMOUNT:	*32B: CURRENCY USD AMOUNT 50000.00
AVAILABLE WITH/BY	*41D: ANY BANK IN CHINA BY DRAFT
DRAFTS AT	*42C: 45 DAYS AFTER B/L DATE
DRAWEE	*42A: HANG SENG BANK, TOKYO BRANCH, TOKYO JAPAN
PARTIAL SHIPMENTS	*43P: ALLOWED
TRANSHIPMENT	*43T: ALLOWED
PORT OF LOADING:	*44E: ANY PORT OF CHINA
PORT OF DISCHARGE	*44F: TOKYO JAPAN

LATEST DATE OF SHIP. *44C: APR. 15, 2009

DESCRIPT. OF GOODS *45A: 42MTS OF GROUNTNUT OIL

QUANTITY (MTS)	SIZE	@USD PER MT
15	GRADE I	1200.00
12	GRADE II	1150.00
15	GRADE III	1100.00

ALL THE GOODS PACKING 5KGS X 6 BOTTLES IN A PACKAGE

AS PER CONTRACT NO. NK9012 DATED FEB. 12, 2009 CFRTOKYO

DOCUMENTS REQUIRED *46A:

+COMMMERCIAL INVOICE IN ONE ORIGINAL AND TWO COPIES CERTIFIED TO BE TRUE AND CORRECT MENTIONING FULL NAME AND ADDRESS OF THE MANUFACTURERS

+FULL SET OF OCEAN BILLS OF LADINGISSUED TO THE ORDER OF ISSUE BANK MARKED FREIGHT PREPAID INDICATION: 1) ISSUE BANK AND APPLICANT AS NOTIFY PARTIES 2) NAME ADDRESS TELEPHONE AND FAX NUMBER OF THE CARRYING VESSEL'S AGENT AT THE PORT OF DESTINATION

+PACKING LIST IN TWO COPIES SHOWING EACH PACKAGE OF N. W/G. W. /MEAS

ADDITIONAL COND. *47A:

+THE DRAFT DRAWN AT 80 PERCENT OF INVOICE VALUE FOR THE HANG SENG BANK, TOKYO BRANCH

+ALL THE AMOUNT AND QUANLITY ALLOWED 10% MORE AR LESS.

+SHOWING CARRIER: CHINA SHIPPING GROUP CO. SHIPPED IN 40 HR CONTAINERS.

+SHIPPING MARK: GRPO/NK9012/PNMA/1-UP APPEAR IN ALL SHIPPING DOCUMENTS.

+REIMBURSEMENT BY T/T IS PROHIBITED

+SUBJECT U. C. P. 2007 ICC PUBLICATION 600

资料2:

INVOICE NO. GK981

VESSEL NAME: COSCO OSAKA V. 32E

B/L NO. COOS4803

CONTAINER NO. TURL583332

SEAL NO. 229862

PER PACKAGE: MEA. 0.028 N. W. 30KGS G. W. 32KGS

MANUFACTURER: QINGDAO FOODS FACTORY, 35 LIAONING ROAD QINGDAO CHINA

VESSEL'S AGENT AT THE PORT OF DESTINATION: YANGMING SHIPPING CO., 25 CHOME TOKYO TEL: 31-88999 FAX: 31-88990

资料3：商业发票

COMMERCIAL INVOICE

Original

To:

Invoice No. :

Date:

L/C No. :

Contract No. :

From: ______________________ To ______________________

Shipping Marks	Quantities & Description	Unit Price	Amount

资料4：装箱单

PACKING LIST

Original

To:

No.

Date:

L/C No. :

CONTRACT:

FROM: ______________________ TO ______________________

Shipping Marks	NO. & Kind of Pkgs: Description of the Goods	Net Weight	Gross Weight	Measurement

资料5：提单

<table>
<tr><td colspan="5"></td><td rowspan="7">B/L No.</td></tr>
<tr><td colspan="5">Shipper</td></tr>
<tr><td colspan="5">Consignee or Order</td></tr>
<tr><td colspan="5">Notify Party</td></tr>
<tr><td colspan="2">Pre – carriage by</td><td colspan="3">Port of Loading</td></tr>
<tr><td colspan="2">Vessel and Voy No.</td><td colspan="3">Port of Discharge</td></tr>
<tr><td colspan="2">Sailing on or about</td><td colspan="3">Final Destination</td></tr>
<tr><td>Marks & Nos.
Container No. & Seal No.</td><td colspan="2">Number and Kind of Packages
Description of Goods</td><td colspan="2">Gross Weight</td><td>Measurement (cbm)</td></tr>
<tr><td colspan="6">TOTAL NUMBER OF CONTAINERS</td></tr>
<tr><td>Freight and Charges</td><td colspan="2">No. of Original B (s) /L</td><td colspan="3">Place and Date of Issue</td></tr>
<tr><td colspan="3"></td><td colspan="3">Signed for the Carrier</td></tr>
</table>

资料6：汇票

No. ______	Qingdao, ______
EXCHANGE FOR	
At sight of this First of EXCHANGE (SECOND OF THE SAME TENOR AND DATE UNPAID) pay to the order of ______	
the sum of	
Drawn under ______	
To ______	

【制单练习五】

根据所给资料，分别填制商业发票、装箱单、提单、汇票和普惠制原产地证。

资料1：信用证

FORM OF DOC. CREDIT: IRREVOCABLE
DOC. CREDIT NUMBER: 0162CDI11007191
DATE OF ISSUE: 131103
EXPRIRY: DATE 140104 PLACE AT YOUR COUNTERS
ADVISING BANK: BANK OF CHINA, WEIHAI BRANCH
ISSUING BANK: BANK OF CEDZAL
APPLICANT: . GLOSERI LTD., CO.
71-192-KINGDOM STREET, MARSEILLE FRANCE
BENEFICIARY: HONGRUNTYRE IMP. & EXP. CO., LTD.
NO. 45 NORTH HAIBIN ROAD, WEIHAI, CHINA
AMOUNT: CURRENCY USD AMOUNT USD130000.00
AVAILABLE WITH ANY BANK BY PAYMENT
PAYMENT: AT SIGHT FOR 98% OF INVOICE VALUE DRAWN ON OURSELVES
PARTIAL SHIPMENTS NOT ALLOWED
TRANSHIPMENTS ALLOWED UNDER DIRECT B/L
LOADING IN CHARGE: QINGDAO PORT IN CHINA
FOR TRANSPORT TO: MARSEILLE FRANCE
LATEST SHIP DATE: 131214

DESCRIPTION OF GOODS：
1800 PIECES（PLUS/LESS 05/05）PNEUS NEUFS DE MARQUE GOODFRIEND
#T6731 800 PIECES @ US $ 57. 00
#6750 600PIECES @ US $ 62. 00
#6785 400PIECES @ US $ 78. 00
PACKED IN WOODEN CASES EACH OF 20PIECES/24KGS N. W /25KGS G. W.
AS PER PERFORMA INVOICE NR：HR2013028 143 DD28. 10. 2013
SALES TERMS：FOB QINGDAO PORT
DOCUMENTS REQUIRED：

1. 3/3 ORIGINALS CLEAN ON BAORD OCEAN BILLS OF LADING （COPY NOT NEGOTIABLE）MADE OUT TO ORDER OF SHIPPER AND NOTIFY APPLICANT AND MARKED FREIGHT PAYABLE AT DESTINATION AND ALSO QUOTING SHIPPED IN 40' CONTAINER.
2. 07 ORIGINALS SIGNED AND DATED COMMERCIAL INVOICE CERTIFYING THAT GOODS STRICTLY CONFORM WITH PROFORMA INVOICE NO：HR2013028 143 DD28. 10. 2013 AND CERTIFYING COUNTRY OF ORIGIN.
3. ORIGINAL CERTIFICATE OF ORIGIN SIGNED AND STAMPED BY CHAMBER OF COMMERCE.
4. ORIGINAL CONFORMITY CERTIFICATE ESTABLISHED BY THE MANUFACTURER
5. 05 ORIGINAL PACKING LISTS
6. ORIGINAL EXISTENCE CERTIFICATE ESTABLISHED BY THE MANUFACTURER AND CERTIFIED BY CHAMBER OF COMMERCE.
7. 02 PHOTOS SHOWING THE ADHESIVE STICKERS ON THE TYRES BEFORE SHIPMENT.

ADDITIONAL COND.

1. INSUTANCE COVERED BY APPLICANT
2. NUMBER OF CREDIT AND NIF NUMBER（000625006694319）MUST BE QUOTED.
3. INVOICE TO SHOW THE MANUFACTURER：LANGHUA FACTORY，284 -7 ZHENGYANGROAD，QINGDAO CHINA，TEL：0532 -89132627
4. DETAILS OF CHARGES：
   ALL BANK CHARGES OUTSIDE ALGERIA ARE FOR ACCOUNT OF BENEFICIARY.

资料 2：

INVOICE NO.：HM125
S/C NO：LTA 5288
VESSEL NAME：S. S. HUMBER V. 066
B/L NO. COSCO1825
CONTAINER NO. DF92301

SEAL NO. 112656
MEASUREMENT OF PACKING：75CM X 125CM X220CM
FORM A NO. K133701100895621

资料3：商业发票

COMMERCIAL INVOICE

Original

To：

Invoice No.：
Date：
L/C No.：
Contract No.：

From： ____________________ **To** ____________________

Shipping Marks	Quantities & Desc Pription	Unit Price	Amount

资料4：装箱单

PACKING LIST

Original

To：

No.
Date：
L/C No.：
CONTRACT：

FROM： ____________________ **TO** ____________________

Shipping Marks	NO. & Kind of Pkgs：Description of the Goods	Net Weight	Gross Weight	Measurement

资料5：提单

<table>
<tr><td colspan="2"></td><td rowspan="7">B/L No.</td></tr>
<tr><td colspan="2">Shipper</td></tr>
<tr><td colspan="2">Consignee or Order</td></tr>
<tr><td colspan="2">Notify Party</td></tr>
<tr><td>Pre - carriage by</td><td>Port of Loading</td></tr>
<tr><td>Vessel and Voy No.</td><td>Port of Discharge</td></tr>
<tr><td>Sailing on or about</td><td>Final Destination</td></tr>
</table>

<table>
<tr><td>Marks & Nos.
Container No. & Seal No.</td><td>Number and Kind of Packages
Description of Goods</td><td>Gross Weight</td><td>Measurement （cbm）</td></tr>
<tr><td></td><td></td><td></td><td></td></tr>
<tr><td colspan="4">TOTAL NUMBER OF CONTAINERS</td></tr>
</table>

<table>
<tr><td>Freight and Charges</td><td>No. of Original B （s） /L</td><td>Place and Date of Issue</td></tr>
<tr><td colspan="2"></td><td>Signed for the Carrier</td></tr>
</table>

资料6：汇票

No. ________ Qingdao, ________

EXCHANGE FOR

At **sight of this First of EXCHANGE (SECOND OF THE SAME TENOR AND DATE UNPAID)** **pay to the order of** ________

the sum of

Drawn under ________

____

To ________

____

资料7：普惠制原产地证

<table>
<tr><td colspan="3">1. Goods Consigned from (Exporter's business name, address, country)</td><td colspan="3" rowspan="2">Reference No.
CENERALIZES SYSTEM OF PREFERENCES
CERTIFICATE OF ORIGIN
(Combined declaration and certificate)
FORM A
issued in

See Notes Overleaf</td></tr>
<tr><td colspan="3">2. Goods Consigned to (Consignee's name, address, country)</td></tr>
<tr><td colspan="3">3. Means of Transport and Route (as far as known)</td><td colspan="3">4. For Official Use</td></tr>
<tr><td>5. Item Number</td><td>6. Marks and Numbers of Packages</td><td>7. Number and Kind of Packages: Description of Goods</td><td>8. Origin Criterion (see Notes Overleaf)</td><td>9. Gross Weight or Other Quantity</td><td>10. Number and Date of Invoices</td></tr>
<tr><td colspan="3">12. Certification
It is hereby certified that the declaration by the exporter is correct.</td><td colspan="3">11. Declaration by the Exporter
The undersigned hereby declares that the above details and statements are correct; that all the goods were produced in

and that they comply with origin requirements specified for those goods in the Generalized System of Preferences for goods exported to

--</td></tr>
<tr><td colspan="3">Place and date, signature and stamp of certifying authority</td><td colspan="3">Place and date, signature and authorized signatory</td></tr>
</table>

任务二 综合审单练习

【审单练习一】

根据合同审核信用证，找到不符之处并加以改正。

资料1：合同

大连泰山箱包有限公司

DALIAN TAISHAN SUITCASE & BAG CO. , LTD.

66 ZHONGSHAN ROAD DALIAN, CHINA

售货确认书

SALES CONFIRMATION

Tel：0086 -0411 -84524789　　编号：No. TSSC0801005

Fax：0086 -0411 -84524799　　日期：Date MAY 18，2013

TO Messrs：

ORTAI CO. , LTD.

30 EAST 40 TH STREET, NEW YORK, US

TEL：001 -212 - 992 -9788

FAX：001 -212 - 992 -9789

谨启者：兹确认授予你方下列货品，其成交条款如下：

Dear Sirs：We hereby confirm having sold to you the following goods on the terms and conditions as specified below：

（1）货物名称及规格 Name of Commodity and Specification	（2）数量 Quantity	（3）单价 Unit Price	（4）总价 Amount
TAISHAN TROLLEY CASES		CIF NEW YORK	
（1）RED －TS503214	1104PCS	USD6. 50/PC	USD7176. 00
（2）BLACK －TS503215	1149PCS	USD6. 00/PC	USD6894. 00
（3）BLUE －TS503216	1440PCS	USD5. 80/PC	USD8352. 00
TOTAL：	3693PCS		USD22422. 00

（5）装运期限：Time of Shipment：LATEST DATE OF SHIPMENT OCT. 2，2013

（6）装运港：Port of Loading：DALIAN

（7）目的港：Port of Destination：NEW YORK

（8）分批装运：Partial Shipment：NOT ALLOWED

（9）转船：Transshipment：ALLOWED

（10）付款条件：Terms of Payment：IRREVOCABLE L/C AT SIGHT

（11）运输标志：Shipping Marks：ORTAI/TSI0601005/NEW YORK/C/NO. 1 - 1231

（12）保险：Insurance：The Seller should cover insurance for 110% of the total invoice value against ALL RISKS as per Ocean Marine Cargo Clauses of PICC dated 1/1/1981.

（13）仲裁

Arbitration：All disputes arising from the execution of, or in connection with this Sales Confirmation, shall be settled amicably through friendly negotiation. In case no settlement can be reached through negotiation, the case shall then be submitted to China International Economic and Trade Arbitration Commission, Shanghai Commission for arbitration in accordance with Rules of Arbitration of China International Economic and Trade Arbitration Commission. The award made by the Commission should be accepted as final and binding upon both parties.

（14）REMARKS：买方须于 2013 年 6 月 1 日前开出本批交易的信用证（或通知售方进口许可证号码）。否则，售方有权不经过通知取消本确认书，或向买方提出索赔。

The Buyer shall establish the covering Letter of Credit (or notify the Import License Number) before JUN. 1, 2013 , falling which the Seller reserves the right to rescind without further notice, or to accept whole or any part of this Sales Confirmation non—fulfilled by the Buyer, or, to lodge claim for direct losses sustained, if any.

凡以 CIF 条件成交的业务，保额为发票价的 110% ，投保险别以售货确认书中所开列的为限，买方如果要求增加保额或保险范围，应于装船前经卖方同意，因此而增加的保险费由买方负责。

For transaction conclude on CIF basis, it is understood that the insurance amount will be for 110% of the invoice value against the risks specified in Sales Confirmation. If additional insurance amount or coverage is required, the buyer must have consent of the Seller before Shipment, and the additional premium is to be borne by the Buyer.

由于发生人力不可抗拒的原因，致使本合约不能履行，部分或全部商品延误交货，卖方概不负责。本合同所指的不可抗力系指不可干预、不能避免且不能克服的客观情况。

The Seller shall not be held liable for failure of delay in delivery of the entire lot or a portion of the goods under this Sales Confirmation in consequence of any Force Majeure incidents.

买方在开给卖方的信用证上请填注本确认书号码。

The Buyer is requested always to quote THE NUMBER OF THIS SALES CONFIRMATION in the Letter of Credit to be opened in favour of the Seller.

买方收到本售货确认书后请立即签回一份，如买方对本确认书有异议，应于收到后五天内提出，否则认为买方已同意接受本确认书所规定的各项条款。

The buyer is requested to sign and return one copy of the Sales Confirmation immediately after the receipt of same, Objection, if any, should be raised by the Buyer within five days after the receipt of this Sales Confirmation, in the absence of which it is understood that the Buyer has accepted the terms and condition of the Sales Confirmation.

买方	卖方
THE BUYER	THE SELLER
PETER SMITH	李华
ORTAI CO., LTD.	DALIAN TAISHAN SUITCASE & BAG CO., LTD.

资料2：信用证

27：SEQUENCE OF TOTAL 1/1

40A：FORM OF DOCUMENTARY CREDIT IRREVOCABLE

20：DOCUMENTARY CREDIT NUMBER N5632405TH11808

31C：DATE OF ISSUE 130522

31D：DATE AND PLACE OF EXPIRY 131001 CHINA

51D：APPLICANT BANK
CITY NATIONAL BANK
133MORNINGSIDE AVE NEW YORK, NY 10027 TEL：001 -212 -865 -4763

50：APPLICANT
ORTAI CO., LTD.
30 EAST 40THSTREET, NEW YORK, US
TEL：001 -212 - 992 -9788
FAX：001 -212 - 992 -9789

59：BENEFICIARY
DALIAN TAISHAN SUITCASE & BAG CO., LTD.
66 ZHONGSHAN ROAD, DALIAN, CHINA
TEL：0086 -0411 -84524789

32B：CURRENCY CODE AMOUNT USD 22422.00

41D：AVAILABLE WITH/BY ADVISING BANK BY NEGOTIATION

42C：DRAFTS AT 30 DAYS SIGHT

42D：DRAWEE ISSUING BANK

43P：PARTIAL SHIPMENTS NOT ALLOWED

43T：TRANSHIPMENTNOT ALLOWED

44E：PORT OF LOADING： DALIAN, CHINA

44F：PORT OF DISCHARGE NEW YORK, U.S.A

44C：LATEST DATE OF SHIPMENT 131002

45A：DESCRIPTION OF GOODS AND/OR SERVICES

"TAISHAN" TROLLEY CASES

ART. NO. QUANTITY UNIT PRICE

RED－TS503214 1104PCS USD6. 50 /PC
BLUE－TS503216 1149PCS USD6. 00 /PC
BLACK－TS503215 1440PCS USD5. 80/PC

CIF NEWYORK
AS PER S/C NO. TKJD2647185
PACKING：1 PC IN 1 PE BAG；3PCS/CTN
46A：DOCUMENTS REQUIRED
+MANUALLY SIGNED COMMERCIAL INVOICE IN 2 COPYES INDICATING L/C NO. AND CONTRACT NO. CERTIFYING THE CONTENTS IN THIS INVOICE ARE TRUE AND CORRECT.
+FULL SET OF ORIGINAL CLEAN ON BOARD MARINE BILLS OF LADING MADE OUT TO ORDER, ENDORSED IN BANK MARKED FREIGHT PREPAID AND NOYIFY APPLICANT
+PACKING LIST IN 2 COPYES ISSUED BY THE BENEFICIARY
+ORIGINAL GSP FORM A CERTIFICATE OF ORIGIN ON OFFICIAL FORM ISSUED BY A TRADE AUTHORITY OR GOVERNMENT BODY
+INSURANCE POLICIES OR CERTIFICATES IN DUPLICATE, ENDORSED IN BLANK FOR 120 PERCENT OF INVOICE VALUE COVERING ICC CLAUSES (A) .
+MANUFACTURER'S QUALITY CERTIFICATE CERTIFYING THE COMMODITY IS IN GOOD ORDER.
+BENEFICIARY'S CERTIFICATE CERTIFYING THAT ONE SET OF COPIES OF SHIPPING DOCUMENTS HAS BEEN SENT TO APPLICANT WHTHIN 5 DAYS AFTER SHIPMENT.
47A：ADDITIONAL CONDITIONS
+UNLESS OTHERWISE EXPRESSLY STATED, ALL DOCUMENTS MUST BE IN ENGLISH.
57D：ADVISE THROUGH BANK：BANK OF CHINA DALIAN BRANCH

信用证不符之处及改正填写在下表中。

序号	信用证不符之处	应改为
1		
2		
3		
4		
5		

【审单练习二】

根据所给资料审核发票、装箱单，找到不符之处并加以改正。

资料1：信用证

DEAR SIRS,

IN ACCORDANCE WITH THE TERMS OF ARTICLE 7（A）OF UCP 600 WE ADVISE HAVING RECEIVED THE FOLLOWING TELETRANSMISSION

FROM：SOUTHEAST BANK LIMITED，PRINCIPAL BRANCH

40A	FORM OF DC：	IRREVOCABLE
20	CREDIT NO：	1335－06－06－0207
31C	DATE OF ISSUE：	11 JUN 2014
31D	EXPIRY DATE AND PLACE：	25 JUL 2014　IN CHINA
50	APPLICANT：	NEPUTUNE GARMENTS LTD. HOUSE NO. 79，3RD FLOOR，BLOCK－H ZIA INT'L AIR PORT ROAD， DHAKA－1213，BANGLADESH
59	BENEFICIARY：	SUNSHINE TRADING CO. LTD. ROOMNO. 865，XIANGGANG ROAD#1， QINGDAO，CHINA
32B	AMOUNT：	GBP56900. 00
41D	AVAILABLE WITH/BY：	ANY BANK IN CHINA BY NEGOTIATION
42C	DRAFTS AT：	120 DAYS SIGHT BY NEGOTIATION.
42D	DRAWEE：	SOUTHEAST BANK LIMITED PRINCIPAL BRANCH DHAKA－1000，BANGLADESH
43P	PARTIAL SHIPMENTS：	NOT ALLOWED
43T	TRANSHIPMENT：	ALLOWED
44A	LOADING/DISPATCH AT/FROM：	ANY SEA PORT OF CHINA
44B	FOR TRANSPORTATION TO：	CHITTAGONG，BANGLADESH.
44C	LATEST DATE OF SHIPMENT：	10 JUL 2014

45A　GOODS：

PRINTED FABRIC

SIZE	QUANTITY	PACKING	UNIT PRICE
DSN#1WHITE / BLUE：	30300YDS	101BALES	GBP1. 00/YD
DSN#2WHITE / RED：	17700YDS	59BALES	GBP1. 50/YD

TERMS OF DELIVERY：CIF CHITTAGONG

PACKING：300 YARDS PER BALES

AS PER S/C NO. QDBJ07115

SHIPPING MARKS：NPT/CHITTAGONG/NO. 1－UP

46A　DOCUMENTS REQUIRED：

01) SIGNED COMMERCIAL INVOICE IN OCTUPLICATE CERTIFYING MERCHANDISE COUNTRY OF ORIGIN

02) FULL SET OF CLEAN SHIPPED ON BOARD MARINE BILL OF LADING MADE OUT TO SHIPPER'S ORDER AND MARKED FREIGHT PREPAID AND NOTIFY APPLICANT AND ISSUING BANK.

47A ADDITIONAL CONDITIONS:

01) THIS L/C NUMBER AND L/C DATE MUST APPEAR ON ALL DOCUMENTS.

02) THE FOLLOWING MUST APPEAR ON THE INVOICES AND BILL OF LADING.

(I) H. S. CODE NO. 5209. 4200. 00

(II) LCA NO. 3180

(III) APPLICANT'S IRC NO. BA - 131610

(IV) EXPORT L/C NO. DCTST115056 DATED 06/06/2014

03) BENEFICIARY MUST CERTIFY ON THE INVOICE THAT THE QUOTED INVOICE PRICE IS NET AND DOES NOT INCLUDE ANY COMMISSION FOR ANY AGENT IN BANGLADESH.

资料 2：

1. INVOICE NO. I06/QD 000117　　DATED JUNE, 27, 2014
2. G. W: 5120KGS
   N. W: 5040KGS
   MEASUREMENT: 12.500CBM
3. B/L NO. COSU82591530 DATED 20140815
   VESSEL &VOY. NO: S. S URU BHUM V. 015
   CONTAINER NO. MT9504
   SEAL NO. 92874

资料 3：商业发票

COMMERCIAL INVOICE

ORIGINAL

To:	NEPUTUNE GARMENTS LTD.	**No.**	I06/QD 000117
	HOUSE NO. 79, 3RD FLOOR, BLOCK - H	**Date:**	JUN. 18, 2014
	ZIA INT'L AIR PORT ROAD,	**L/C No.:**	1335 - 06 - 06 - 0207
	DHAKA - 1213, BANGLADESH	**CONTRACT:**	QDBJ07115
FROM:	QINGDAO, CHINA	**TO**	CHITTAGONG, BANGLADESH

Shipping Marks	Quantities & Description	Unit Price	Amount

NPT	PRINTED FABRIC			CIF CHITTAGONG	
CHITTAGONG	SIZE	QUANTITY	PACKING		
NO. 1 – UP	DSN#1 WHITE/BLUE	30300YDS	101BALES	@ GBP1. 00/YD	GBP30300. 00
	DSN#2 WHITE/RED	17700YDS	59BALES	@ GBP1. 50/YD	GBP26550. 00
	TOTAL	48000YDS	160BALES		GBP56800. 00

PACKED IN 160BALES AND 300YARDS PER BALES

AS PER S/C NO. QDBJ07115

H. S. CODE NO. 5209. 4200. 00

LCS NO. 3180

APPLICANT'S IRC NO. BA – 131610

EXPORT L/C NO. DCTST115056 DATED 06/06/2014

WE HEREBY CERTIFY THAT THE QUOTED INVOICE PRICE IS NET AND DOES NOT INCLUDE ANY COMMISSION FOR ANY AGENT IN BANGLADESH

L/C NO.: 1335 – 06 – 06 – 0207　DATED JUN. 11, 2014

SUNSHINE TRADING CO. LTD.

TOM

资料4：装箱单

PACKING LIST

ORIGINAL

To: NEPUTUNE GARMENTS LTD.
HOUSE NO. 79, 3RD FLOOR, BLOCK – H
ZIA INT'L AIR PORT ROAD,
DHAKA – 1213, BANGLADESH

No. I06/QD 000117
Date: JUN. 18, 2014
L/C No.: 1335 – 06 – 06 – 0207
CONTRACT: QDBJ07115

FROM: QINGDAO, CHINA　**TO** CHITTAGONG, BANGLADESH

Shipping Marks	NO. & Kind of Pkgs: Description of the Goods	Net Weight	Gross Weight	Measurement

NPT	PRINTED FABRIC					
CHITTAGONG	SIZE	QUANTITY	PACKING	@31.50KGS/BALE	@32.00KGS/BALE	@0.078CBM/BALE
NO.1 - UP	DSN#1WHITE/BLUE	30300YDS	101BALES	3181.50KGS	3232.00KGS	7.891CBM
	DSN#2WHITE/RED	17700YDS	59BALES	1858.50KGS	1888.00KGS	4.609CBM
	TOTAL	48000YDS	160BALES	5040.00KGS	5120.00KGS	12.500CBM

PACKED IN 160BALES AND 300YARDS PER BALES

SUNSHINE TRADING CO. LTD.

TOM

单据不符之处及改正填写在下表中。

序号	单据不符之处	应改为
1		
2		
3		
4		
5		

【审单练习三】

根据所给资料审核提单，找到不符之处并加以改正。

资料1：信用证

ISSUING BANK: YOKOHAMA SHINKIN BANK, YOKOHAMA JAPAN
ADVISING BANK: BANK OF CHINA, SHANDONG BRANCH
L/C NO. 9723MH00163
DATE SEP. 12, 2012
EXPIRY DATE AND PLACE:
OCT. 31, 2012—CHINA
APPLICANT: INADA ASSOCIATES INTERNATIONAL CO.
YOKOHAMA CITY JAPAN
BENEFICIARY: QINGDAO HOPE IMP. AND EXP. CO.
82 YANAN ROAD QINGDAO CHINA
……
PARTIAL SHIPMENTS: ALLOWED
TRANSHIPMENT: PROHIBITED
SHIPMENT FROM ANY PORT IN CHINA TO YOKOHAMA JAPAN AT LATEST

OCT. 20 2012

DESCRIPTION OF GOODS:
GREEN BEAN VERMICELLI
450 CASES OF 25 -27CM AT USD15. 25 PER CASE
250 CASES OF 30 -32 CM AT USD17. 25 PER CASE
300 CASES OF 33 -35 CM AT USD18. 50 PER CASE
CIF YOKOHAMA
PACKED IN 20KGS NET /21KGS GROSS PER CASE
AS PER CONTRACT NO. HFJVS2012 -11

DOCUMENTS:
+SIGNED COMMERCIAL INVOICE IN TRIPLICATE CERTIFYING MERCHANDISE COUNTRY OF ORIGIN
+FULL SET ORIGINAL CLEAN ON BOARD BILLS OF LADING MADE OUT TO SHIPPER'S ORDER AND ENDORSED IN BLANK AND MARKED FRIEIGHT PREPAID AND NOTIFY APPLICANT AND ISSUING BANK

SPECIAL CONDITIONS:
+DOCUMENTS TO EVIDENCE THE SHIPPING MARKS: ISI/YOKOHAMA/1 -UP
+ALL DOCUMENTS MUST EVIDENCE THIS L/C NO.
+THE B/L SHOWING LINER B/L
+THE GOODS HAVE SHIPPED IN CONTAINER APPEAR IN B/L
+THE IMPORT REGISTRATION NO W -6389 APPEAR ON INVOICE
+BILL OF LADING MUST SHOW NAME ADDRESS AND TELEPHONE NUMBER OF LOCAL SHIPPING AGENT AT PORT OF DESTINATION

资料2:

1. B/L NO. SITT5463792
   B/L DATE: OCT. 19, 2012
2. VESSEL NAME: SITC YANT V. 021
   CONTAINER NO. COSU261825
   SEAL NO. 561774
3. MEASUREMENTSOF PACKING: 250MM X 400MM X 500MM
4. SHIPPING AGENT ATYOKOHAMA: MIT JAPAN SHIPPING CO.
   3 -19 -4 HONGO YOKOHAMA
   TEL: 332 -7299

资料3：提单

Shipper QINGDAO HOPE IMP. AND EXP. CO. 82 YANAN ROAD QINGDAO CHINA	**B/L No.** SITT5463792
Consignee or Order TO SHIPPER'S ORDER AND ENDORSED IN BLANK	
Notify Party INADA ASSOCIATES INTERNATIONAL CO. YOKOHAMA CITY JAPAN AND BANK OF CHINA, SHANDONG BRANCH	

Pre－carriage by	**Port of Loading** QINGDAO, CHINA	
Vessel and Voy No. SITC YANT V. 021	**Port of Discharge** YOKOHAMA, JAPAN	
Sailing on or about OCT. 20, 2012	**Final Destination**	

Marks & Nos. **Container No. & Seal No.**	**Number and Kind of Packages** **Description of Goods**	**Gross Weight**	**Measurement (cbm)**
ISI YOKOHAMA 1－1000	GREEN BEAN VERMICELLI 1000CASES	21000. 00KGS	50. 000CBM
CONTAINER NO. COSU261825 SEAL NO. 561774	L/C NO. 9723MH00163 THE GOODS HAVE SHIPPED IN CONTAINER.		ON BOARD

TOTAL NUMBER OF CONTAINERS OR PACKAGES (IN WORDS)	SAY ONE THOUSAND CASES ONLY

Freight and Charges FREIGHT PREPAID	**No. of Original B (s) /L** THREE	**Place and Date of Issue** QINGDAO CHINA OCT. 19, 2010
		Signed for the Carrier ***

提单不符之处及改正填写在下表中。

序号	提单不符之处	应改为
1		
2		
3		
4		
5		

【审单练习四】

根据所给资料审核下列汇票，找到不符之处并加以改正。

资料1：商业发票

COMMERCIAL INVOICE

ORIGINAL

To: TOKAI SUISAN KAISHA LTD.,
6 - CHOME CHUO - KU TOKYO JAPAN

No. TTF0751
Date: AUG. 28, 2013
L/C No.: S - 043 - 2007096
CONTRACT: S18007

FROM: QINCDAO, CHINA **TO** TOKYO, JAPAN

Shipping Marks		**Quantities & Description**			**Unit Price**	**Amount**
TST		DRIED SEA TANGLE			CIF TOKYO	
TOKYO	SIZE	QUANTITY	PACKING/	PACKAGE		
NO. 1 - 500	WAA	2MTS	4 * 5KGS	100PKGS	USD6800.00/MT	USD13600.00
	WBB	3MTS	2 * 10KGS	150PKGS	USD7900.00/MT	USD23700.00
	WCC	5MTS	1 * 20KGS	250PKGS	USD8200.00/MT	USD41000.00
						USD78300.00
					LESS COMMISSION OF 2%	USD1566.00
		TOTAL	10MTS	500PKGS		USD76734.00

PACKED IN 500PKGS AND 20KGS NET WEIGHT 22KGS GROSS WEIGHT PER PACKAGE
AS PER CONTRACT NO. S18007
WE HEREBY CERTIFY THAT THE GOODS ARE OF CHINA ORIGIN

SHANDONG TRADING CO.
ERIC

资料2：信用证条款

ISSUING BANK: BANK OF TOKYO－MITSUBISHI UFJ LTD. , TOKYO JAPAN
ADVISING BANK: BANK OF CHINA, SHANDONG BRANCH
L/C NO. PGH000348DC
DATE: AUG. 21 2013
EXPIRY DATE AND PLACE: SEP. 30, 2013—CHINA
APPLICANT:
SOO HUP SENG TRADING CO. ,
165 DOWING STREET TOKYO
BENEFICIARY:
SHANDONG TRADING CO.
50 ZHONGSHAN ROAD QINGDAO CHINA
AVAILABLE WITH ADVISING BANK BY NEGOTIATION
DRAFTS: AT 30 DAYS AFTER SIGHT FOR 80% INVOICE VALUE OF GOODS
DRAWN ON OURSELVES

资料3：汇票

No. S18007 **Qingdao**, AUG. 20, 2013
EXCHANGE FOR USD76734. 00
At 30 DAYS sight of this First of EXCHANGE (SECOND OF THE SAME TENOR AND DATE UNPAID) pay to the order of BANK OF CHINA, SHANDONG BRANCH
the sum of SAY U. S. DOLLARS SEVENTY SIX THOUSAND SEVEN HUNDRED AND THIRTY－FOUR ONLY
Drawn under BANK OF TOKYO－MITSUBISHI UFJ LTD. , TOKYO JAPAN
L/C NO. : S－043－2007096 DATED AUG. 21, 2013

To BANK OF TOKYO－MITSUBISHI UFJ LTD
TOKYO JAPAN

SHANDONG TRADING CO.
ERIC

汇票不符之处及改正填写在下表中。

序号	汇票不符之处	应改为
1		
2		
3		
4		
5		

【审单练习五】

根据所给资料审核发票、装箱单、提单、汇票，找到不符之处并加以改正。

资料1：信用证

BASIC HEADER	F01 BKCHCNBJA940 0588 550628
APPLICATION HEADER	HSBC BANK CANADA
SEQUENCE OF TOTAL	27：1/1
FORM OF DOC. CREDIT	40A：IRREVOCABLE
DOC. CREDIT NUMBER	20：KL21909
DATE OF ISSUE	31C：MAR. 25. 2012
DATE/PLACE EXP.	31D：120530 CHINA
APPLICANT	50：PARMIX SPORTSWEAR INC 591EAST LAMEN STREET, TORONTO, CANADA
BENEFICIARY	59：NANJING ZHENHUA TEXTLE GARMENT CO. , LTD. NANJING CHINA
AMOUNT	32B：USD 10000. 00
AVAILABLE WITH/BY	41D：ANY BANK BY NEGOTIATIONG
DRAFTST AT···	42C：AT SIGHT 90 PCT OF INVOICE
DRAWEE	42A：US
RARTIAL SHIPMETS	43P：ALLOWED
TRANSSHIPMENT	43T：ALLOWED
LOADING ON BRD	44A：PORT OF DALLAN
FOR TRANSPORTATION TO	44B：TORONTO
GOODS DESCRIPT	45A：

50PCT NYLON/50PCT RAYON, WOVEN LADIES 2PCE SUIT - JACKET
STYLE 167C/168C TTL500SETS AT USD10/SET
STYLE 585A/169C TTL500SETS AT USD8/SET
STYLE 167C/168C PACKING 5KGS * 5SETS IN A PACKAGE PLUS 1 KGS G. W.

STYLE 585A/169C PACKING 4KGS * 10SETS IN A PACKAGE PLUS 2KGS G. W.
LATEST SHIPMENT DATE: APR. 27. 2012
TRADE TERMS: CFR CANADA PORT.
ALL OTHER DETAILS ARE AS PER S/C NO . IMMZ - 10 - 1 DATED 11/11/2012
DOCUMENTS REQUIRED 46A:
+ COMMERCIAL INVOICES IN QUADRUPLICATE SIGNED BY BENEFICAIARY'S REPRESENTATIVE SHOWING FOB VALUE SEPERATELY QUOTING INDENT NO. 9545
+ FULL SET OF ORIGINAL MARINE BILLS OF LADING CLEAN ON BOARD PLUS 2 NON NEGOTIABLE COPIES MADE OUT OR ENDORSED TO ORDER OF BNP PARIBAS (CANADA) MARKED FREIGHT PREPAID AND NOTIFY APPLICANT'S FULL NAME AND ADDRESS.
+ PACKING LIST ISSUED BY SELLER: 3 ORIGINALS AND 3 ORIGINAL COPIES STATING GROSS WEIGHT, NET WEIGHT, QUANTITY AND MEASUREMENT AND CERTIFYING THAT ALL EXPORT CARTONS MARKED WITH APPLICANT SHIPPPING MARK AND SIDE MARK MUST CONFORM WITH APPLICANT PURCHASE ORDER ACCORDINGLY
ADDITIONL CONDITIONS 47A;
+ IF DOCUMENTS PRESENTED ARE FOUND BY US NOT TO BE UNFULL COMEPLIANCE WITH CREDIT TEARMS WE WILL ASSESS A CHARGE OF USD55. 00 PER SET OF DOCUMENTS.
+ ALL CHARGES IF ANY RELATED TO SETTLEMENTS ARE FOR ACCOUNT OF BENEFICIARY.
+ 3PCS MORE OR LESS IN AMOUNT AND QUANTITY IS ALLOWED
+ ALL CERTIFICATES /LETTERS/ STATEMENTS MUST BE SIGNED AND DATED
+ P/L CERTIFYING THAT THE CONTENTS AND QUANTITY ARE MARKED ON THE OUTSIDE OF EACH CARTON.
+ SHIPMENT COVERED BY K LINE CO.
+ ORIGINAL INVOICE AND PACKING LIST CERTIFIED BY CHAMBER OF COMMERCE IN THE EXPORT TOWN WITH DATE

资料2:

INVOICE NO. LBE485 DATED MAR. 29, 2012
B/L NO. COOS4803
FREIGHT CHARGE: USD2500. 00
VESSEL NAME: COSCO OSAKA V. 32E
CONTAINER NO. TURL583332
SEAL NO. 229862
MEASUREMENTS OF PACKING: 150MMX230MMX450MM/PKG

资料3：商业发票

COMMERCIAL INVOICE

ORIGINAL

To: PARMIX SPORTSWEAR INC
591EAST LAMEN STREET,
TORONTO, CANADA

No. LBE485
Date: MAR. 29, 2012
L/C No.: KL21909
CONTRACT: IMMZ - 10 - 1

FROM: QINGDAO, CHINA　**TO** TORONTO, CANADA

Shipping Marks	Quantities & Description				Unit Price	Amount
P. S. I.	50PCT NYLON/50PCT RAYON,				CFR CANADA PORT	
IMMZ - 10 - 1	WOVEN LADIES 2PCE SUIT - JACKET					
TORONTO	STYLE	TTL	PACKAGE			
NO. 1 - 150	167C/168C	500SETS	100PKGS		@ USD10. 00/SET	USD5000. 00
	585A/169C	500SETS	50PKGS		@ USD8. 00/SET	USD4000. 00
	TOTAL	1000SETS	150PKGS			USD9000. 00

PACKED IN 150PKGS

STYLE 167C/168C PACKING 5KGS * 5SETS IN A PACKAGE PLUS 1 KGS G. W.

STYLE 585A/169C PACKING 4KGS * 10SETS IN A PACKAGE PLUS 2KGS G. W.

LATEST SHIPMENT DATE APR 27. 2012

ALL OTHER DETAILS ARE AS PER S/C NO. IMMZ - 10 - 1 DATED 11/11/2012

INDENT NO. 9545

DALIAN, CHINA
CHAMBER OF COMMERCE

NANJING ZHENHUA TEXTLE GARMENT CO. , LTD.
TOM

资料4：装箱单

PACKING LIST

ORIGINAL

To: PARMIX SPORTSWEAR INC
591EASTLAMEN STREET,
TORONTO, CANADA

No. LBE485
Date: MAR. 29, 2012
L/C No.: KL21909
CONTRACT: IMMZ - 10 - 1

FROM: QINGDAO, CHINA **TO** TORONTO, CANADA

Shipping Marks	NO. & Kind of pkgs: Description of the Goods			Net Weight	Gross Weight	Measurement
P. S. I.	50PCT NYLON/50PCT RAYON,					
IMMZ - 10 - 1	WOVEN LADIES 2PCE SUIT - JACKET					
TORONTO	STYLE	TTL	PACKAGE	@25. 00KGS/PKG	@26. 00KGS/PKG	@0. 015525CBM/PKG
NO. 1 - 150	167C/168C	500SETS	100PKGS	2500. 00KGS	2600. 00KGS	1. 5525CBM
				@40. 00KGS/PKG	@41. 00KGS/PKG	@0. 015525CBM/PKG
	585A/169C	500SETS	50PKGS	2000. 00KGS	2050. 00KGS	0. 77625CBM
	TOTAL	1000SETS	150PKGS	4500. 00KGS	4650. 00KGS	2. 329CBM

PACKED IN 150PKGS AND STYLE 167C/168C PACKING 5KGS * 5SETS

IN A PACKAGE PLUS 1 KGS G. W.

STYLE 585A/169C PACKING 4KGS * 10SETS IN A PACKAGE PLUS 2KGS G. W.

MEASUREMENTS OF PACKING: 150MM X 230MM X 450MM/PKG

WE HEREBY CERTIFY THAT ALL EXPORT CARTONS MARKED WITH

APPLICANT SHIPPING MARK AND SIDE MARK HAS BEEN CONFORMED

WITH APPLICANT PURCHASE ORDER ACCORDINGLY.

DALIAN, CHINA
CHAMBER OF COMMERCE

NANJING ZHENHUA TEXTLE GARMENT CO., LTD.
TOM

资料5：提单

B/L No.
COOS4803

Shipper
NANJING ZHENHUA TEXTLE GARMENT CO., LTD.
NANJING CHINA

Consignee or Order
TO ORDER OF SHIPPER

Notify Party
PARMIX SPORTSWEAR INC
591EAST LAMEN STREET, TORONTO, CANADA

Pre – carriage by	**Port of Loading** QINGDAO, CHINA
Vessel and Voy No. COSCO OSAKA V. 32E	**Port of Discharge** TORONTO, CANADA
Sailing on or about APR. 26, 2012	**Final Destination**

Marks & Nos. Container No. & Seal No.	Number and Kind of Packages Description of Goods	Gross Weight	Measurement (cbm)
P. S. I. IMMZ – 10 – 1 TORONTO NO. 1 – 150 CONTAINER NO. TURL583332 SEAL NO. 229862	50PCT NYLON/50PCT RAYON, WOVEN LADIES 2PCE SUIT – JACKET 150PKGS	4650. 00KGS	2. 329CBM ON BOARD

TOTAL NUMBER OF CONTAINERS OR PACKAGES (IN WORDS)　SAY ONE HUNDRED AND FIFTY PACKAGES ONLY

Freight and Charges FREIGHT PREPAID	**No. of Original B (s) /L** THREE	**Place and Date of Issue** DALIAN, CHINA APR. 26, 2012
		Signed for the Carrier ***

资料6：汇票

No. LBE485	**Qingdao**, APR. 28，2012
EXCHANGE FOR USD9000.00	
At **sight of this First of EXCHANGE（SECOND OF THE SAME TENOR AND DATE UNPAID）** **pay to the order of** BANK OF CHINA，NANJING BRANCH	
the sum of SAY U.S. DOLLARS NINE THOUSAND ONLY	
Drawn under HSBC BANK CANADA	
L/C NO.：KL21909 DATED MAR. 25，2012	
To US	
	NANJING ZHENHUA TEXTLE GARMENT CO.，LTD. TOM

单据不符之处及改正填写在下表中。

序号	单据不符之处	应改为
1		
2		
3		
4		
5		
6		
7		
8		
9		
10		

附录：

ICC跟单信用证统一惯例（UCP600）

国际商会
ICC跟单信用证统一惯例（UCP600）
（2006年国际商会修订，2007年7月1日生效）

第一条　UCP的适用范围

《跟单信用证统一惯例——2007年修订本，国际商会第600号出版物》（简称“UCP”）乃一套规则，适用于所有的其文本中明确表明受本惯例约束的跟单信用证（下称信用证）（在其可适用的范围内，包括备用信用证）。除非信用证明确修改或排除，本惯例各条文对信用证所有当事人均具有约束力。

第二条　定义

就本惯例而言：

通知行指应开证行的要求通知信用证的银行。

申请人指要求开立信用证的一方。

银行工作日指银行在其履行受本惯例约束的行为的地点通常开业的一天。

受益人指接受信用证并享受其利益的一方。

相符交单指与信用证条款、本惯例的相关适用条款以及国际标准银行实务一致的交单。

保兑指保兑行在开证行承诺之外做出的承付或议付相符交单的确定承诺。

保兑行指根据开证行的授权或要求对信用证加具保兑的银行。

信用证指一项不可撤销的安排，无论其名称或描述如何，该项安排构成开证行对相符交单予以承付的确定承诺。

承付指：

a. 如果信用证为即期付款信用证，则即期付款。

b. 如果信用证为延期付款信用证，则承诺延期付款并在承诺到期日付款。

c. 如果信用证为承兑信用证，则承兑受益人开出的汇票并在汇票到期日付款。

开证行指应申请人要求或者代表自己开出信用证的银行。

议付指指定银行在相符交单下，在其应获偿付的银行工作日当天或之前向受益人预付或者同意预付款项，从而购买汇票（其付款人为指定银行以外的其他银行）及/或单据的行为。

指定银行指信用证可在其处兑用的银行，如信用证可在任一银行兑用，则任何银行均为指定银行。

交单指向开证行或指定银行提交信用证项下单据的行为，或指按此方式提交的单据。

交单人指实施交单行为的受益人、银行或其他人。

第三条　解释

就本惯例而言：

如情形适用，单数词形包含复数含义，复数词形包含单数含义。

信用证是不可撤销的，即使未如此表明。

单据签字可用手签、摹样签字、穿孔签字、印戳、符号或任何其他机械或电子的证实方法为之。

诸如单据须履行法定手续、签证、证明等类似要求，可由单据上任何看似满足该要求的签字、标记、印戳或标签来满足。

一家银行在不同国家的分支机构被视为不同的银行。

用诸如“第一流的”、“著名的”、“合格的”、“独立的”、“正式的”、“有资格的”或“本地的”等词语描述单据的出单人时，允许除受益人之外的任何人出具该单据。

除非要求在单据中使用，否则诸如“迅速地”、“立刻地”或“尽快地”等词语将被不予理会。

“在或大概在（on or about）”或类似用语将被视为规定事件发生在指定日期的前后五个日历日之间，起讫日期计算在内。

“至（to）”、“直至（until/till）”、“从……开始（from）”及“在……之间（between）”等词用于确定发运日期时包含提及的日期，使用“在……之前（before）”及“在……之后（after）”时则不包含提及的日期。

“从……开始（from）”及“在……之后（after）”等词用于确定到期日时不包含提及的日期。

“前半月”及“后半月”分别指一个月的第一日到第十五日及第十六日到该月的最后一日，起讫日期计算在内。

一个月的“开始（beginning）”、“中间（middle）”及“末尾（end）”分别指第一到第十日、第十一日到第二十日及第二十一日到该月的最后一日，起讫日期计算在内。

第四条　信用证与合同

a. 就其性质而言，信用证与可能作为其开立基础的销售合同或其他合同是相互独立的交易，即使信用证中含有对此类合同的任何援引，银行也与该合同无关，且不受其约束。因此，银行关于承付、议付或履行信用证项下其他义务的承诺，不受申请人基于与开证行或与受益人之间的关系而产生的任何请求或抗辩的影响。

受益人在任何情况下不得利用银行之间或申请人与开证行之间的合同关系。

b. 开证行应劝阻申请人试图将基础合同、形式发票等文件作为信用证组成部分的做法。

第五条　单据与货物、服务或履约行为

银行处理的是单据，而不是单据可能涉及的货物、服务或履约行为。

第六条　兑用方式、截止日和交单地点

a. 信用证必须规定可在其处兑用的银行，或是否可在任一银行兑用。规定在指定银行兑用的信用证同时也可以在开证行兑用。

b. 信用证必须规定其是以即期付款、延期付款、承兑还是议付的方式兑用。

c. 信用证不得开成凭以申请人为付款人的汇票兑用。

d. i. 信用证必须定一个交单的截止日。规定的承付或议付的截止日将被视为交单的截止日。

ii. 可在其处兑用信用证的银行所在地即为交单地点。可在任一银行兑用的信用证其交单地点为任一银行所在地。除规定的交单地点外，开证行所在地也是交单地点。

e. 除非如第二十九条 a 款规定的情形，否则受益人或者代表受益人的交单应在截止日当天或之前完成。

第七条　开证行责任

a. 只要规定的单据提交给指定银行或开证行，并且构成相符交单，则开证行必须承付，如果信用证为以下情形之一：

i. 信用证规定由开证行即期付款、延期付款或承兑；

ii. 信用证规定由指定银行即期付款但其未付款；

iii. 信用证规定由指定银行延期付款但其未承诺延期付款，或虽已承诺延期付款，但未在到期日付款；

iv. 信用证规定由指定银行承兑，但其未承兑以其为付款人的汇票，或虽然承兑了汇票，但未在到期日付款。

v. 信用证规定由指定银行议付但其未议付。

b. 开证行自开立信用证之时起即不可撤销地承担承付责任。

c. 指定银行承付或议付相符交单并将单据转给开证行之后，开证行即承担偿付该指定银行的责任。对承兑或延期付款信用证下相符交单金额的偿付应在到期日办理，无论指定银行是否在到期日之前预付或购买了单据。开证行偿付指定银行的责任独立于开证行对受益人的责任。

第八条　保兑行责任

a. 只要规定的单据提交给保兑行，或提交给其他任何指定银行，并且构成相符交单，保兑行必须：

i. 承付，如果信用证为以下情形之一：

a）信用证规定由保兑行即期付款、延期付款或承兑；

b）信用证规定由另一指定银行延期付款，但其未付款；

c）信用证规定由另一指定银行延期付款，但其未承诺延期付款，或虽已承诺延期付款但未在到期日付款；

d）信用证规定由另一指定银行承兑，但其未承兑以其为付款人的汇票，或虽已承兑汇票未在到期日付款；

c）信用证规定由另一指定银行议付，但具未议付。

ii. 无追索权地议付，如果信用证规定由保兑行议付。

b. 保兑行自对信用证加具保兑之时起即不可撤销地承担承付或议付的责任。

c. 其他指定银行承付或议付相符交单并将单据转往保兑行之后，保兑行即承担偿付该指定银行的责任。对承兑或延期付款信用证下相符交单金额的偿付应在到期日办理，无论指定银行是否在到期日之前预付或购买了单据。保兑行偿付指定银行的责任独立于保兑行对受益人的责任。

d. 如果开证行授权或要求一银行对信用证加具保兑，而其并不准备照办，则其必须毫不延误地通知开证行，并可通知此信用证而不加保兑。

第九条 信用证及其修改的通知

a. 信用证及其任何修改可以经由通知行通知给受益人。非保兑行的通知行通知信用证及修改时不承担承付或议付的责任。

b. 通知行通知信用证或修改的行为表示其已确信信用证或修改的表面真实性，而且其通知准确地反映了其收到的信用证或修改的条款。

c. 通知行可以通过另一银行（“第二通知行”）向受益人通知信用证及修改。第二通知行通知信用证或修改的行为表明其已确信收到的通知的表面真实性，并且其通知准确地反映了收到的信用证或修改的条款。

d. 经由通知行或第二通知行通知信用证的银行必须经由同一银行通知其后的任何修改。

e. 如一银行被要求通知信用证或修改但其决定不予通知，则应毫不延误地告知自其处收到信用证、修改或通知的银行。

f. 如一银行被要求通知信用证或修改但其不能确信信用证、修改或通知的表面真实性，则应毫不延误地通知看似从其处收到指示的银行。如果通知行或第二通知行决定仍然通知信用证或修改，则应告知受益人或第二通知行其不能确信信用证、修改或通知的表面真实性。

第十条 修改

a. 除第三十八条另有规定者外，未经开证行、保兑行（如有的话）及受益人同意，信用证既不得修改，也不得撤销。

b. 开证行自发出修改之时起，即不可撤销地受其约束。保兑行可将其保兑扩展至修改，并自通知该修改时，即不可撤销地受其约束。但是，保兑行可以选择将修改通知受益人而不对其加具保兑。若然如此，其必须毫不延误地将此告知开证行，并在其给受益人的通知中告知受益人。

c. 在受益人告知通知修改的银行其接受该修改之前，原信用证（或含有先前被接受的修改的信用证）的条款对受益人仍然有效。受益人应提供接受或拒绝修改的通知。如果受益人未能给予通知，当交单与信用证以及尚未表示接受的修改的要求一致时，即视为受益人已做出接受修改的通知，并且从此时起，该信用证被修改。

d. 通知修改的银行应将任何接受或拒绝的通知转告发出修改的银行。

e. 对同一修改的内容不允许部分接受，部分接受将被视为拒绝修改的通知。

f. 修改中关于除非受益人在某一时间内拒绝修改否则修改生效的规定应不予理会。

第十一条 电讯传输的和预先通知的信用证和修改

a. 以经证实的电讯方式发出的信用证或信用证修改即被视为有效的信用证或修改文据，任何后续的邮寄确认书应不予理会。

如电讯声明“详情后告”（或类似用语）或声明以邮寄确认书为有效信用证或修改，则该电讯不被视为有效信用证或修改。开证行必须随即不迟延地开立有效信用证或修改，其条款不得与该电讯矛盾。

b. 开证行只有在准备开立有效信用证或做出有效修改时，才可以发出关于开立或修改信用证的初步通知（预先通知）。开证行做出该预先通知，即不可撤销地保证不迟延地开立或修改信用证，且其条款不能与预先通知相矛盾。

第十二条　指定

a. 除非指定银行为保兑行，对于承付或议付的授权并不赋予指定银行承付或议付的义务，除非该指定银行明确表示同意并且告知受益人。

b. 开证行指定一银行承兑汇票或做出延期付款承诺，即为授权该指定银行预付或购买其已承兑的汇票或已做出的延期付款承诺。

c. 非保兑行的指定银行收到或审核并转递单据的行为并不使其承担承付或议付的责任，也不构成其承付或议付的行为。

第十三条　银行之间的偿付安排

a. 如果信用证规定指定银行（"索偿行"）向另一方（"偿付行"）获取偿付时，必须同时规定该偿付是否按信用证开立时有效的 ICC 银行间偿付规则进行。

b. 如果信用证没有规定偿付遵守 ICC 银行间偿付规则，则按照以下规定：

i. 开证行必须给予偿付行有关偿付的授权，授权应符合信用证关于兑用方式的规定，且不应设定截止日。

ii. 开证行不应要求索偿行向偿付行提供与信用证条款相符的证明。

iii. 如果偿付行未按信用证条款见索即偿，开证行将承担利息损失以及产生的任何其他费用。

iv. 偿付行的费用应由开证行承担。然而，如果此项费用由受益人承担，开证行有责任在信用证及偿付授权中注明。如果偿付行的费用由受益人承担，该费用应在偿付时从付给索偿行的金额中扣取。如果偿付未发生，偿付行的费用仍由开证行负担。

c. 如果偿付行未能见索即偿，开证行不能免除偿付责任。

第十四条　单据审核标准

a. 按指定行事的指定银行、保兑行（如果有的话）及开证行须审核交单，并仅基于单据本身确定其是否在表面上构成相符交单。

b. 按指定行事的指定银行、保兑行（如有的话）及开证行各有从交单次日起的至多五个银行工作日用以确定交单是否相符。这一期限不因在交单日当天或之后信用证截止日或最迟交单日届至而受到缩减或影响。

c. 如果单据中包含一份或多份受第十九、二十、二十一、二十二、二十三、二十四或二十五条规制的正本运输单据，则须由受益人或其代表在不迟于本惯例所指的发运日之后的二十一个日历日内交单，但是在任何情况下都不得迟于信用证的截止日。

d. 单据中的数据，在与信用证、单据本身以及国际标准银行实务参照解读时，无须与该单据本身中的数据、其他要求的单据或信用证中的数据等同一致，但不得矛盾。

e. 除商业发票外，其他单据中的货物、服务或履约行为的描述，如果有的话，可使用与信用证中的描述不矛盾的概括性用语。

f. 如果信用证要求提交运输单据、保险单据或者商业发票之外的单据，却未规定出单人或其数据内容，则只要提交的单据内容看似满足所要求单据的功能，且其他方面符合第十四条 d 款，银行将接受该单据。

g. 提交的非信用证所要求的单据将被不予理会，并可被退还给交单人。

h. 如果信用证含有一项条件，但未规定用以表明该条件得到满足的单据，银行将视为未做规定并不予理会。

i. 单据日期可以早于信用证的开立日期，但不得晚于交单日期。

j. 当受益人和申请人的地址出现在任何规定的单据中时，无须与信用证或其他规定单据中所载相同，但必须与信用证中规定的相应地址同在一国。联络细节（传真、电话、电子邮件及类似细节）作为受益人和申请人地址的一部分时将被不予理会。然而，如果申请人的地址和联络细节为第十九、二十、二十一、二十二、二十三、二十四或二十五条规定的运输单据上的收货人或通知方细节的一部分时，应与信用证规定的相同。

k. 在任何单据中注明的托运人或发货人无须为信用证的受益人。

l. 运输单据可以由任何人出具，无须为承运人、船东、船长或租船人，只要其符合第十九、二十、二十一、二十二、二十三或二十四条的要求。

第十五条　相符交单

a. 当开证行确定交单相符时，必须承付。

b. 当保兑行确定交单相符时，必须承付或者议付并将单据转递给开证行。

c. 当指定银行确定交单相符并承付或议付时，必须将单据转递给保兑行或开证行。

第十六条　不符单据、放弃及通知

a. 当按照指定行事的指定银行、保兑行（如有的话）或者开证行确定交单不符时，可以拒绝承付或议付。

b. 当开证行确定交单不符时，可以自行决定联系申请人放弃不符点。然而这并不能延长第十四条 b 款所指的期限。

c. 当按照指定行事的指定银行、保兑行（如有的话）或开证行决定拒绝承付或议付时，必须给予交单人一份单独的拒付通知。

该通知必须声明：

i. 银行拒绝承付或议付；及

ii. 银行拒绝承付或者议付所依据的每一个不符点；及

iii. a）银行留存单据听候交单人的进一步指示；或者

b）开证行留存单据直到其从申请人处接到放弃不符点的通知并同意接受该放弃，或者其同意接受对不符点的放弃之前从交单人处收到其进一步指示；或者

c）银行将退回单据；或者

d）银行将按之前从交单人处获得的指示处理。

d. 第十六条 c 款要求的通知必须以电讯方式，如不可能，则以其他快捷方式，在不迟于自交单之翌日起第五个银行工作日结束前发出。

e. 按照指定行事的指定银行、保兑行（如有的话）或开证行在按照第十六条 c 款 iii 项 a）或 b）发出了通知后，可以在任何时候将单据退还交单人。

f. 如果开证行或保兑行未能按照本条行事，则无权宣称交单不符。

g. 当开证行拒绝承付或保兑行拒绝承付或者议付，并且按照本条发出了拒付通知后，有权要求返还已偿付的款项及利息。

第十七条　正本单据及副本

a. 信用证规定的每一种单据须至少提交一份正本。

b. 银行应将任何带有看似出单人的原始签名、标记、印戳或标签的单据视为正本单据，除非单据本身表明其非正本。

c. 除非单据本身另有说明，在以下情况下，银行也将其视为正本单据：

i. 单据看似由出单人手写、打字、穿孔或盖章；或者

ii. 单据看似使用出单人的原始信纸出具；或者

iii. 单据声明其为正本单据，除非该声明看似不适用于提交的单据。

d. 如果信用证要求提交单据的副本，提交正本或副本均可。

e. 如果信用证使用诸如“一式两份（in duplicate）”、“两份（in two fold）”、“两套（in two copies）”等用语要求提交多份单据，则提交至少一份正本，其余使用副本即可满足要求，除非单据本身另有说明。

第十八条　商业发票

a. 商业发票：

i. 必须看似由受益人出具（第三十八条规定的情形除外）；

ii. 必须出具成以申请人为抬头（第三十八条 g 款规定的情形除外）；

iii. 必须与信用证的货币相同；且

iv. 无须签名

b. 按指定行事的指定银行、保兑行（如有的话）或开证行可以接受金额大于信用证允许金额的商业发票，其决定对有关各方均有约束力，只要该银行对超过信用证允许金额的部分未做承付或者议付。

c. 商业发票上的货物、服务或履约行为的描述应该与信用证中的描述一致。

第十九条　涵盖至少两种不同运输方式的运输单据

a. 涵盖至少两种不同运输方式的运输单据（多式或联合运输单据），无论名称如何，必须看似：

i. 表明承运人名称并由以下人员签署：

* 承运人或其具名代理人，或

* 船长或其具名代理人。

承运人、船长或代理人的任何签字，必须标明其承运人、船长或代理人的身份。

代理人签字必须表明其系代表承运人还是船长签字。

ii. 通过以下方式表明货物已经在信用证规定的地点发送、接管或已装运。

* 事先印就的文字，或者

* 表明货物已经被发送、接管或装船日期的印戳或批注。

运输单据的出具日期将被视为发送、接管或装运的日期，也即发运的日期。然而如单据以印戳或批注的方式表明了发送、接管或装船日期，该日期将被视为发运日期。

iii. 表明信用证规定的发送、接管或发运地点，以及最终目的地，即使：

a）该运输单据另外还载明了一个不同的发送、接管或发运地点或最终目的地，或者

b）该运输单据载有“预期的”或类似的关于船只、装货港或卸货港的限定语。

iv. 为惟一的正本运输单据，或者，如果出具为多份正本，则为运输单据中表明的全套单据。

v. 载有承运条款和条件，或提示承运条款和条件参见别处（简式/背面空白的运输单据）。银行将不审核承运条款和条件的内容。

vi. 未表明受租船合同约束。

b. 就本条而言，转运指在从信用证规定的发送、接管或者发运地点最终目的地的运输过程中从某一运输工具上卸下货物并装上另一运输工具的行为（无论其是否为不同的运输方式）。

c. i. 运输单据可以表明货物将要或可能被转运，只要全程运输由同一运输单据涵盖。

ii. 即使信用证禁止转运，注明将要或者可能发生转运的运输单据仍可接受。

第二十条　提单

a. 提单，无论名称如何，必须看似：

i. 表明承运人名称，并由下列人员签署：

＊承运人或其具名代理人，或者

＊船长或其具名代理人。

承运人、船长或代理人的任何签字必须标明其承运人、船长或代理人的身份。

代理人的任何签字必须标明其系代表承运人还是船长签字。

ii. 通过以下方式表明货物已在信用证规定的装货港装上具名船只：

＊预先印就的文字，或

＊已装船批注注明货物的装运日期。

提单的出具日期将被视为发运日期，除非提单载有表明发运日期的已装船批注，此时已装船批注中显示的日期将被视为发运日期。

如果提单载有“预期船只”或类似的关于船名的限定语，则需以已装船批注明确发运日期以及实际船名。

iii. 表明货物从信用证规定的装货港发运至卸货港。

如果提单没有表明信用证规定的装货港为装货港，或者其载有“预期的”或类似的关于装货港的限定语，则需以已装船批注表明信用证规定的装货港、发运日期以及实际船名。即使提单以事先印就的文字表明了货物已装载或装运于具名船只，本规定仍适用。

iv. 为惟一的正本提单，或如果以多份正本出具，为提单中表明的全套正本。

v. 载有承运条款和条件，或提示承运条款和条件参见别外（简式/背面空白的提单）。银行将不审核承运条款和条件的内容。

vi. 未表明受租船合同约束。

b. 就本条而言，转运系指在信用证规定的装货港到卸货港之间的运输过程中，将货物从一船卸下并再装上另一船的行为。

c. i. 提单可以表明货物将要或可能被转运，只要全程运输由同一提单涵盖。

ii. 即使信用证禁止转运，注明将要或可能发生转运的提单仍可接受，只要其表明货物

由集装箱、拖车或子船运输。

d. 提单中声明承运人保留转运权利的条款将被不予理会。

第二十一条　不可转让的海运单

a. 不可转让的海运单，无论名称如何，必须看似：

i. 表明承运人名称并由下列人员签署：

* 承运人或其具名代理人，或者

* 船长或其具名代理人。

承运人、船长或代理人的任何签字必须标明其承运人、船长或代理人的身份。

代理签字必须标明其系代表承运人还是船长签字。

ii. 通过以下方式表明货物已在信用证规定的装货港装上具名船只：

* 预先印就的文字，或者

* 已装船批注表明货物的装运日期。

不可转让海运单的出具日期将被视为发运日期，除非其上带有已装船批注注明发运日期，此明已装船批注注明的日期将被视为发运日期。

如果不可转让海运单载有“预期船只”或类似的关于船名的限定语，则需要以已装船批注表明发运日期和实际船名。

iii. 表明货物从信用证规定的装货港发运至卸货港。

如果不可转让海运单未以信用证规定的装货港为装货港，或者如果其载有“预期的”或类似的关于装货港的限定语，则需要以已装船批注表明信用证规定的装货港、发运日期和船只。即使不可转让海运单以预先印就的文字表明货物已由具名船只装载或装运，本规定也适用。

iv. 为惟一的正本不可转让海运单，或如果以多份正本出具，为海运单上注明的全套正本。

v. 载有承运条款的条件，或提示承运条款和条件参见别处（简式/背面空白的海运单）。银行将不审核承运条款和条件的内容。

vi. 未注明受租船合同约束。

b. 就本条而言，转运系指在信用证规定的装货港到卸货港之间的运输过程中，将货物从一船卸下并装上另一船的行为。

c. i. 不可转让海运单可以注明货物将要或可能被转运，只要全程运输由同一海运单涵盖。

ii. 即使信用证禁止转运，注明转运将要或可能发生的不可转让的海运单仍可接受，只要其表明货物装于集装箱、拖船或子船中运输。

d. 不可转让的海运单中声明承运人保留转运权利的条款将被不予理会。

第二十二条　租船合同提单

a. 表明其受租船合同约束的提单（租船合同提单），无论名称如何，必须看似：

i. 由以下人员签署：

* 船长或其具名代理人，或

* 船东或其具名代理人，或

＊租船人或其具名代理人。

船长、船东、租船人或代理人的任何签字必须标明其船长、船东、租船人或代理人的身份。

代理人签字必须标明其系代表船长、船东还是租船人签字。

代理人代表船东或租船人签字时必须注明船东或租船人的名称。

ii. 通过以下方式表明货物已在信用证规定的装货港装上具名船只：

＊预先印就的文字，或者

＊已装船批注注明货物的装运日期

租船合同提单的出具日期将被视为发运日期，除非租船合同提单载有已装船批注注明发运日期，此时已装船批注上注明的日期将被视为发运日期。

iii. 表明货物从信用证规定的装货港发运至卸货港。卸货港也可显示为信用证规定的港口范围或地理区域。

iv. 为惟一的正本租船合同提单，或如以多份正本出具，为租船合同提单注明的全套正本。

b. 银行将不审核租船合同，即使信用证要求提交租船合同。

第二十三条　空运单据

a. 空运单据，无论名称如何，必须看似：

i. 表明承运人名称，并由以下人员签署：

＊承运人，或

＊承运人的具名代理人。

承运人或其代理人的任何签字必须标明其承运人或代理人的身份。

代理人签字必须标明其系代表承运人签字。

ii. 表明货物已被收妥待运。

iii. 表明出具日期。该日期将被视为发运日期，除非空运单据载有专门批注注明实际发运日期，此时批注中的日期将被视为发运日期。

空运单据中其他与航班号和航班日期相关的信息将不被用来确定发运日期。

iv. 表明信用证规定的起飞机场和目的地机场。

v. 为开给发货人或托运人的正本，即使信用证规定提交全套正本。

vi. 载有承运条款和条件，或提示条款和条件参见别处。银行将不审核承运条款和条件的内容。

b. 就本条而言，转运是指在信用证规定的起飞机场到目的地机场的运输过程中，将货物从一飞机卸下再装上另一飞机的行为。

c. i. 空运单据可以注明货物将要或可能转运，只要全程运输由同一空运单据涵盖。

ii. 即使信用证禁止转运，注明将要或可能发生转运的空运单据仍可接受。

第二十四条　公路、铁路或内陆水运单据

a. 公路、铁路或内陆水运单据，无论名称如何，必须看似：

i. 表明承运人名称，并且

＊由承运人或其具名代理人签署，或者

* 由承运人或其具名代理人以签字、印戳或批注表明货物收讫。

承运人或其具名代理人的收货签字、印戳或批注必须标明其承运人或代理人的身份。

代理人的收货签字、印戳或批注必须标明代理人系代表承运人签字或行事。

如果铁路运输单据没有指明承运人，可以接受铁路运输公司的任何签字或印戳作为承运人签署单据的证据。

ii. 表明货物的信用规定地点的发运日期，或者收讫待运或待发送的日期。运输单据的出具日期将被视为发运日期，除非运输单据上盖有带日期的收货印戳，或注明了收货日期或发运日期。

iii. 表明信用证规定的发运地及目的地。

b. i. 公路运输单据必须看似为开给发货人或托运人的正本，或没有任何标记表明单据开给何人。

ii. 注明“第二联”的铁路运输单据将被作为正本接受。

iii. 无论是否注明正本字样，铁路或内陆水运单据都被作为正本接受。

c. 如运输单据上未注明出具的正本数量，提交的份数即视为全套正本。

d. 就本条而言，转运是指在信用证规定的发运、发送或运送的地点到目的地之间的运输过程中，在同一运输方式中从一运输工具卸下再装上另一运输工具的行为。

e. i. 只要全程运输由同一运输单据涵盖，公路、铁路或内陆水运单据可以注明货物将要或可能被转运。

ii. 即使信用证禁止转运，注明将要或可能发生转运的公路、铁路或内陆水运单据仍可接受。

第二十五条　快递收据、邮政收据或投邮证明

a. 证明货物收讫待运的快递收据，无论名称如何，必须看似：

i. 表明快递机构的名称，并在信用证规定的货物发运地点由该具名快递机构盖章或签字；并且

ii. 表明取件或收件的日期或类似词语，该日期将被视为发运日期。

b. 如果要求显示快递费用付讫或预付，快递机构出具的表明快递费由收货人以外的一方支付的运输单据可以满足该项要求。

c. 证明货物收讫待运的邮政收据或投邮证明，无论名称如何，必须看似在信用证规定的货物发运地点盖章或签署并注明日期。该日期将被视为发运日期。

第二十六条　“货装舱面”、“托运人装载和计数”、“内容据托运人报称”及运费之外的费用

a. 运输单据不得表明货物装于或者将装于舱面。声明货物可能被装于舱面的运输单据条款可以接受。

b. 载有诸如“托运人装载和计数”或“内容据托运人报称”条款的运输单据可以接受。

c. 运输单据上可以以印戳或其他方法提及运费之外的费用。

第二十七条　清洁运输单据

银行只接受清洁运输单据，清洁运输单据指未载有明确宣称货物或包装有缺陷的条款或

批注的运输单据。“清洁”一词并不需要在运输单据上出现，即使信用证要求运输单据为“清洁已装船”的。

第二十八条　保险单据及保险范围

a. 保险单据，如保险单或预约保险项下的保险证明书或者声明书，必须看似由保险公司或承保人或其代理人或代表出具并签署。

代理人或代表的签字必须表明其系代表保险公司或承保人签字。

b. 如果保险单据表明其以多份正本出具，所有正本均须提交。

c. 暂保单将不被接受。

d. 可以接受保险单代替预约保险项下的保险证明书或声明书。

e. 保险单据日期不得晚于发运日期，除非保险单据表明保险责任不迟于发运日生效。

f. i. 保险单据必须表明投保金额并以与信用证相同的货币表示。

ii. 信用证对于投保金额为货物价值、发票金额或类似金额的某一比例的要求，将被视为对最低保额的要求。

如果信用证对投保金额未做规定，投保金额须至少为货物的 CIF 或 CIP 价格的百分之一百一十。

如果从单据中不能确定 CIF 或者 CIP 价格，投保金额必须基于要求承付或议付的金额，或者基于发票上显示的货物总值来计算，两者之中取金额较高者。

iii. 保险单据须表明承保的风险区间至少涵盖从信用证规定的货物接管地或发运地开始到卸货地或最终目的地为止。

g. 信用证应规定所需投保的险别及附加险（如有的话）。如果信用证使用诸如“通常风险”或“惯常风险”等含义不确切的用语，则无论是否有漏保之风险，保险单据将被照样接受。

h. 当信用证规定投保“一切险”时，如保险单据载有任何“一切险”批注或条款，无论是否有“一切险”标题，均将被接受，即使其声明任何风险除外。

i. 保险单据可以援引任何除外条款。

j. 保险单据可以注明受免赔率或免赔额（减除额）约束。

第二十九条　截止日或最迟交单日的顺延

a. 如果信用证的截止日或最迟交单日适逢接受交单的银行非因第三十六条所述原因而歇业，则视截止日或最迟交单日中何者适用，顺延至其重新开业的第一个银行工作日。

b. 如果在顺延后的第一个银行工作日交单，指定银行必须在其致开证行或保兑行的面函中声明交单是在根据第二十九条 a 款顺延的期限内提交的。

c. 最迟发运日不因第二十九条 a 款规定的原因而顺延。

第三十条　信用证金额、数量与单价的伸缩度

a. “约”或“大约”用于信用证金额或信用证规定的数量或单价时，应解释为允许有关金额或数量或单价有不超过百分之十的增减幅度。

b. 在信用证未以包装单位件数或货物自身件数的方式规定货物数量时，货物数量允许有百分之五的增减幅度，只要总支取金额不超过信用证金额。

c. 如果信用证规定了货物数量，而该数量已全部发运，及如果信用证规定了单价，而该单价又未降低，或当第三十条 b 款不适用时，则即使不允许部分装运，也允许支取的金额有百分之五的减幅。若信用证规定有特定的增减幅度或使用第三十条 a 款提到的用语限定数量，则该减幅不适用。

第三十一条　部分支款或部分发运

a. 允许部分支款或部分发运。

b. 表明使用同一运输工具并经由同次航程运输的数套运输单据在同一次提交时，只要显示相同目的地，将不视为部分发运，即使运输单据上表明的发运日期不同或装货港、接管地或发运地点不同。如果交单由数套运输单据构成，其中最晚的一个发运日将被视为发运日。

含有一套或数套运输单据的交单，如果表明在同一种运输方式下经由数件运输工具运输，即使运输工具在同一天出发运往同一目的地，仍将被视为部分发运。

c. 含有一份以上快递收据、邮政收据或投邮证明的交单，如果单据看似由同一快递或邮政机构在同一地点和日期加盖印戳或签字并且表明同一目的地，将不视为部分发运。

第三十二条　分期支款或分期发运

如信用证规定在指定的时间段内分期支款或分期发运，任何一期未按信用证规定期限支取或发运时，信用证对该期及以后各期均告失效。

第三十三条　交单时间

银行在其营业时间外无接受交单的义务。

第三十四条　关于单据有效性的免责

银行对任何单据的形式、充分性、准确性、内容真实性、虚假性或法律效力，或对单据中规定或添加的一般或特殊条件，概不负责；银行对任何单据所代表的货物、服务或其他履约行为的描述、数量、重量、品质、状况、包装、交付、价值或其存在与否，或对发货人、承运人、货运代理人、收货人、货物的保险人或其他任何人的诚信与否、作为或不作为、清偿能力、履约或资信状况，也概不负责。

第三十五条　关于信息传递和翻译的免责

当报文、信件或单据按照信用证的要求传输或发送时，或当信用证未做指示，银行自行选择传送服务时，银行对报文传输或信件或单据的递送过程中发生的延误、中途遗失、残缺或其他错误产生的后果，概不负责。

如果指定银行确定交单相符并将单据发往开证行或保兑行，无论指定银行是否已经承付或议付，开证行或保兑行必须承付或议付，或偿付指定银行，即使单据在指定银行送往开证行或保兑行的途中，或保兑行送往开证行的途中丢失。

银行对技术术语的翻译或解释上的错误，不负责任，并可不加翻译地传送信用证条款。

第三十六条　不可抗力

银行对由于天灾、暴动、骚乱、叛乱、战争、恐怖主义行为或任何罢工、停工或其无法控制的任何其他原因导致的营业中断的后果，概不负责。

银行恢复营业时，对于在营业中断期间已逾期的信用证，不再进行承付或议付。

第三十七条　关于被指示方行为的免责

a. 为了执行申请人的指示，银行利用其他银行的服务，其费用和风险由申请人承担。

b. 即使银行自行选择了其他银行，如果发出的指示未被执行，开证行或通知行对此亦不负责。

c. 指示另一银行提供服务的银行有责任负担被指示方因执行指示而发生的任何佣金、手续费、成本或开支（“费用”）。

如果信用证规定费用由受益人负担，而该费用未能收取或从信用证款项中扣除，开证行依然承担支付此费用的责任。信用证或其修改不应规定向受益人的通知以通知行或第二通知行收到其费用为条件。

d. 外国法律和惯例加诸于银行的一切义务和责任，申请人应受其约束，并就此对银行负补偿之责。

第三十八条　可转让信用证

a. 银行无办理信用证转让的义务，除非其明确同意。

b. 就本条而言：

可转让信用证系指特别注明“可转让（transferable）”字样的信用证。可转让信用证可应受益人（第一受益人）的要求转为全部或部分由另一受益人（第二受益人）兑用。

转让行系指办理信用证转让的指定银行，或当信用证规定可在任一银行兑用时，指开证行特别如此授权并实际办理转让的银行。开证行也可担任转让行。

已转让信用证指已由转让行转为可由第二受益人兑用的信用证。

c. 除非转让时另有约定，有关转让的所有费用（诸如佣金、手续费、成本或开支）须由第一受益人支付。

d. 只要信用证允许部分支款或部分发运，信用证可以分部分地转让给数名第二受益人。

已转让信用证不得应第二受益人的要求转让给任何其后受益人。第一受益人不视为其后受益人。

e. 任何转让要求须说明是否允许及在何条件下允许将修改通知第二受益人。已转让信用证须明确说明该项条件。

f. 如果信用证转让给数名第二受益人，其中一名或多名第二受益人对信用证修改的拒绝并不影响其他第二受益人接受修改。对接受者而言，该已转让信用证即被相应修改；而对拒绝改的第二受益人而言，该信用证未被修改。

g. 已转让信用证须准确转载原证条款，包括保兑（如果有的话），但下列项目除外：

——信用证金额，

——规定的任何单价，

——截止日，

——交单期限，或

——最迟发运日或发运期间。

以上任何一项或全部均可减少或缩短。

必须投保的保险比例可以增加，以达到原信用证或本惯例规定的保险金额。

可用第一受益人的名称替换原证中的开证申请人名称。

如果原证特别要求开证申请人名称应在除发票以外的任何单据出现时，已转让信用证必须反映该项要求。

h. 第一受益人有权以自己的发票和汇票（如有的话）替换第二受益人的发票的汇票，其金额不得超过原信用证的金额。经过替换后，第一受益人可在原信用证项下支取自己发票与第二受益人发票间的差价（如有的话）。

i. 如果第一受益人应提交其自己的发票和汇票（如有的话），但未能在第一次要求时照办，或第一受益人提交的发票导致了第二受益人的交单中本不存在的不符点，而其未能在第一次要求时修正，转让行有权将从第二受益人处收到的单据照交开证行，并不再对第一受益人承担责任。

j. 在要求转让时，第一受益人可以要求在信用证转让后的兑用地点，于原信用证的截止日之前（包括截止日），对第二受益人承付或议付。本规定并不损害第一受益人在第三十八条 h 款下的权利。

k. 第二受益人或代表第二受益人的交单必须交给转让行。

第三十九条　款项让渡

信用证未注明可转让，并不影响受益人根据所适用的法律规定，将该信用证项下其可能有权或可能将成为有权获得的款项让渡给他人的权利。本条只涉及款项的让渡，而不涉及在信用证项下进行履行行为的权利让渡。

参考文献

1. 王海欧:《外贸单证实务》,清华大学出版社、北京交通大学出版社2011年版。

2. 韩宇红、李志勇:《外贸单证缮制任务书》,北京理工大学出版社2011年版。

3. 吴穗山:《外贸单证实务》,电子工业出版社2011年版。

4. 顾建华:《外贸单证实务》,清华大学出版社2010年版。

5. 全国国际商务单证专业培训考试办公室:《国际商务单证理论与实务》、《国际商务单证专业培训考试大纲与复习指南》,中国商务出版社2013年版。